THE CATHOLIC U
STUDIES IN]
NE.
VOLUME V

PAUL ALBAR OF CORDOBA: STUDIES ON HIS LIFE AND WRITINGS

A DISSERTATION

SUBMITTED TO THE FACULTY OF THE GRADUATE SCHOOL OF ARTS
AND SCIENCES OF THE CATHOLIC UNIVERSITY OF AMERICA
IN PARTIAL FULFILLMENT OF THE REQUIRE-
MENTS FOR THE DEGREE OF DOCTOR
OF PHILOSOPHY

BY

CARLETON M. SAGE

OF

THE SOCIETY OF ST. SULPICE

THE CATHOLIC UNIVERSITY OF AMERICA PRESS
WASHINGTON, D. C.
1943

Nihil Obstat:
    A. K. Ziegler, S.T.D.
        Censor Deputatus
        Washingtonii, D. C., die XV Septembris, 1943

Imprimatur:
    ✠ Michael J. Curley, D.D.
            Archiepiscopus Baltimorensis et Washingtoniensis
        Baltimorae, die XVII Septembris, 1943

MURRAY & HEISTER—WASHINGTON, D. C.

PRINTED IN THE UNITED STATES

9

TABLE OF CONTENTS

v

PREFACE

In the seventh century, Visigothic Spain had been a leader in preserving the ancient culture of western Christendom. When internal decay and repeated waves of barbarian invasion had gone far to bury the culture of Italy, Gaul, and Africa, Spanish churchmen with St. Isidore at their head had been able, if not to continue the creativeness of earlier centuries, at least to cherish their inheritance and to preserve it in a compendious and simplified form which could make it available to darker ages to come. Saved from some of the later waves of northern invasion, Spain was able to merge and assimilate the Suevi and Visigoths with the Hispano-Roman population, so that both in religion and culture they formed in the seventh century a united people which rejoiced in their Catholic and Roman heritage. It is possible that the latter part of the century saw the beginning of a decline; but the endemic inability of the early Germanic tribes to achieve a political constitution which would fix the succession to the throne first weakened the state with civil wars, and then was the occasion of the sudden catastrophe of 711, when almost by accident Berber and Arab adventurers from Africa conquered the Peninsula. Only the backward mountain district of the far north remained free and in Christian hands. Elsewhere the Spanish Christians became a subject population, free to practise their religion, but burdened with extra taxes and subjected to various disabilities. At first there was considerable variation from place to place in the conditions in which the Spanish found themselves, according to whether the locality had been conquered by force, or had surrendered without resistance. But in the course of decades, as the Moslem population increased and the new rulers felt their rule more assured, the terms of early treaties were not always observed, and the lot of the Christians became more unfavorable. They remained personally free and retained the ownership of their property, and churches and monasteries remained open; but both legal and social pressure weighed more heavily upon them.

Some, a small minority of course, migrated to the free prin-
cipalities in the north; but those who remained at home found
themselves cut off from Christendom. Not that travel across the
frontiers was wholly impossible—doubtless there was always some
of it—but in all the affairs of ordinary life the Christians now
found themselves engulfed in an entirely alien, Oriental world.
Córdoba, the seat in turn of Arab governors, emirs, and caliphs,
belonged to the world of Fez, Cairo, Damascus, and Bagdad, not
to that of Lyons, Trier, Milan, and Rome. In each generation
weaker Christians apostatized and joined the Moslem ranks.
Arabic culture displaced Christian, and in time the Mozarabs, or
those who retained their Christian faith, seem to have adopted
the Arabic language. In the only passage of his writings which
is frequently quoted in modern times,[1] the ninth-century Paul
Albar complains bitterly that Christian youths now disdain Latin
literature and surpass the very Moslems in their devotion to
Arabic writings. A century later the Bible was translated into
Arabic for the use of the Mozarabs.

This current of Arabization was not alone in tending to sever
the Mozarabs from intercourse with their fellow Christians elsewhere. On both sides of the frontier political conditions were
turbulent through most of the eighth and ninth centuries. In
Spain there were frequent revolts of both Mozarabs and apostate
Christians or Renegades, and constant personal and tribal feuds
and struggles for power among Berbers and Arabs. North of
the Pyrenees, Charlemagne's reign marked only a partial and
transitory halt in the long descent from the ancient world to the
bottom of the Dark Age. Even within western Christendom itself, there was less intercourse of part with part, and culture
found its last refuge behind monastery walls until the eleventh
century should bring a new dawn.

Thus the Mozarab Church lived on memories. Lacking the
stimulation of new life from without—for there is no evidence
of any influence from the Carolingian renaissance—and without a
creative impulse of its own, it lived on its inheritance of Isidorian
culture. How much did it inherit? How much survived, not just

---

[1] *Indiculus luminosus*, n. 35, PL 121:555f.

in old manuscripts waiting unused until a later age should rediscover them, but actually used and assimilated by the Mozarabs themselves? When today we come to assemble what has survived from the early Mozarab centuries, it seems disappointingly small: a few Bibles and liturgical books, some scattered writings of the Fathers, three or four collections of canon law, some of the Christian poets of the late Roman Empire. Many folios are like copy-books, filled with miscellaneous fragments that struck the copyist's fancy—extracts, etymologies taken from Augustine and Isidore, a law of a Visigothic king, a list of the episcopal sees of Spain and other geographical facts, unknown sermons ascribed to famous doctors like Augustine, a fragment of a chronicle, a list of books in some unknown library. Most of these writings are survivals from the patristic age. But the manuscripts preserve also a few works of the early Mozarab period. The paucity of written documents coming to us from the conquered Christians makes the first centuries following the conquest dark to us. But by good fortune we have a group of interconnected texts which throw light on the Christians in the Moslem capital in the two middle decades of the ninth century. The most important of these belong to the two friends, Paul Albar and St. Eulogius, and to Abbot Samson; smaller driftwood comes from Abbot Speraindeo, the priest Leovigild, and the archpriest Cyprian. Taken together these furnish us with a connected narrative of a period of martyrdom, and throw much light on personalities, on churches and monasteries, and on the conditions in which the Spanish Christians lived. They also show us something of the controversies and theology of the time, and supply material which can be used to assay the quality of its Christian-Latin culture.

These materials have long been known in Spain, and some were printed as early as the sixteenth century. The martyrs, especially, have been held in honor, and their story has been written many times since Ambrosio de Morales first published Eulogius' works, and retold the story in his *Corónica*. Recently a life of St. Eulogius [2] has been written, and an adaptation of

---

[2] Justo Pérez de Urbel, *San Eulogio de Córdoba*, Madrid, 1928; *A Saint Under Moslem Rule*, Milwaukee, 1937, is an abbreviated translation.

it has appeared in English; here again the purpose is chiefly to tell
the story of the martyrs, and to bring the background and personalities to life. Outside of Spain, something has been done,
notably in Germany, mostly from a narrative or philological
point of view. The old dissertation of Count Baudissin,[3] though
academic, is still rather general, and the historical narrative
retains a prominent place. In all these studies St. Eulogius is
given the center of the stage. This is natural, since he is a more
attractive personality, more facts are known of his life, his writings are easier to read, and it is they which tell most of the story
of the martyrs. Albar is treated as the darker component of a
double star, as a complement and foil to Eulogius. This is not
entirely fair, and to the present writer it seems somewhat unfortunate. If Eulogius is the more winning and romantic figure, his
writings are less rich; except for the letter to Wiliesind, they
are devoted wholly to the martyrs, and consist largely of a series
of short biographical sketches. Albar covered a wider field:
not only the martyrs, but philosophical and theological problems
with a marshalling of quotations from other writers, a debate on
the importance of rhetoric and another against Judaism, some
verses, a highly developed biography, a book of devotion, and
finally the *Indiculus luminosus,* which is a defense of the voluntary martyrs constructed on a larger scale than Eulogius' *Liber
apologeticus.* Thus Albar offers a more fruitful field than
Eulogius for a study of the quality of the Latin culture achieved
in their day. It may be supposed that all modern writers on the
period have read Albar's works; but apart from the *Vita Eulogii,*
and a few passages of the other writings, particularly the oft-
cited conclusion of the *Indiculus* lamenting the defection of Christian youths to Arabic literature, comments tend to limit themselves
to generalizations. The only exception is the critical edition of
the poems made by Ludwig Traube for the Monumenta Germaniae historica.[4]

The present study is an effort to examine the character, and as
far as possible to discover the sources of some of Albar's writings. It has not been possible to treat them all; the *Indiculus*

---

[3] Wolf Wilhelm Graf von Baudissin, *Eulogius und Alvar,* Leipzig, 1872.
[4] MGH, *Poetae Latini aevi carolini,* III, i, 122–142.

luminosus, and the correspondence with Bodo are omitted, though both hold out a hope of interesting results. The verses are also passed over, as they are few and of slight merit, and not much is likely to be gleaned in the wake of Traube. But the *Vita Eulogii,* the *Confessio,* and the correspondence with John of Seville offer a varied fare; it is hoped that a careful examination of them will give evidence of a richer culture among the Mozarabs of ninth-century Córdoba than sometimes they get credit for. This is not a philological study; that is impossible, as the printed text has been partly normalized by the editor. Primarily, the work has been done as a search for sources and parallels, though along the road various other aspects have received attention. In some of his writings such as his correspondence, Albar names his authors, and editors have done much to identify the citations; even here it is hoped that this study has made some further contribution. In other works, such as the *Vita* and *Confessio,* Albar follows a different literary method, weaving quotations and allusions into his text without formal quotation; and it is here that the present writer believes he has accomplished most. But he is well aware that he can make no claim to completeness; some passages which he is confident Albar has borrowed he has been unable to trace, while there are doubtless others that have escaped him entirely.

The various editions are described in an appendix; here it is enough to explain that the texts used are that of Lorenzana for the *Vita Eulogii,* that of Traube for the poems, and that of Flórez for the remaining works. However all of these are rather rare, and so for the convenience of the reader footnote references are normally given to the reprints in Migne's Patrologia Latina. All of Albar's writing except the *Vita* are in Volume 121 of Migne, and whenever a reference to Migne gives the column but omits the number of the volume, this volume is to be understood.

The author is especially happy to thank the Reverend Dr. Aloysius K. Ziegler who not only suggested and directed the dissertation, but who was constant in his kind encouragement. He is grateful also to Dr. Martin R. P. McGuire and the Reverend Dr. James A. Geary for their helpful criticism of the manuscript.

And to Dom Anselm Strittmatter O.S.B. he is indebted for having come to his aid more than once in matters connected with the early liturgy. He wishes also to express his deep gratitude to his Sulpician superiors, the Very Reverend John F. Fenlon and the Very Reverend Anthony Vieban, for their unfailing kindness.

FEAST OF OUR LADY OF MOUNT CARMEL, 1943.

PART ONE

ALBAR'S LIFE AND WORKS

CHAPTER I

Early Life, Before the Martyr Movement

Our only knowledge of Paul Albar [1] comes to us from his own writings and those of Eulogius. Abbot Samson, who was active in the years following Eulogius' martyrdom and a protagonist in a later controversy, does not mention Albar in his polemical *Apologeticus*.[2] Flórez brought together the available biographical references in the introduction to his edition of Albar's works,[3] and little can be added to it.[4]

---

[1] The name is commonly spelled Alvarus, or in Spanish, Paulo Alvaro or Alvaro Cordobès, and in French, Alvare; but it is certain that he himself spelled it in its Latin form Albarus, for so it is regularly given in the Cordovan MS. (cf. the transcript of contents and facsimile in Artiles' article, *Rev. bibl. arch. mus.*, IX (1932), 208ff, and the headings of Epistles 11–13 in Gomez Bravo, *Catál. obisp. Córd.*, I, 145ff, and the hymn he wrote for Eulogius gives the acrostic "Albarus te rogat salves" (the text in Flórez and Migne has been "improved," spoiling the acrostic; see the original form in MGH, *Poet. lat.*, III, i, 139ff, and *Analecta hymnica*, XXVII, 169ff). The spelling with the original *b* has been restored to use by some recent scholars; Dom Lambert uses "Albar," omitting the Latin ending, *DHGE*, VI, 66.

[2] Printed by Flórez, ES, XI, 325ff.

[3] "Vida de Alvaro Cordobès," ES, XI, 10–31.

[4] Earlier than Flórez, Ambrosio de Morales had included Albar's life in the narrative of the period in his continuation of Florian Ocampo's *Corónica general de España* (new ed., Madrid, 1791–92, Vol. 7; the first ed. had appeared at Alcala, 1574–77), and Nicolas Antonio had given him an important article in his *Bibliotheca hispana vetus* (Rome, 1696, I, 348–53; second ed., Madrid, 1788, I, 475–81); Gomez Bravo had also included most that could be said, though scattered through his treatment of the period,

1

Albar's own writings supply three precise dates: the correspondence with Bodo was in 840 A. D.[5]; the *Indiculus luminosus* was written in 854[6]; and his friend Eulogius was martyred on Saturday, March 11,[7] and this it is safe to say was in 859. Eulogius was more interested in chronology, and furnishes many dates for events, all of them, however, lying in the few years between 850 and 857, the period of the martyrdoms. A few other dates can be inferred with more or less probability.

Thus the productive period of Albar's life falls in the middle of the ninth century. The year and place of his birth are unknown, but all that we know of him associates him with Córdoba—his schooling, his lifelong friendship with Eulogius, his connection with the martyrs. Twice he speaks of his ancestry, both times in his correspondence with Bodo, and he gives different accounts in the two places. In the former, replying to some boasting of his newly acquired Jewish faith that Bodo had apparently given expression to, Albar claims a better title to the name of Hebrew.

> Which of us better deserves the name of Israelite? You who, as you say, have been converted from idolatry to the worship of the supreme God, and are a Jew not by race but by faith, or I who am a Hebrew both by faith and race? But I am not called a Jew because a new name has been given me which the mouth of the Lord has named. Abraham is my father, for my forbears descended from that stem; for looking for the Messias who was to come, and receiving him when he came, they are more truly Israel than those who were expecting him but rejected him at his coming, and have not ceased to hope for him; for you are still awaiting one whom you have already rejected. The Gentiles who daily are being converted to the faith of Israel take their place in the

in *Catál. obisp. Córd.* (Córdoba, second ed., 1778, I, 104–161; the first ed. had appeared 1739). Subsequent writers have largely followed Flórez (e. g., J. R. de Castro, *Bibliteca española*, Madrid, 1786, II, 446ff; Baudissin, *Eulogius und Alvar;* F. J. Simonet, *Historia de los Mozárabes,* Madrid, 1903; Z. García Villada, *Historia eclesiástica de España,* Vol. III, 1936).

[5] *Ep.* 16, n. 6, 7; PL 121:488f.

[6] *Ind. lum.,* n. 21, PL 536C.

[7] *Vita,* c. 5, n. 15, PL 115:717C.

people of God, while you have adhered to the error of the Jews.[8]

There is enough obscurity in this passage to enable some to hold that Albar's claim of a Jewish origin was only metaphorical; that since the Christian Church is the " people of God " in succession to, or rather in continuation of, the Israel of the old covenant, Albar really means no more than that by being a Christian he is a member of the true " Israel." [9] Albar's meaning is not very clear when he says that his ancestors had looked for the Messias' coming, and accepted him when he came; it is hard to accept it in its obvious meaning, as it would strain the imagination to believe that a family would remember such a fact after a lapse of eight hundred years. Be this as it may, Albar seems very definitely to claim Jewish blood in such phrases as " ex Israelis stirpe descendens," " ego qui et fide et gente Hebraeus sum " (this precisely in contrast with Bodo who is a Jew in faith, not in blood—" non gente, sed fide Judaeus es "), and " pater meus Abraham est, quia majores mei ex ipsa descenderunt traduce." But whenever it was that his family became Christian, it was clearly before Albar's own day; he admits to Bodo he does not know the Hebrew language; [10] as a boy he had gone to school under the Christian Abbot Speraindeo; and there is no hint in any of his writings that he had ever been anything but a Christian.[11] In fact, in a different and wholly unpolemical book, Albar lets slip a phrase that is rather antisemitic.[12]

---

[8] *Ep.* 18, n. 5, PL 121 :496.

[9] cf. Gomez Bravo, " claramente . . . ingenioso artificio para convencer al Apostata," *op. cit.,* I, 120.

[10] *Ep.* 16, n. 4: scis nos ignaros linguae Hebraeae, PL 487A.

[11] Baudissin, *op. cit.,* pp. 43f., says his father must also have been a Christian, as he made gifts to a monastery located on his property. The reference is to *Ep.* 9, n. 3, 4, PL 465f., and Albar's style leaves the exact sense a little less than clear. The monks were accusing Albar of having recently sold some property he had formerly given them, apparently including the church or monastery itself. The monks at least thought Albar's father had given them the church, but Albar insists he had himself made the gift (" sed terminum ecclesiae, quem non genitor meus sed ego dederam, indicavi." PL 466C). Speaking of his many gifts to the monastery, Albar says, " Et quod genitor meus divae memoriae, nec ante me

The other reference to his ancestry is in his final missive to Bodo, in which he warns Bodo he has a terrible Goth to deal with; after quoting three lines of verse that mention the Getes, he says, " I am, I am one of those whom Alexander advised to avoid, whom Pyrrhus feared, at whom Cæsar was terrified. Of us our Jerome said, He has a horn on his forehead, run for your life." [13] As the Visigoths had entered Spain four centuries earlier, it may be presumed that by Albar's time a large part of the Spanish people had some Gothic blood in them. It is probable that Albar had both Gothic and Jewish strains in his ancestry; but as both his statements are made in the heat of an argument in order to make points against an opponent, there is no assurance that either strain was so predominant that it characterized the family. It even remains possible that both statements are metaphorical, the Gothic claim meaning only that he is a Spaniard, and the Hebrew referring to the Christian Church as the new Israel.

There is no mention of parents, brother or sister,[14] but it is

---

ex nostris fecerat ullus, ego spontanea mente impleveram solus " (PL 465C) ; here though the *nec* comes only in the following clause, Albar seems to mean that neither his father nor others of the family had done what Albar himself had done in making the gifts. A third clause is more uncertain—" Juste namque confessor (i.e., the monk Julian) dixerat quia illi qui a genitore meo vel a me empta habebant vendere cupiebant " (PL 465D) ; here perhaps it is admitted that his father had a share in the disposal; the property which here "had been bought" is shown by the context to be the same as that which elsewhere Albar says he had "given," and the forced sale of which to the unnamed *princeps* was the cause of the monks' complaint. Perhaps the conclusion is that while Albar was more generous than his father, the latter had made some transfers to the monastery of a kind, whether "sale" or not, that caused the monks to think of him as a benefactor; so it is legitimate to infer he was a Christian.

[12] Judaeorum foetores. *Conf.,* n. 4, PL 410B.

[13] *Ep.* 20, PL 514A. Albar: Noster Hieronymus dicit, cornu habet in fronte, longe fuge. This is a variant of Horace' " faenum habet in cornu, longe fuge " (*Satires*, I, 4, l. 34) which Braulio of Zaragoza quotes, *Ep.* II, PL 80 :657. On the word *Getae* applied to the Goths, v. Sister Genevieve Marie Cook, *Life of St. Epiphanius by Ennodius*, pp. 168ff.

[14] Mabillon (*AASSOSB,* saec. IV, ii, 592) mistakenly identifies Paul Albar with an Alvarus who was a brother of St. Eulogius (Eulog., *Ep. ad Wiliesindum*, n. 1, PL 115 :845B). But Paul Albar and Eulogius first met at school; and the words used by Albar to describe Eulogius' trip

generally accepted that the family was one of some prominence, some like Morales and Flórez even placing it among the higher nobility. The evidence usually advanced for such a claim is the high-sounding names and titles which appear in the headings and addresses of his correspondence. He and John of Seville, in addressing each other, add Aurelius Flavius to their names, though neither uses them of himself.[15] It is reminiscent of the Roman emperors and Visigothic kings;[16] but probably Flórez is right in seeing only friendly good nature in their use by Albar and John.[17] Then there is a sprinkling of honorific adjectives in the letters sent him—" Inlustri eximio celsoque Alvaro Joannes; " " Inlustrissimo mihi domino ac venerabili . . . inclyto Alvaro Speraindeo ; " " Vale in Domino Jesu Christo, serenissime frater."[18] There have been times and places where such words as *illustrissimus* and *serenissimus* were strictly limited to the nobility, but it has been in countries where this nobility was in unchallenged power, not as in ninth-century Córdoba where the Spanish people had been a subject race for almost a century and a half. Morales,[19] Gomez Bravo,[20] and Flórez[21] are willing to see in these titles a sure proof of Albar's nobility; but the present writer feels safer in following Nicolas Antonio,[22] who believed they may have been less formally precise in Córdoba in the ninth century than they

---

to the north are incompatible with his being one of the brothers of whom Eulogius was in search, or, indeed, a brother at all (occasione fratrum suorum qui ipsis diebus in Franciae finibus exulabant. *Vita,* c. 3, n. 9, PL 115:712B).

[15] Aurelio Flavio Alvaro . . . minimi Joannis suggessio (*Ep.* 3). Aurelio Flavio Joanni Paulus Alvarus (*Ep.* 4).

[16] The acta of Spanish councils show the use of Flavius by Kings Chintila, Receswinth, Erwig, Gundemar, and Egica; e.g., at the fifth Council of Toledo: In nomine Domini Flavius Chintila rex (PL 84:393B).

[17] They were "efecto de urbanidad," and "tratamientos políticos honoríficos," ES, XI, 11, n. 2. Cf. Baudissin, *op. cit.,* p. 66, n. 2; Nic. Antonio, *op. cit.,* (1696), I, 349.

[18] Speraindeo's letter is full of them: serenitas vestra, excellentia vestra, vestra benignitas, celsitudo vestra. Eulogius commonly uses only carissimus.

[19] PL 115:706B.

[20] *Op. cit.,* I, 160.

[21] ES, XI, 14.

[22] *Op. cit.,* (1696), I, 349.

were in the seventeenth. But after refusing to see in them the observance of a rigid noble etiquette, we may well admit that even their loose use in dignified, friendly intercourse would be more natural among members of the upper classes. The only correspondent to whom Albar applies such words is the physician Romanus,[23] who had at one time held the position of *Conde de los christianos* under the Moslem government, and whom Albar was now urging to use his influence on his behalf with the present holder of the office, Servandus.[24] The very profusion of such words here, shows they were acceptable to those in prominent position. And, in regard to Albar, though it is hard to find a clinching proof of high position, we may well agree with Baudissin [25] that the whole situation of his life suggests he was of a well-to-do and well-known family.

There is nowhere any hint of a trade or profession exercised by Albar or his forefathers, and his writings show no interest other than religion and Latin literature. But in these he was proficient, and that means that he had devoted much leisure to them; for even then Latin was a dead language to be learned painfully from books and teachers, and the ability to write a " fine style " in it was the result of long years of study. A priest would get much of this as a part of his professional training, but not so a layman. And that Albar had acquired the culture, and then was able to give himself without apparent distraction to erudite correspondence and careful composition—even to writing poor specimens of drawing-room verse—strongly hints a gentleman of assured position and easy circumstances. We know from his letter to Romanus that he, and his father before him, had some country property [26] on a part of which they had built, and seemingly

---

[23] The only other person to whom he might have applied them was John of Seville. Saul, Eulogius, and Speraindeo were clergy and were given more religious titles. The apostate Bodo could hardly expect such address.

[24] *Ep.* 9. Serenissimo omnium catholicorum summo domino meo Romano Alvarus. Ac deinde, mi sublimissime domine. . . . Quid nunc agendum est, serenissime domine?

[25] *Op. cit.,* p. 45.

[26] Cf. limites agrorum nostrorum. PL 121 :466A.

endowed, a monastery, the rest presumably remaining as a home.[27] We do not know whether he lived there or in the city; there is one indication that he had a home that was conveniently located for friends to drop in to see him, for St. Eulogius tells of going to his *atrium* to see him one day, and finding St. Aurelius there ahead of him in quest of Albar's advice about martyrdom. This passage is also interesting as showing the esteem in which Albar was held, and as it is Eulogius' fullest reference to him it may be given here in full:

> One day when I sought the atrium of our serene master Albar for a conference according to our common purpose of studying Scripture problems, for he is praised throughout the West for his knowledge of the Scriptures, I found Christ's knight, Aurelius, with him seeking advice about martyrdom, and begging to know how he might obtain an omen of martyrdom. The great doctor and our day's fountain of wisdom, basing his words in the examples of the Fathers, told him . . .[28] [29]

For schooling Albar had gone as a boy to Abbot Speraindeo, and it was there that he met and formed his lifelong friendship with Eulogius. Both men later wrote of their old teacher in

---

[27] Even after the monastery had been built, Albar has a patrimony he is unwilling to sell (haereditatem meam ne traducerem multis suggessionibus deprecavi. PL 466B) ; when he was forced to sell it he marked off the boundary of the monastery so it would be given special consideration (sed terminum ecclesiae, quem non genitor meus sed ego dederam, indicavi. PL 466C).

[28] Eulogius, *Mem. SS.,* II, c. 10, n. 18, PL 115:785A.

[29] There is an obscure passage, *Ep.* 16, n. 2, PL 484C, not hitherto brought up in connection with his wealth. Albar is expostulating with Bodo for accusing him of avarice and lust—. . . et quem scis parentum praedia reliquisse, vel opes largas, amore pecuniae dicas injectum? necnon et libidinibus arguis virum etiam conscientia castum, qui ob virginitatis studium jejunia, squalorem et oblectamenta mundialium respuit facultatum? qui enim sua dimisit, qualiter amore pecuniae aliena quaesivit? Though the text seems corrupt, and some verb like " adoptavit " seems to belong after " squalorem," the general sense is clear, and from it we might almost infer that in 840 Albar had become a monk if we had not other evidence to the contrary.

terms of highest praise.[30]　As a translation of the *Vita* is included
in this volume, it will not be necessary to repeat here the details
which it gives.　The friendship of Eulogius was perhaps Albar's
greatest treasure, and after Eulogius' maryrdom he paid him a
noble tribute; he felt towards him not only love but reverence.
But Baudissin goes too far in his belittling of Albar when he
calls him a dazzled satellite, and intimates that he thrust himself
upon Eulogius.[31]　Albar outlived his friend and wrote a *Vita* and
some verses in his honor, in which he makes no secret of his admiration and devotion.　By the nature of the case, Eulogius was
not in a position to reciprocate.　But apart from this biography,
and apart from two letters which are answers to Eulogius and
which Eulogius prefixed to his *Memoriale sanctorum* and *Documentum martyriale,* there is only a single reference, and that a
passing one,[32] to Eulogius in his writings.　Albar shows he has
other interests and other friends.　And on his part, Eulogius
shows he fully returns Albar's devotion; his letters to Albar are
very affectionate, and in each case Eulogius took the initiative in
writing; before publishing, he submitted his books to Albar for
criticism, and placed Albar's enthusiastic letters as an introduction.　There is not a shred of evidence that Eulogius found Albar's
friendship a little trying.　Each had a special respect as well as
affection for the other.　Eulogius clearly had a great esteem for
his friend's learning; Albar had a certain religious awe for
Eulogius, not merely because of his clerical status but for the
holiness of his character.　In the *Vita* Albar is at pains to show
that the privilege of martyrdom was the fitting crown of a holy
life.

---

[30] Albar: abbatem bonae recordationis et memoriae Speraindeum, opinabilem et celebritate doctrinae praeconabilem virum saepius invisebat (i.e.,
Eulogius), auditorioque more ex illius ore disertissimo dependebat. Qui
ipso tempore totius Baeticae fines prudentiae rivulis dulcorabat (*Vita,* c.
1, n. 2, PL 115:708); cf. also his letter to the Abbot (*Ep.* 7). Eulogius:
Vir disertissimus, magnum temporibus nostris Ecclesiae lumen, Speraindeo
abbas (*Mem. SS.,* I, n. 7, PL 115:745A); Senex et magister noster, atque
illustrissimus doctor . . . beatae recordationis et memoriae Speraindeo
abbas (*op. cit.,* II, c. 8, n. 9, PL 115:839C).

[31] *Op. cit.,* pp. 47f.

[32] *Ep.* 13, a part of his recrimination of Bishop Saul.

Eulogius was not alone in appreciating his friend's learning. When Albar wrote in his mature years to Speraindeo, asking him to write a controversial treatise against some heretics of the day, his former teacher replied a little querulously that Albar could have done it better himself, and the abbot submits his composition for correction before publication.[33] John of Seville, too, uses some laudatory phrases, but possibly in his case they contain an element of friendly banter.[34] But as the chief purpose of this study is to examine his learning, we need not linger on it here. It will be enough to point out, as does Flórez,[35] that in the incident already quoted in part, Albar gave Aurelius advice which showed good judgment and a knowledge of human nature, and thus justified the fact that some looked to him for guidance and leadership.[36]

While we have no direct statement of the fact, it is certain that Albar was a layman and married.[37] . Not only is there no hint of his performing clerical functions, but a number of allusions concur in pointing to the lay state. In the preface to the *Vita,* after speaking of their close union in boyhood, Albar writes, " He, adorned with the gift of the priesthood and borne aloft on the wings of virtue, flew the higher; while overcome by the mud of luxury and lust, I am still creeping along the ground." [38] The contrast here is not primarily between virtue and vice, but between two states—the celibate priesthood, and the married state. Again,

---

[33] *Ep.* 8, n. 3, PL 464.

[34] O magne domine, et sapientium multorum sapientissime . . . he begins *Ep.* 3; Cum diebus omnibus et momentis studium sapientiae vestrae, et sollicitudinem pervigilem circa utilitatem fidei Catholicae comprobaremus . . . opens *Ep.* 6.

[35] ES, XI, n. 21–22, pp. 23–24.

[36] Briefly, it was that Aurelius should consider the matter carefully, meanwhile keeping it secret; that he should try to determine whether he could face death without flinching when it should be at hand; that his motives should be pure, not the seeking of human glory. *Mem. SS.,* II, c. 10, n. 18, PL 115 :785.

[37] The seventeenth-century Bollandists argued from the fact that Albar, in the presence of Bishop Saul and Eulogius, had a deacon read a letter (*Vita,* c. 2, n. 7), that Albar had some ecclesiastical rank. Flórez shows this is another indication he was a layman (ES, XI, n. 13, pp. 17f.).

[38] *Vita,* preface, n. 1, PL 115 :707A.

at the end of his two letters, John of Seville sends his greetings
to the " ornament· of your home," [39] which can hardly mean any
but a wife,[40] unless we follow Flórez in proposing to include
daughters.[41] Another pair of obscure references are usually taken
to refer to the death of three daughters. In concluding his first
letter, John of Seville writes, " I have heard from our common
father of the death of your three girls," and adds a few words
of Christian comfort and hope. Towards the end of his next
letter Albar merely speaks of his great grief: " I have received
your letter, sad and sunk almost to hell, and I know the little
consolation a friend's writing brings to us in anguish. Tears have
made it impossible for me to answer, as we read it said by our
elders, A tale out of time is like music in mourning (Ecclus.
22: 6)." [42]

In the *Vita* we are told that while yet studying with Speraindeo,
Eulogius and Albar wrote rhythmical verses to each other and
composed volumes on Scriptural subjects beyond their depth, but
a consideration for posterity later led them to destroy them.[43]
The verses that survive are the work of Albar's mature age; they
are metrical, and so are subsequent to Eulogius' study of metrics
while in prison in 851 A. D.[44]

[39] Salutare praesumo per os vestrum omnem decorem domus vestrae
(*Ep.* 3, n. 9, PL 427A). Si ausum datis, salutamus omnem pulchritudinem
domus vestrae (*Ep.* 6, n. 10, PL 461A).

[40] Baudissin, *op. cit.,* pp. 49f., gives a Biblical parallel: Et speciei domus
dividere spolia (Ps. 67:13).

[41] ES, XI, n. 14, p. 18. John may imply more than one person by
" omnem."

[42] *Ep.* 3, n. 9, PL 427A; *Ep.* 4, n. 36, PL 447D. John's word was " trium
ancillarum vestrarum " which properly means a servant or slave; but
Albar's sorrow and John's sympathy imply rather that they were daughters, and so modern writers commonly understand them. Though dictionaries give no evidence for it, *Ancilla* may have risen in the social scale,
at least in familiar endearment. Baudissin, *op. cit.,* p. 50, suggests John
means " ancillae Domini " which would make them nuns; this is pure
hypothesis. Cf. the English " maid."

[43] *Vita,* c. 1, n. 2, PL 115:708. Ita ut volumina conderemus quae postea
aetas matura abolenda, ne in posteros remanerent, decrevit.

[44] So Traube, MGH, *Poet. lat.,* III, i, 124. The hymn to Eulogius was
of course written after 859.

It seems that the earliest written of Albar's surviving works is the correspondence with Bodo, Epistles 14–20.[45] One of these is explicitly dated 840 A. D.[46] The Frankish *Annales Bertiniani,* under the year 839, tell us the strange story of the German deacon Bodo.[47] He had been brought up from childhood at the imperial court and there had received such education as he possessed. The previous year he had received permission to make a pilgrimage to Rome and was entrusted with gifts from the emperor; but somewhere along the way he suddenly became a Jew, selling his companions into slavery—except for a nephew whom he constrained also to become a Jew. Of his motives we know nothing, unless Albar was right in implying it was concupiscence.[48] Be that as it may, the Annals go on to say that he was circumcised, let his hair and beard grow, adopted a military costume, changed his name to Eleazar, married a Jewess, and betook himself about the middle of August to Zaragoza. Some years later, in 847, the same Annals show him still in Spain, where he tried to rouse the Moslem people against the Christians, and sought to have the emir rule that all Christians should become either Moslems or Jews under pain of death. While no such decree was issued, he aroused enough trouble for the Christians to cause them to send a letter to Charles the Bald begging him to recall his former subject.[49] After this date nothing more is heard of Bodo-Eleazar. It is reasonably sure that this is Albar's correspondent in *Epistles* 14–20. Though the titles of the letters call him only Transgressor, the salutations of the first three give the name Eleazar,[50] which was the name Bodo adopted on becoming a Jew. And in the body of the letters Albar refers to his having been in the court

---

[45] A. Lukyn Williams has a short chapter on the Albar—Bodo correspondence, *Adversus Judaeos,* pp. 224ff., considering it as an example of Christian apologetic. Cf. Gams, *Kirchengesch. v. Span.,* II, ii, 316ff.

[46] *Ep.* 16, n. 6, 7, PL 488A, 489A.

[47] Ed. G. Waitz, MGH, *in usum scholarum,* pp. 17f.

[48] *Ep.* 18, n. 15, 16, PL 503f.; cf. *Ep.* 16, n. 2, PL 484.

[49] *Annal. Bertin.,* 847 A. D., pp. 35ff.

[50] E.g., Dilecto mihi Eleazaro Alvarus, *Ep.* 14, PL 478.

of the Frankish king,[51] and to his having married a Jewess.[52] And since the date of the letters, 840, is in the midst of the time Bodo was in Spain, and finally as Bodo must have been in Córdoba as the Annals tell us he tried to influence the emir, there could scarcely be anyone else who would fulfill all the conditions.

This correspondence contains seven letters, four by Albar and three by Bodo. But those by Bodo are only fragments, as long ago someone removed folios and erased lines in the codex in order to destroy Bodo's work; so his style and arguments have to be reconstructed in part from Albar's replies to them. Albar took the initiative, opening the correspondence with the most correct politeness, and even with charity, in a genuine effort to induce Bodo to return to the Church. In later epistles there are passages which are neither calm nor charitable, and we know from *Epistle* 13 to Bishop Saul that Albar had a bad temper, under the influence of which he did not weigh his words. But it seems that Albar's outbursts are the result of Bodo's provocations. Thus, while Albar's first letter was courteous, the second he opens by remonstrating against the spirit of Bodo's reply, and against his personal attacks.[53] Albar's next letter shows a shortening of temper at what he implies are additional false personal charges, this time of blasphemy, and other insults.[54] Another aspect of Bodo's letters that roused Albar to fury and to a regrettable coarseness of language, was the attacks on Jesus and Mary. The first such passage is aroused by the suggestion of a substitute for Christ;[55]

---

[51] *Ep.* 18, n. 14: dicis te in Francorum regis palatio vidisse quattuordecim viros . . . PL 503B.

[52] *Ep.* 18, n. 16, PL 504.

[53] *Ep.* 16, n. 1: Responsionis tuae, reverendissime frater, litteras legi, et praepostero ordine invectionem mihi latam probavi. Objectiones enim meae minime extenuatae existunt, nec unicuique oppositioni responsio obvia fuit; sed tantum animus in praeceps stylum blasphoemum gessit . . . (PL 483C). *Ibid.,* n. 2: Sed priusquam incipiam singulorum interpretum editiones conferre, aequumne tibi est, vir bone, ut non solum absentem, verum etiam quietudine aeterna fruentem, ita canibus morsibus lanies? etc. (PL 484C).

[54] *Ep.* 18, n. 1: Confectam mendacio, contumeliis foetidam tuam coenerosam epistolam vidimus . . . (PL 492B). *Ibid.,* n. 9: Venimus ad epilogos tuos, id est, ad maledicta tua, ubi me miserum vocas . . . (PL 499B).

[55] *Ep.* 16, n. 11, PL 490f.

a longer one, by foul attacks on our Lord and his Mother.[56] As we see Bodo through the medium of Albar's rebuttals, we are prepared to believe Albar's further statements of his bad character.[57] Bodo was an ornament of neither the Christian nor the Jewish religion.[58] The final exchange of letters between them, *Epistles* 19 and 20, is short and vituperative. The reason for mentioning this unpleasant aspect of these letters here is to extenuate Albar's evident shortcomings; we have his letters in full, and only the briefest excerpts from Bodo's, and a rapid reader might not notice that Albar's lapses were reactions against earlier offenses on the part of his correspondent.

The constructive part of Albar's argument is an honest effort to prove from the Old Testament that Jesus was the expected Messias. However he does not use the kind of fulfilment of prophecy that is pointed out in the Gospels. Rather he begins by calculating chronology from the weeks of Daniel, showing that the Messias was to come about the time of Jesus; and again he is at pains to show that Jewish princes continued until our Lord's time, but that there has been none after, in fulfilment of a verse in the blessing of the patriarch Jacob (Gen. 49: 10). A number of other points come up, ending with many quotations from the Old Testament about the sin, the blindness, and the rejection of Israel. Presumably in preparing his arguments Albar leaned heavily upon patristic material; indeed, Bodo's parting thrust was that Albar was only a compiler, and in his final sentence Albar scarcely denies it.[59]

The exchange of letters between Albar and Speraindeo, *Epistles*

---

[56] *Ep.* 18, n. 10–12, PL 500ff.

[57] *Ep.* 16, n. 2: Tu vero, mi frater, quomodo alium incusare non dubitas in rem quam tibi abundasse in dogmate nostro omnibus clamitas, ita ut passim per diversarum feminarum concubitus in templo nostro te glories dulces tibi habuere complexus. (PL 484D. Cf. *Ep.* 18, n. 16).

[58] There is nothing to show that in his activity in Spain Bodo spoke for the Jewish community, or for anyone but himself.

[59] *Ep.* 19: tu qui compilator es (PL 512D). *Ep.* 20: Et ideo noli canes rabidos dicere, sed te vulpeum gannientem cognosce; neque me compilatorem veterum, quod magnarum est virium, asseras. (PL 514A).

7 and 8,[60] offers little or nothing to help us fix a date.[61] They must be earlier than 853, for in writing the passion of Flora and Mary Eulogius speaks of Speraindeo as already dead.[62] Albar here asks his former teacher to write a treatise against some unnamed heretics whom Baudissin [63] would identify with the Cassianists condemned in the Council of Córdoba in 839,[64] thus placing these letters sometime before the Council. However, as Baudissin says in another place,[65] Albar's description of their heresy may come to no more, if we discount the violence of his language, than to a determined distinction of the two natures in Christ,[66] and so be akin to the adoptianism of the late eighth century. As there is a trace of this in John of Seville a little later, no ground is left for placing these letters before the Council of 839.[67]

---

[60] These two letters are also printed PL 115:859–861, with two fragments of Speraindeo's writings cols. 962–966.

[61] So Traube, MGH, *Poet. lat.*, III, i, 122, n. 1.

[62] *Mem. SS.*, II, c. 8, n. 9, PL 115:839C. This latter part of Bk. II of *Mem. SS.* was written not before 853, and not later than 856 when the whole work, including Bk. III was complete; cf. Flórez, ES, XI, p. 38. Flórez has a fuller discussion of the composition of *Mem. SS.*, ES, X, 434ff.

[63] *Op. cit.*, pp. 43f.; also Pérez de Urbel, *San Eulogio*, p. 144.

[64] The acta are published, ES, XV, the unnumbered pp. at beginning.

[65] *Op. cit.*, p. 71.

[66] Spanish theology continued to use Christological formulas which had earlier been common in the West, but which were becoming archaic, and in which there was latent a certain tendency towards adoptianism (cf. Amann, *L'époque carolingienne*, pp. 132f.). This might crop out here or there in a virulent form, perhaps mixed with other errors, as in the Cassianists. But Albar does not mention the special, crude, disciplinary errors which characterized the Cassianists; while the Council of Córdoba does not accuse these heretics of any Trinitarian or Christological heresy.

[67] The following passage occurs near the end of Speraindeo's letter (PL 464A): Quidquid enim absque norma veritatis paternitas ibidem praesenserit domni nostri, vestri genitoris, mox illud emendet velocitas scriptoris; et me iterum clam instruat, ut olim fecit alios, gratia vestri honoris, et celet inscium atque ignarum vestra solertia cordis ita ut errorem nemo sentiat foris. At the close, "vestra solertia cordis" surely refers to Albar, and modern writers who mention the passage as displaying the abbot's humility, assume that the whole sentence applies to Albar, and that it was he who was to correct the abbot's composition (thus Gomez Bravo, *op. cit.*, I, 118; Flórez, ES, XI, 5). But how can the earlier phrase, "paternitas

Before taking up Albar's correspondence with John of Seville, it will be necessary to make an excursus on Eulogius' trip to Navarre. Albar tells of this in the *Vita*,[68] and refers us to the fuller account that Eulogius himself gave in his bread-and-butter letter to Bishop Wiliesind.[69] Two of Eulogius' brothers, Alvar and Isidore, were merchants, and had journeyed north into the Frankish Empire. After a time Eulogius set out in search of them, but border wars prevented him from crossing into France. In Catalonia a certain William was, with the aid of the emir Abd ar-Rahman II, conducting a war against Charles the Bald. Turning west along the Pyrenees, Eulogius found the frontier from Navarre blocked by another local war of Count Sancho Sanchez. So he resigned himself to visiting Bishop Wiliesind of Pamplona and a number of monasteries in the neighborhood. Besides making acquaintances which he remembered with pleasure afterward, he was given a number of valuable books which were not at that time available in Córdoba—St. Augustine's *City of God*, Vergil's *Aeneid*, Horace, and Juvenal among them. It is this literary treasure trove that has caught the interest of modern non-Spanish writers, and leads them to mention this trip more than any other part of Eulogius' life; Eulogius himself was perverse enough, judging from his letter, to be more interested in what he saw of the Church in free Spain and in the holy men he met there.[70]

. . . domni nostri, vestri genitoris," be reconciled with this? The "vestri genitoris" clearly refers to Albar's father; and the use of the third person in the verbs praesenserit, emendet, instruat, and fecit, points to the same conclusion. Nothing is known of the date of Albar's father's death, so this would give no more help in dating these letters than to suggest Albar himself is not yet an old man. But if this interpretation is true, it throws a little additional light upon the Latin culture of the Mozarabs. The father also was trained in it, and was competent in Speraindeo's judgment to criticize and correct his treatise; indeed, he had performed a similar service for others. Albar would not then be a singular figure, but a member of a family in which such interests and training were hereditary, even for the laymen. And again, it would be another indication that Albar belonged to the gentry or aristocracy.

[68] C. 3, n. 9, PL 115:712.

[69] PL 115:845–852.

[70] Baudissin (*Eulog. u. Alvar*, pp. 90ff.; also "Eulogius," Herzog's *Realencyklopädie*, V, 595), followed by some others, keeps insinuating that

It is the date of this trip that concerns us at the present. Morales at first placed it in 839, then altered it to 840,[71] and his influence has led others to accept this dating. Recently Millares Carlo [72] and Urbel [73] have placed it in 845. However Gomez Bravo [74] made the historical background quite clear, and he has been followed by Flórez [75] and most later writers.[76] The rebel William mentioned by Eulogius was the son of the Marquis Bernard and his wife Dhuoda. Bernard had been restless and ambitious, and in frequent hostility to the Carolingian emperors. Finally he was captured, and Charles the Bald had him condemned to death in May 844.[77] It was only after this that the youthful William began to follow in his father's footsteps as a rebel, and so Morales' date is already impossible. In June 844 Pepin II of Aquitaine won a battle against Charles the Bald, William being among the nobles of the Midi who aided Pepin.[78] After some negotiations,

---

Eulogius had a political motive in making the trip, namely, to arouse the Franks to drive the Moslems out of Spain and free the Christians there from their yoke. This is a gratuitous assumption with no evidence to offer in support. On the other hand, both Eulogius and Albar give a sufficient motive in the search for the overdue brothers; and when finally on his return trip Eulogius gets news of them (*Ep. ad Wiliesind*, n. 6), he seems satisfied. Again, while he was in Navarre, which was a part of free Christian Spain, his visits were not to political leaders, but to the bishop and monasteries. Finally, in their writings neither Eulogius nor Albar gives any indication of hoping or planning for any violent riddance of the Moslem power, however much they would doubtless have rejoiced at it.

[71] *Corónica general*, VII, 393–396.

[72] *Nuevos estudios*, p. 94.

[73] *San Eulogio*, pp. 155f.

[74] *Catál. obisp. Córd.*, I, 121f.

[75] ES, X, 443–445.

[76] The best recent political historians give the same date as Flórez: Cotarelo y Valledor, *Hist. Alfonso III el Magno*, p. 137; Léonce Auzias, *L'Aquitaine caroling.*, pp. 259ff.

[77] Auzias, *op. cit.*, pp. 187f. The *Annales Bertiniani*, ed Waitz, MGH, *in usum scholarum*, p. 30, gives the following under 844: Bernardus comes marcae Hispanicae, iam dudum grandia moliens summisque inhians, maiestatis reus Francorum iudicio, iussu Karoli in Aquitania capitalem sententiam subiit.

[78] Auzias, *op. cit.*, p. 209.

Charles was forced to make an unfavorable peace with Pepin at Saint-Benoît-sur-Loire in June 845. Nothing is known of William during the next three years; but it was a period of external peace during which Pepin enjoyed his position as a sovereign king independent of Charles, while Charles was busy diplomatically trying to get the help of his brothers, the friendly Ludwig and the hostile Lothar.[79] In 847 the Emir Abd ar-Rahman II sent ambassadors to Charles to establish peace between them.[80] In 848 Charles took preliminary military steps against Pepin; but it was only in the summer of 849 that the full invasion began, leading to the speedy capture of Toulouse.[81] The *Annales Bertiniani* now bring William back into the light; the entry for 848 tells us that William broke into warfare and by guile seized Ampurias and Barcelona; the entry for 850 completes the story: " William, son of Bernard, by trickery seized Counts Aledramnus and Isembardus in the Spanish March; but he himself was captured with greater guile, and put to death in Barcelona." [82] After taking Toulouse, Charles moved in October 849 to Narbonne to prevent William's rebellion from spreading north of the Pyrenees. Auzias cites an Arab chronicler to show that Saracens aided William in this rebellion.[83]

Conditions in Gascony and Navarre at this period are very obscure; however, in June 850 two nobles of Navarre are known to have gone to Charles to make peace.[84] This sketch of political events shows how well the story of Eulogius' journey fits into Frankish history. The truce between Pepin and Charles from 845 to 848, and the peace between Charles and Abd ar-Rahman made in 847 would give Eulogius reason to believe that a journey into the Frankish Empire was possible. If he started in 848, he could reach Catalonia after William had burst into action; the trip

---

[79] *Ibid.*, pp. 218–249.

[80] *Annal. Bertin.*, p. 34.

[81] Auzias, *op. cit.*, pp. 249–259.

[82] *Op. cit.*, pp. 36, 38. The story here separated under the years 848 and 850 is told completely under 849 in the *Fragmentum chronici Fontanellensis,* Bouquet, VII, 40–43; Pertz reprinted Bouquet's text in MGH, *Scriptores,* II, 301–304.

[83] *Op. cit.*, p. 261, n. 39.

[84] *Ibid.*, pp. 263f.

probably lasted several months, and he would have returned home at the end of 848 or in 849.[85]

With the date of Eulogius' northern journey fixed, we can come to Albar's correspondence with John of Seville, which took place subsequent to the journey. It consists of the first six letters of the collection, and together they are half again as long as the correspondence with Bodo. Though controversial, they are very different in tone, as Albar and John were personal friends. The correspondence grew out of a conversation they had;[86] Albar had disagreed with John on an important theological question, and John had objected to Albar's attitude toward rhetoric. Since their meeting, Albar has looked up authorities and now comes to the charge with a salvo of quotations. Thus opened, the correspondence continues with more quotations and less reasoned argument than in the letters to Bodo.

Like Albar, John was a married layman of literary tastes and attainments.[87] He was notably older than Albar.[88] It would

---

[85] On the other hand, Urbel's suggestion of 845–46 is less probable. We have no knowledge of William at that time, but it was a time of peace when it would be less likely for a single noble to enter into hostility against Charles. Urbel chose the earlier date because Eulogius says the Moslems aided William, and Urbel pointed to the treaty of peace of 847. However Auzias shows they did in fact help William at the later time.

[86] Ep. I, n. I: quae vobiscum verbo tenus disputavi, penes me in magnorum virorum volumina disquisivi; et quae de his invenire potui, manu propria ipse in procincto conscripsi. PL 413B.

[87] As in Albar's case, a proof that he was married is found in the greeting sent to his wife: Opto per te decorem domus vestrae salutare (*Ep.* 2, n. 3). In the past there has been some confusion about John's identity. An early chronicler speaks of a Bishop John of Seville who was an Arabic scholar and wrote commentaries on Scripture in that language. Again, one of the signatures to the acts of the Council of Córdoba in 839 is: "Joannes Ispalensis sedis epis. et metrop. haec statuta subscripsi." Nicolas Antonio (*Bibliotheca hisp. vet.*, I, first ed., p. 355, second ed., p. 483f.) suggested the possibility of identifying the Arabic-writing bishop with Albar's friend, and since then various authors have spoken of Albar's John as a bishop (e.g., Baudissin, *op. cit.*, p. 43; L. Serrano, *Revista arch. bibl. y mus.*, XXIV [1911], 494). But the only reason for identifying them is that both lived in Seville and bore the name John. Albar's friend shows no interest in Arabic, but much in Latin; and more interest in rhetoric than

seem that the two men had some sort of family connections, probably being brothers-in-law. Each of them in writing to the other
speaks of their common father, Albar adding the fact that his
name also was John.[89] It does not seem likely they would speak
in this way if they were blood-brothers; brothers-in-law is more
probable.[90] Albar had other kinsmen in Seville,[91] the lady Froisinda and her children, " rich in wheat," perhaps being among
them.[92] Writers sometimes speak of John as a grammarian or
rhetorician;[93] if these terms are taken in the old professional
sense, the evidence at hand is not enough to justify them, but it
does point to what appears to be his cast of mind, whatever his
vocation may have been. As we shall see later, his greatest in-
interest in the correspondence seems to be to defend the value of
Latin rhetoric against Albar's moderate disparagement. And on
his part, Albar calls him " chief of Roman dialectic," and alludes
unfavorably to " your grammarians." [94]

It is difficult to determine the date of this group of letters.
There are three hints which offer a foothold for investigation.
The one that caught the attention of earlier scholars is a refer-
ence to an otherwise unknown Bishop Teudula, presumably of

---

in Scripture; and he was married. After all, John is not an uncommon
name.

[88] Albar writes to him: crede mihi, frater, imo aetate pater, *Ep.* 5, n. 2,
PL 450B.

[89] Albar to John: Patrem nostrum communem domnum Joannem salutari
expecto (*Ep.* 2, n. 3). John to Albar: De trium vero ancillarum vestrarum migratione ex ore patris communis audivi integre (*Ep.* 3, n. 9).

[90] Flórez, ES, XI, 35: Baudissin, *op. cit.,* p. 50, n. 2; Pérez Urbel, *op.
cit.,* p. 95.

[91] *Ep.* 2, n. 3: omnemque cognationem nostram vice nostra osculato. PL
420A.

[92] John sends her greetings to Albar: Salutat vos domna Froisinda cum
filiis suis, sani et incolumes, et tritici multitudine locupletes. *Ep.* 3, n. 9,
PL 427B.

[93] E.g., Baudissin, *op. cit.,* pp. 65f.; Lambert, " Bachiarius," *DHGE,* VI,
66.

[94] *Ep.* 4, n. 3: Audi ergo vir prudentissime, et Romanae dialecticae
caput . . . (PL 428B). *Ep.* 5, n. 4: . . . nec vestri potuerunt scire gram-
matici . . . (PL 451B). *Ep.* 4, n. 24: . . . tibi tanto et tali viro scientia
et liberalibus artibus inlustrato . . . (PL 441C).

Seville.[95] Taken in its context, Albar's reference means that Teudula was active against Elipandus' adoptianism, which raged during the last fifteen years of the eighth century. Assuming that "requisitus" implied the bishop was still living, it was necessary to place this correspondence fairly early, so Gomez Bravo located it between 820 and 830,[96] Flórez about 830,[97] and Baudissin sometime before 839, when the acts of the Council of Córdoba show that a John was Metropolitan of Seville.[98] But as Traube says,[99] far from implying that Teudula was still alive, Albar's "nunc requisitus" means that he is now dead and his absence regretted; this is borne out by the context which says in effect: Back in the time when the savage fury of Elipandus lay waste our province, your Bishop Teudula, now regretted, after writing much on the nature of Christ, summarized his teaching as follows. . . . This removes the only reason for holding to so early a date for these letters. Traube then points to two places which make use of two of the books which Eulogius obtained in a monastery of Navarre

---

[95] *Ep.* 4, n. 27: vester nunc requisitus episcopus Teudula post multa et varia de proprietate Christi veneranda eloquia . . . (PL 443D).

[96] *Op. cit.,* I, 115.

[97] ES, XI, 37f.

[98] *Op. cit.,* p. 43, n. 3. Baudissin (p. 69) thinks *Epp.* 5 and 6 were written a decade later than *Epp.* 1 to 4, for he thinks John's notice of Mahomet (*Ep.* 6, n. 9) is dependent upon the one that Eulogius discovered in Navarre and reproduced in his *Liber apologeticus* (n. 15, 16, PL 115:859f). (The *Lib. apolog.* narrates martyrdoms of 857, and so was written 857–859.) Possibly this is true, and if so, it would strengthen the arguments for accepting the position of Traube, to be advanced next. But weakening the probative force of the passage on Mahomet are the following considerations: 1). It comes from John in Seville, not from Albar who ought to have immediate access to Eulogius in Córdoba; 2). While the texts are similar, and in places identical, in other places they differ; and the form given in Eulogius is more than five times as long, including much of interest we should expect John and Albar to want to keep if they knew it; 3). Flórez says (ES, XI, 36) that such notices on the beginning and end of Mahomet are common in ancient chronicles. Hence we may infer that even though the two texts are related, it is not necessary that John is indebted to Eulogius for it.

[99] MGH, *Poet. lat.,* III, ii, 122, n. 1.

and brought back to Córdoba in 848 or 849.[100] This seems conclusive. The writing of the six letters was spread out over some time, perhaps many months, for Albar complains of John's slowness in answering, and in apologizing, John asserts he " would have written seven weeks ago if . . ." But they must be given a date which would allow Albar time to have read and learned phrases of the *Aeneid* before he composed the fourth letter. Thus they cannot be before 849. On the other hand they are probably not much later, for there is no hint of persecution or of martyrdoms; they have an air of academic calm, not of the nervous excitement of later years. As June 3, 851 was the day of the death of St. Isaac, the first of the voluntary martyrs, and the beginning of a period of unusual excitement which lasted until after the martyrdom of St. Eulogius in 859, it seems likely the correspondence with John was completed before June 851. Apart from these six letters, we know nothing of John or of Albar's connections with Seville.

---

[100] *Ep.* 4, n. 10 quotes the *Aeneid; Ep.* 5, n. 7 twice cites *The City of God.*

CHAPTER II

THE LATER YEARS

It is no part of this study to retell the story of the Cordovan martyrs. But it is necessary to say a few words of explanation of the movement in order to place some of Albar's works in their setting. Legally, the Christians enjoyed freedom of worship, but this was with certain limitations. They were allowed to keep and use those churches which the Moslems had not confiscated for use as mosques;[1] but they were not allowed to build new ones or repair the old, so that in time the churches would fall into ruin. This law was not always strictly enforced, and the Christians were able to make improvements; however the law remained, and any emir could put it into execution, as did Mahomet when he came to the throne in 852.[2] Again, the emir usurped some control over the appointment of bishops,[3] and men were chosen for other than their Christian qualifications; Recafred of Seville was not admirable, Hostegesis of Malaga and Samuel of Elvira were scandalous, Saul of Córdoba was not unblemished, while on the other hand it was presumably the emir who prevented Eulogius' consecration to Toledo. Another law that worked much harm was the prohibition under pain of death for a Moslem to become a Christian. This meant that the many Christians who in a moment of weakness apostatized to Islam, and later repented, were unable to return to the Church; it also meant that children of mixed marriages were unable to profess Christianity. This law made martyrdom possible at any time. Many of the unfortunate renegades lived publicly as Moslems while they tried to remain Christians in the secrecy of their homes. But if at any time they

---

[1] Cf. Dozy, *Hist. Musulm. Esp.*, I, 280–283. For a study of this topic in general, but with only passing references to Spain, cf. A. S. Tritton, *The Caliphs and Their Non-Muslim Subjects*, London, 1930.

[2] Eulog., *Mem. SS.*, III, 3. *Ind. lum.*, n. 7: dum ecclesiae Dei destruuntur, et antiqua soliditate templa firmata terratenus coaequantur. PL 522A.

[3] Dozy, *loc. cit.*

or their children, through conscience or accident, let their Christian faith be known, it meant death.   There were martyrs of this kind both before and after [4] the years with which we are concerned, and many of the martyrs of the 850's were secret Christians of this kind who at last made a public profession of their faith, as they were bound to do by Christian teaching.

Just as hard to endure was the hostility of the Moslem populace, with its mingled contempt and hatred.   When feeling rose, sticks and stones as well as names were hurled at the clergy, whose special dress marked them as Christians.   It was this popular hatred rather than any action of the government which brought about the death of St. Perfectus April 18, 850,[5] and the near-death of the merchant John.[6]   The next year St. Isaac began a series of a different kind: those who voluntarily sought martyrdom by going to the magistrates and publicly proclaiming their Christian faith and condemning Mahomet.   Feeling ran high; the more enthusiastic party of the Christians supplied fifty martyrs in the course of the next few years—some, secret Christians who published their faith; some, Christians who spontaneously sought death.[7]   The government was disturbed; it preferred the Church to suffer an unobtrusive and unprotested strangulation, and it caused a council of bishops to forbid the voluntary martyrdoms, it imprisoned many of the clergy, and did what it could to end the movement.   An important part of the Christians also objected bitterly to what they believed was the fanaticism of their fellow-churchmen, which was bringing increased pressure and hostility upon all.

Albar and Eulogius gave their full support to the movement. They did not originate it; it seems to have been a spontaneous outgrowth from the reaction of the Christians to their general religious situation, and to the death of Perfectus.   This latter had

---

[4] E.g., SS. Adulfus and John, martyred at Córdoba Sept. 27, 824 (*Mem. SS.*, II, 8; Férotin, *Lib. ordinum,* pp. 480f). San Pelayo or Pelagius, 925 A. D.; Argentea, 931 A. D.

[5] *Mem. SS.*, II, 1.

[6] *Ind. lum.*, n. 5.

[7] Eulogius wrote the passions of those who died before him in his *Mem. SS.* and *Lib. apologeticus.*

roused the zeal of the more fervent, and Eulogius and Albar quickly lent the movement their support. For a moment in its early period Eulogius seems to have wavered; but Albar encouraged him,[8] and thereafter both were wholeheartedly behind the movement. It is impossible to say how great their influence was in stimulating the martyrs, or how long the fervor might have lasted without them. We know these years only in their own writings, and so usually assume that they were the heart and soul of the movement. But as far as we can tell from Eulogius' narratives of the martyrs, only a minority of them had any personal contact with Eulogius, and still fewer with Albar. Both wrote books to justify voluntary martyrdom against the attacks of those they considered weak brethren, and undoubtedly they and their writings were influential.

Not only in their time but in ours has there been a strong difference of opinion about the martyrs of those years.[9] The arguments against voluntary martyrdom are sufficiently clear not to need underlining. From the earliest times the normal teaching of the Church has been opposed to it, and the Fathers and early councils denounced it.[10] On the other hand, Albar is able to claim the example of some early saints,[11] and Eulogius names Felix of Gerona, Sebastian, Thyrsus, Hadrian, Justus and Pastor, Eulalia of Barcelona, and Babylas.[12] The Bollandist, Père Delehaye, says that all the writers of the early Church condemned voluntary martyrdom in principle; but once a man had courageously suffered

---

[8] Letter of Eulog. to Albar prefixed to *Doc. mart.*, PL 115:819A.

[9] E.g., Baudissin; Dozy, *op. cit.*, I, 317–362; Levi-Provençal, *Esp. musul.*, pp. 33ff. are opposed to them as fanatics. Flórez, ES, X, 340–351 gives the defence, as do most Spanish writers.

[10] Cf. Augustine, *Tractatus 51 in Joannem*, n. 10, PL 35:1767; Leclercq, "Martyr," *DACL*, X, ii, 2381–84. On the other hand, Isidore, *Sentent.*, I, 23 (PL 83:590f) would give support to Eulogius and Albar.

[11] *Ind. lum.*, n. 3: Legite sanctorum martyrum diversorum passionum agones, agmina Domini praeliantes, verbi gladio hostes Domini detruncantes, et liquide videbitis multos ultronee prosilisse; non expectantes persecutorum jussa nec delatorum decipula, furentium intentata, sed ad exemplum Domini spontanea propria grata offerentes libamina, seque super altare Christi Dei aeterni cruore sacratum adportantes hostiam puram. PL 517.

[12] *Mem. SS.*, I, 24.

and died, he was generally, and even by these same authors, honored as a holy martyr.[13]

Since to appreciate Albar and Eulogius it is necessary to have at least some sympathy with the martyrs of Córdoba, it may be well to say à word in their defence. They were not seeking death for its own sake, nor merely as a speedy way of gaining heaven. Judging from the remaining records, they viewed it as an emergency measure for an emergency situation. The Moslem world, both government and people, was gradually closing down upon the remnant of the Christians, crushing them.[14] In face of this, we may see in voluntary marytrdom a twofold purpose: it was a militant affirmation of Christian faith against an overpowering Islam; and it was meant to exert a moral pressure on the Moslem government, somewhat parallel to modern hunger-strikes and campaigns of non-resistance. The Cordovan Christians of those years either did not hope for, or did not think of, relief by war or rebellion. Others, Christian and Moslem, tried rebellions at frequent intervals; but there is no evidence that these had in their mind the political overthrow of the Moslem power. This was a

---

[13] *Sanctus,* pp. 166–169; *Origines du culte des martyrs,* p. 21. Prospero Lambertini (Benedict XIV), *De servorum Dei beatificatione . . . ,* III, 167–182, (Lib. III, c. 16), discusses Eulogius and the Cordovan martyrs with approval on the ground that voluntary martyrdom is praiseworthy when the faith would be endangered by continued silence. He gives the derogatory name " conciliabulum " to the council of bishops which, at the emir's instigation, met in Córdoba in 852 and condemned the martyr movement.

[14] Cf. Dozy: En d'autres termes, il arriva en Espagne ce qui arriva dans tous les pays que les Arabes avaient conquis: leur domination, de douce et humaine qu'elle avait été au commencement, dégénéra en un despotisme intolérable. Dès le IXème siècle, les conquérants de la Péninsule suivaient à la lettre le conseil du calife Umar, qui avait dit assez crûment: " Nous devons manger les chrétiens et nos descendants doivent manger les leurs tant que durera l'islamisme." *Hist. Musulm. Esp.* I, 282f. So also A. S. Tritton: Though *dhimmis* (Christians) might enjoy great prosperity, yet always they lived on suffrance, exposed to the caprices of the ruler and the passions of the mob. . . . But in later times the position of the *dhimmis* did change for the worse. They were much more liable to suffer from the violence of the crowd, and the popular fanaticism was accompanied by an increasing strictness among the educated. *The Caliphs and Their Non-Muslim Subjects,* p. 232.

religious movement, using spiritual means to gain a spiritual end. They did not succeed in obtaining any notable alleviation of the Moslem yoke, and they did succeed in pushing some weak Christians into apostasy to avoid persecution. Yet they strengthened the faith of others; their memory was cherished in Córdoba, and they were honored as saints by Spanish Christians of the free north as well as of the subject south; [15] and their spirit helped sustain the struggle of Christendom against Islam for a long time to come. Even today all their names are included in the Roman Martyrology.

Little is known of Albar's course of action during the decade of martyrdoms. From his two exchanges of letters with Eulogius we know he encouraged him with all the vehemence of his own nature. Again, the *Vita* [16] shows Albar supplying to Eulogius the hint to stop saying Mass in order, as he thought, to avoid being in communion with the Erastian Reccafred. If this latter action seems rather extreme and far-fetched, Eulogius records an episode from which we get a more favorable impression of his judgment.[17] When St. Aurelius consulted him about seeking martyrdom, Albar advised him to think carefully of the matter, to be sure that his motive was good, to try to foresee whether, as death should draw near, he would be able to stand firm; and in the meantime, to keep the matter secret. It was presumably in harmony with Albar's counsel that this group of martyrs chose an entirely unobjectionable way of winning the death sentence: being secret Christians, they merely went publicly to Church, thereby making known that they had lapsed from Islam. Neither Albar nor Eulogius was himself a voluntary martyr. The *Vita* shows that Eulogius firmly persevered in doing his duty; but it was only when doing his duty led to his arrest by the police that he was sentenced to death. Earlier he had written that martyrdom was a high honor of which he felt unworthy, and he waited for God's

---

[15] Cf. The Mozarabic calendars printed by Férotin, *Lib. Ordinum*, pp. 450ff. Also, the translation of Eulogius' relics to Oviedo in 884 (Flórez, ES, X, 457; Cotarelo y Vallador, *Hist. Alfonso III*, pp. 287–291). They were returned to Córdoba in 1737 (Flórez, *ibid.*, p. 459).

[16] C. 2, n. 7.

[17] *Mem. SS.*, II, c. 10, n. 18, PL 115:285A–C.

providence to bring him to the scaffold. Of Albar we can only say that the very fact that the circumstances of his death are unknown makes it unlikely he was a martyr. Yet, amid all the self-recrimination of the *Vita* and the *Confessio*, there is no hint that he feels himself a coward for not rushing to the scaffold. These facts, together with Albar's advice to Aurelius, should make us cautious in condemning the two men as fanatics; they approved and supported the movement, but not as a wave of excited mass emotion; it was for heroic volunteers acting after prudent thought and prayer. There was no shame in not stepping forward; the only disgrace was through fear for one's own safety to disown and attack the heroes of the faith.

LETTERS TO EULOGIUS

So far as we know, the first works written by Albar in this period are two letters to Eulogius. Both in manuscripts and editions the things Albar wrote for Eulogius appear with Eulogius's works, not with those of Albar.[18] The letters were written in 851. The death of St. Isaac led to a wave of great enthusiasm among the Christians of Córdoba, and he was quickly followed by several other voluntary martyrs. Thereupon Bishop Saul, his clergy, and some of the laity, were thrown into prison. Eulogius improved his time there by completing the first part of his *Memoriale sanctorum,*[19] defending the martyr movement and chronicling its first heroes, and in writing the smaller *Documentum martyriale* to encourage his fellow prisoners, Flora and Mary. From prison he sent both of these to Albar for correction and approval, and for each Albar wrote back a little rhetorical letter of high praise. These replies of Albar were both written while Eulogius was still in prison,[20] that is, before November 29, 851, when the clergy were released.[21]

---

[18] Letter for *Mem. SS.*, PL 115:734-36; that for *Doc. mart., ibid,* 819f.

[19] I.e., Bk. I, and Bk. II, cc. 1-6; cf. Flórez, ES, X, 432ff.

[20] Albar's letter prefixed to *Mem. SS.*: et inter saeva claustra et arcta custodiae verbum regni serens, feliciori polles victoria. PL 115:736C. His letter prefixed to *Doc. mart:* Peto autem ut in alio quaternione apertiori manu illis sororibus scribatur. *Ibid.,* 820C. Flora and Mary were martyred Nov. 24, 851.

[21] *Mem. SS.,* II, c. 8, n. 16, PL 115:842C.

These little notes show us that Albar's admiration for Eulogius was just as great in his lifetime as it was after his death; and they express a very exaggerated opinion of the literary excellence of Eulogius' writings—they are greater than Livy, Cato, Demosthenes, Cicero, and Quintilian, nay, even inspired by the Holy Ghost. They are examples of Albar's own style at its most florid.

INDICULUS LUMINOSUS

Albar's most extensive composition is the *Indiculus luminosus* which he wrote in 854 [22] to defend the martyrs against the hostile clamor of those Christians who wanted to avoid for themselves the additional persecution that was the first Moslem reaction to the martyrs. For this same purpose Eulogius had written the first book of his *Memoriale sanctorum* [23] in 851, and would later write the *Liber apologeticus* in 857 or 858. Albar's work is more ambitious than either of those of Eulogius, and even so, we have only half of what Albar planned; for he promised [24] a second book that would bring together passages from the " doctors " to confirm what he had himself said in the first book. This second book is unknown in modern times, and it may be assumed that it was never written, for the copyist of the Cordovan codex had more leaves at the end of his volume [25] and could hardly have failed to copy a second book if he had known it.

The enigmatic title means that the author intends his book to be a bright light showing that Mahomet was a precursor of Antichrist, and that it is the duty of Christians to oppose him by every means. It is in Albar's characteristic style—ornate, and sometimes obscure; but it has all his fire. After an opening prayer

---

[22] *Ind. lum.*, n. 21, PL 121 :536C.

[23] The first book of this work is an argued defence of the martyrs; the second and third consist largely of chapters narrating the passions of the several martyrs.

[24] *Op. cit.*, n. 21: ac in secundo libello doctorum sententias congregemus, nostrasque operosas, fabellas (Flórez: favillas?) veracium stellatione firmemus. PL 535B. Cf. n. 1: Et quam haec universalis sit nostra credulitas, in secundo huius operis libro majorum firmavit auctoritas. PL 516A. Cf. also n. 11, PL 527B.

[25] The *Ind. lum.* ends on fol. 164v; the codex continues to fol. 208. Artiles, *Rev. bibl. arch. mus.*, IX (1932), 212–215.

much in the spirit of the *Confessio,* and an exordium which warns
that he intends to be a dog barking for the Lord (Isaias 56: 10),
he comes to the onset:

> But there are some unworthy to be fervent, frigid in
> their love for the faith, terrified with an earthly fear of
> a swordstroke, who with no subdued voice but with
> raucous throat, with distended mouth, and with a con-
> torted tongue disparage and revile with unbecoming in-
> sults the martyr movement of our time; and are willing,
> as far as in them lies, to give the palm of victory to the
> devil.[26]

After this emphatic beginning, he assures the reader that he wishes
to discuss the matter not haughtily, though firmly, as with brethren.

The contents of the surviving book fall into two parts. The
first (nn. 2–20) is somewhat loosely constructed, moving back and
forth as his passionate arguing leads him. The main thought is
that it is the duty of Christians to publish the truth of the Gospel.
Our Lord said that the Gospel must first be preached to all
peoples before the end could come, and Albar doubts if the
descendants of Ishmael have yet heard the preaching. It is not
at all necessary that everyone be converted; many will not be;
but all peoples must hear it. It is this proclamation which the
martyrs are making, and which the timid Christians who oppose
them are trying to hamper. These unworthy members of the
Church say there was no persecution until the headstrong fanatics
stirred up trouble. To this Albar replies that persecutions are
the result of Christian teaching: the heathen do not persecute us
until we reveal to them the unwelcome truth, so that it is a normal
concomitant of the Church in a sinful world. If there was no
persecution, it was a proof of our compromising half-heartedness.
But there *was* a persecution, and Albar points to Perfectus and
John, and to Moslem oppression; and now a part of the sufferings
you complain of is God's punishment for your sinful cowardice
in opposing the heroes of the faith.

The latter part of the book (nn. 21–35) is somewhat more

---

[26] *Ind. lum,* n. 2, PL 516B.

systematic, seeking to prove that Mahomet fulfils some of the
Old Testament prophecies of Antichrist. Albar uses Daniel
(nn. 21ff.) and Job (nn. 26–31), following St. Gregory's *Moralia*
for the interpretation of Behemoth and Leviathan. Albar does
not think Mahomet was himself Antichrist—he will appear only
at the end—but the prophecies have a meaning for every age, and
have various partial fulfilments, so Mahomet is a forerunner of
the final Antichrist. Along the way Albar points to some specific
contrasts between Christianity and Islam (n. 33), and denounces
Mahomet for his lust, both in his life and in his notion of Para-
dise (nn. 23ff.). The Christians of Spain had no love for Islam,
and their conception of Mahomet was perhaps truer ontologically
than historically.[27] In the closing section Albar points to certain
fulfilments of the prophecies of St. John in the Apocalypse: some
Mozarabs by their compromises with Islam—adoption of circum-
cision, use of Arabic names and clothes, seeking for wealth and
position in the Moslem state, accepting Arabic culture [28]—bear
upon them the mark of the beast. The ending is abrupt, showing
that a second book was planned.

There can be no valid doubt about the authenticity of this work,
though in the codex it does not happen to have a title or Albar's
name affixed to it.[29] However it is given together with his other
writings, and is entirely in his style. But it will be well to mention the fact that Ambrosio de Morales, the first editor of
Eulogius, did doubt it for a while, and that his influence misled a
few others. He gave two reasons for thinking Albar did not
write it: that it contains no mention of Eulogius, though it treats
subjects in which the saint was deeply concerned,[30] and that Albar
would not have written this when only three years earlier Eulogius
had treated the same subject in the first book of the *Memoriale
sanctorum*.[31] But these were weak negative arguments; a mention

---

[27] Eulogius fully agrees with Albar; cf. *Mem. SS.*, I, 7; II, 16, 2;
Doc. mart., n. 15; *Lib. apol.*, nn. 16, 19.

[28] It is here that comes the oft-quoted passage about Christian youths
rushing to study Arabic literature and ignoring Latin; n. 35, PL 555f.

[29] Artiles, *op. cit.*, p. 212.

[30] Final scholion to the " Oratio " appended to the *Vita*, PL 115:732B.

[31] Scholion n. 23 to the first book of *Mem. SS.*, PL 115:878A.

of Eulogius was not essential to Albar's argument, and he may have had many reasons for not naming him. There is no reason why he should not write after Eulogius had already produced one work—not many controversies are quieted by a single pamphlet, and three years is a long time at the height of a controversy. Later, however, Morales changed his mind, concluding it was Albar's work,[32] and since Flórez' time all agree with his final opinion.

VITA EULOGII

As the *Vita*, like the *Confessio*, will be treated much more fully in later chapters, it will receive only a mention here in its chronological place. It gives us Albar's last word on the martyr movement. Eulogius died on March 11, 859,[33] and the *Vita*, with its three attendant poems,[34] was written some time thereafter—not too soon after, for both the *Vita* and Hymn must have required much time for their rhetorical composition; not too long after, for the impression of the saint's life and death is still freshly vivid. Perhaps they were completed in 860.

VERSES

The other poems are ten in number, and alone of Albar's writings have received the care of modern critical editing.[35] All strive

---

[32] *Corónica general*, Vol. 7, p. 272. Flórez seems to think Morales' arguments pro and con more weighty than does the present writer. Like all more recent authors, he holds it is certainly by Albar; but he goes to considerable length to urge that though written in 851, Eulogius did not publish Bk. I until the whole of the *Mem. SS.* was completed at a time not earlier than June 856. Cf. ES, XI, 42–47. This may be true, but is not essential to Albar's authorship.

[33] The year is nowhere given in the surviving records. Albar says the martyrdom occured quinto Idus Martii, die sabbato (*Vita*, c. 5, n. 15). V Idus Martii is March 11; the years on which this day fell on Saturday are 853, 859, 864, etc. As Eulogius wrote his *Lib. apol.* not earlier than 857, 859 is the earliest possible date for his death. On the other hand, to place his death in one of the later years would leave that number of years empty of any known facts about him. So all writers agree in taking 859 as the year of his death.

[34] "Hymnus in diem S. Eulogii," "Epitaphium S. Eulogii," "Oratio Alvari," PL 115:720ff. They are also in Traube's ed. of Albar's verses.

[35] By Ludwig Traube, MGH, *Poetae latini aevi carolini*, III, i, 122–142.

to be, and proudly proclaim they are, metrical in structure, so Traube [36] considers them all to have been composed after Eulogius' study of metrics during his imprisonment in 851.[37]   Their poetical inspiration is slight; but they have a certain interest as showing us the deadly-earnest Albar trying his hand at such conventional themes of an earlier and more classic age as the nightingale, the cock, and the peacock.   However, most of the verses are on religious themes: on a Bible, in honor of St. Jerome, in praise of the Cross, and on his sickness.   The first three are in elegiac couplets, the rest in hexameters.

EPISTLES 9–13

These epistles appear to be a unit and to belong to the end of Albar's life.   Number 9 is a letter from Albar to the physician Romanus begging for the help of his political influence.   Number 10 is from one bishop to another alluding to the decision of an unknown council.   Numbers 11–13 are an exchange between Albar and Bishop Saul over Albar's request for a commutation of his penance.

The letter to Romanus tells us more of Albar's life than any other work except the *Vita*.   Poverty and weakness keep Albar from coming to Romanus in person; [38] he has had a severe illness, and in danger of death he received the sacrament and accepted the disabilities of ecclesiastical penance; [39] now he is constrained by the law of penance, and his feebleness shows he is about to die.[40]   But instead of having quiet at such a time, accusations of injustice are being brought against him.   A certain monk, Julian, and Felix, son of judge Gratiosus, whom Albar

---

[36] *Op cit.*, p. 124.

[37] Cf. *Vita*, c. 2, n. 4, PL 115:709C. For the rhythmical verses of their school-days, cf. *Vita*, c. 1, n. 2.

[38] *Ep.* 9, n. 6: quia paupertas et debilitas me a vobis fecit absentem, bonitas vestra me semper animo reddat praesentem. PL 467B.

[39] *Ep.* 9, n. 3: certe ante aegritudinis meae dispendium, et poenitentiae quam in ultima necessitate accepi remedium . . . PL 465B.

[40] *Ibid.*: Et nunc quando poenitentiae lex miserrimum curbat, et debilitas jam jamque moriturum incurrat . . .

calls a Manichee [41] had brought complaints to Count Servandus, under the Moslem government the political head of the Mozarabs, and to Romanus who had formerly held that position (nn. 2, 6). They represented the monks of a monastery which either Albar or his father,[42] or both, had built and endowed on their property. The monks claimed that now Albar had sold the property without sufficient safeguards for the monastery; the community was suffering invasions of their land (and they may have felt their very existence was imperiled). Not only the monks were laying formal complaints before the officials, but Albar was incurring widespread ill-will [43] for his action. Now Albar writes to Romanus, reminding him of his own parents' friendship for Romanus (n. 1), and that Romanus had known all about him since his infancy (n. 2); in closing he begs Romanus to embrace him as a son. Albar gives his version of the transaction (n. 4), and it is one which throws some light on conditions of the time. In former days Albar had given many gifts to the monastery (n. 3); more recently, however, there had been unexplained troubles with *Romani* [44] against whom Albar apparently had no effective police protection or legal remedy. So, in agreement with the monks, Albar arranged a feigned sale to an unnamed *princeps* whom he thought he could trust, and whose position made him able to protect the estate. The *princeps* agreed, and the sale was made; but the *princeps* was busy, and for some time gave little attention to the estate of which he had become the nominal owner. Meantime, the privileged *Romani* increased their plundering, and threatened to occupy the whole place. Albar was grieved, but could do nothing since in the public eye he had no longer any connection with it. After six months the *princeps* asked to buy the property in full ownership. Albar at first demurred; but seeing he was helpless in the matter, he at last reluctantly made the sale, though not until

---

[41] *Ibid.*, n. 2: Manichaeus Felix . . . confessor Julianus. No. 6: Felix Gratiosi judicis filius.

[42] Albar's father is now dead: genitor meus divae memoriae (n. 3).

[43] *Ibid.*, n. 5: Culpamur ab omnibus et incusamur.

[44] Scholars usually follow Gomez Bravo (*Catál. obisp. Córd.*, I, 140) and Flórez (ES, XI, 39) in thinking the *Romani* were Frankish servants or soldiers, mercenary or slave, in the service of the emir.

he had before witnesses earnestly commended the monks to the *princeps'* protection. Such is Albar's case; he is desperately sorry, and admits he is somewhat to blame; yet what else could he have done? He has tried to buy the place back, but without success. He had honestly sought to protect the monks, but the scheme had not worked out as planned. So he begs Romanus' help in his need, both for the justice of his cause, and for their old friendship.

Epistles 11–13 are an exchange between Albar and Bishop Saul. But the correspondence is not complete, for there are evidences that each had written at least once before the first of the surviving letters,[45] which may help to explain, if not to excuse, Albar's tone. In number 11 Albar reminds the bishop of the recent illness which brought Albar to the verge of death, during which he had received " the remedy of penance." [46] This reference to a nearly fatal illness and the reception of penance makes it clear that these letters are contemporary with the letter to Romanus, for penance of this type could be received only once in a lifetime. But in his mercy God has spared Albar's life, and now he is bound to observe the severe laws of the penitential state. He makes no complaint about its austerities, he is even willing to add to them if Saul will commute to fasting, alms-giving, or mortification the one burden which he finds unbearable—the inability to receive Holy Communion.[47] So he begs Saul to delegate a priest to come and absolve him from excommunication; indeed, he is most urgent about it; he asks for an answer within the week, or he will go to some other bishop for reconciliation, because he cannot endure

---

[45] Albar: Nunc quae agenda sunt iterum humiliter cupio implorare (*Ep.* 11, n. 2). Saul: Nam ut vobis intimavimus . . . Sed ut dulcedini tuae prius notui . . . Sed plane nescio quos salsuginosas asseritis, et prope Migentianos, Donatistas, et Luciferianos notatis (there is nothing of this in *Ep.* 11) . . . Prius quidem amantissime idcirco scripsimus vobis semi-plene, quia characteres ignoravimus epistolae vestrae. (*Ep.* 12, n. 2.)

[46] Death-bed penance, which was the common form at this time, will be explained later in connection with Albar's *Confessio.*

[47] *Ep.* 11, n. 2: Paratus enim sum in omnibus obedire, et praeceptis vestris salutaribus me totum dedere; tantum non privet communionis remedio, quia plane ingenti afficior taedio, dum extorrem me doleo a nuptiarum Agni convivio. Qualem vero mihi legem posueritis jejunii, eleemosynarum, seu temperantiae operis boni perficere cupio.

going so long without the Body and Blood of the Lord.[48] Earlier in the letter Albar had said he could obtain reconciliation elsewhere, but preferred to obey the canons and seek it from his own bishop.[49] These last not-too-submissive sentiments seem to imply that Albar felt he was asking what was his due, not suing for a favor; was such a commutation of penitential excommunication when the sick recovered the custom in ninth-century Córdoba?

Saul's reply, Epistle 12, has an air of sweet reasonableness, but the answer is definitely no. As for sending a priest, it is against the canons for a priest to reconcile when the bishop is available, and Albar has Saul right at hand.[50] But there is something else behind this which is more serious and not very clear. After quoting Scripture to the effect that "he that toucheth pitch shall be defiled with it" (Ecclus. 13: 1), Saul asks what good it would do him to receive the sacraments if the next day he were joined with a pseudo-bishop (PL 475D). Saul does not pre-judge or condemn anyone (PL 475A), but he intends to wait until the situation has been clarified by a decision of a legitimate council (PL 475B), and he cannot see why a prudent man like Albar is so vehement against him, talking about Migentians, Donatists, and Luciferians, when Saul is only observing the prescriptions of canon law. The bishop suggests, I suppose with irony, that since Albar knows and approves the mind and intention of these other people from whom he had received penance, he should go to them for absolution from it; for if their penance was valid, their ab-

---

[48] *Ibid.,* n. 3: Tamen rescriptum nostrum hac hebdomada praestolabor, quem si recipere non meruero, a fratribus vestris et episcopis reconciliationem ipsam implorare dispono, quia tanto tempore a corpore Dei mei et sanguine privatus stare non valeo.

[49] *Ibid.,* n. 2: . . . licet reconciliationem aliunde valerem frui, si vellem, tamen ea quae auctoritate patrum sacrata sunt implere desiderans permissum vestrum inquirere volui, atque per jussionem paternitatis vestrae ad communionem reditum habere disposui.

[50] *Ep.* 12, n. 2: . . . notesco quod interdictum sit hoc negotium omni clero praesente episcopo. Tunc dicit regularis instituta hoc cui injunctum fuerit licere, cum aut longinquitas itineris, aut imbecillitas corporis id episcopo denegaverit posse. Nunc vero quid ad haec opponere potestis, cum me habetis praesentem? cur praesentiam recusantes litteras petitis? PL 475B.

solution would be, too (PL 475A). In conclusion, the bishop hopes Albar will quietly consider the matter of the bad company he has been in, and so be admitted to reconciliation; but if Albar will stubbornly follow his own will, let him do what seems to him proper. "*His explosis,*" writes Saul, I have said all I can. God's saints remember you, as I always do. I salute your household with a holy kiss, and I hope to see you in joy. (PL 476A.) [51]

Albar's last word, Epistle 13, is one of bad temper and bad taste. He descends to name-calling and recrimination, though this would not seem so unbecoming to an admirer of Jerome as it does today. But underneath, it is a cry of pain. Apparently Albar set more store in Saul's reconciliation, and less in that of the " other bishops," than his previous letter indicated. Whether he believes it, or whether it is a literary fiction, Albar professes to see in Saul's letter, not Saul's own hand but that of another ignorant and malicious disturber of the peace,[52] and he uses it as a means of lashing out at the literary ineptitude of Epistle 12, and of denouncing the author: if only the writer would fight openly like a man, and not hiddenly like a tortoise, woman-wise, covertly whetting his sword; he is self-condemned, neither truly monk nor priest—his clothing proclaims a monk, but his tongue a scoffer; his woolen garments bespeak a religious, but his full-grown beard a layman; his sanctity is hypocrisy, and his slandering shows him a Pharisee.[53] Elsewhere he speaks directly to the bishop: " When I wrote you with my own hand, sincerely and simply begging a remedy for my soul, you replied bitingly and deceitfully, not from your mind, but from a stomach overcome with much drinking,

---

[51] This whole paragraph is from *Ep.* 12, n. 2, PL 475f.

[52] *Ep.* 13, n. 1: Epistolam ex nomine vestro nobis directum suscepimus, et recitationem non vestram sed illius homunculi esse cognovimus, quem patriae exturbatorem et multarum haeresum satorem saepe probavimus (PL 476B). N. 3: remedium postulavi; et vos non ex vobis pure, sed qui mihi quasi inimico responderet sophistam inquiritis, imo non sophistam sed sollecistam rogatis (PL 477A). N. 4: quid contra se in hoc dumtaxat dixerit loco sciolus ille . . . (PL 478A). Cf. also the last sentence of the letter.

[53] *Ibid.,* n. 2: . . . quem simulatio operis sanctum, et aemulatio detractionis ostendit elatum. PL 476C.

and you offered me poison in place of the drink of life." [54] However, it is of greater interest to history when Albar's wrath leads him to remind Saul of some of the shadows in his own past—how through friendship he had often been in communion with a certain excommunicated priest, even helping him to vest for the liturgy; that without any council he had absolved many whom the fathers had excommunicated; that simony had besmirched his consecration, for he had publicly paid to eunuchs of the court four hundred solidi of the Church's money, presumably to gain the government's consent to his consecration; that he had ordained priests without proper credentials, and bishops without the approval of the clergy and faithful (at the order of the government?); [55] and in the first onset of the persecution he commanded Eulogius to say Mass. [56] Albar expresses the pious hope that the council awaited by Saul may indeed meet, and opines that the result might not be that anticipated by the bishop; it might put a check on the mouth which, not knowing how to talk, has up till now been hissing around the caverns (PL 477D). An allusion to the parable of the Good Samaritan, with its callous priest and Levite, supplies the sting to the tail of this remarkable letter. Yet there is no suggestion of Albar seeking absolution elsewhere, and there are wistful hints of his sad plight and his desire that Saul would help him. But we may doubt that Saul was mollified by this epistle.

These three letters tell us much, and at the same time leave much unexplained. First, there is no certain indication of date; and second, we have no other light to clarify the ecclesiastical situation at which the letters hint. Flórez has made a reconstruction of events which is somewhat hypothetical, [57] yet is commonly

---

[54] *Ibid.*, n. 1.

[55] *Ibid.*, n. 3, PL 477A–C.

[56] *Ibid.*, n. 4, PL 477D. There are hints that Albar is not the only one Saul is at odds with; Saul thinks his whole flock is sick, and instead of nursing them with healing medicines, he tears them to pieces with teeth and hands (PL 476B); he separates himself from his own people (PL 478A).

[57] As regards Saul, ES, X, 276–79; as regards Albar, ES, XI, 28–30.

accepted and in the main will be followed here. Since no datable
writing of Albar [58] makes any reference to Albar's temporal and
spiritual misfortunes, Epistles 9, 11–13 are placed after the writing of the *Vita Eulogii,* probably in 860 or 861.

For the ecclesiastical conditions Flórez goes back to 852. To
the extent that Albar's recriminations in Epistle 13 can be trusted
—and if we discount Albar's bias, the underlying facts may not
have been so much to Saul's discredit—Saul's record was not
wholly unblemished. Yet there is nothing at all to show that he
was an unworthy or disedifying bishop.[59] Like Eulogius and
Albar, he was a proponent of the martyrs; in 850 he presided
at the burial of St. Perfectus,[60] and as late as 857 he buried St.
Roderick; on the latter occasion Eulogius speaks well of him,
venerabilis pontifex, inclytus papa.[61] In 858 he helped Usuard
get relics of SS. George and Aurelius, and when Aimoin wrote
up their journey, he called Saul *vir modestus.*[62] Twice he had
been imprisoned for the faith; first, in 851 when Reccafred's storm
landed Saul, Eulogius, and other clergy in jail;[63] the second
time in 852, when the emir raged against the Christians.[64] Perhaps his second release came when Abd ar-Rahman II died,
September 22, 852 [65] and, says Eulogius, *aeterno clibano deputatus
est.*[66] A third time, in 853, the government tried to arrest him,
but he was able to make his escape.[67] So there is no reason to

---

[58] Passing over the *Confessio,* and two of the verses, which give no clue
to date.

[59] Eulogius does not mention his name, nor does Albar in the *Vita;* they
speak only of "the bishop." The identification of this bishop with Saul
comes through Albar's *Ep.* 13, where he reproves Saul for having required
Eulogius to say Mass, an incident narrated in the *Vita.*

[60] *Mem. SS.,* II, 1, PL 115:768A–B.

[61] *Lib. apol.,* n. 34, PL 115:867C.

[62] *Translatio SS. Georgii, Aurelii, et Nathaliae,* n. 10, PL 115:945C: ad
episcopum ejusdem urbis virum modestum, nomine Saulem. This represents
a first-hand witness of Saul as the bishop's name, independent of the
testimony of Albar.

[63] *Vita,* c. 2, n. 4, PL 115:709; cf. *Mem. SS.,* II, 8.

[64] *Mem. SS.,* II, 16, 2, PL 115:797.

[65] For date, cf. *Mem. SS.,* II, 13; Dozy, *Hist. musul. Esp.,* I, 346.

[66] *Mem. SS.,* II, 16, 2, PL 115:797C.

[67] *Ibid.,* III, 7, 4.

suppose Albar and Saul were divided in their attitude towards the martyrs. Eulogius tells us [68] that in 852 a council of bishops assembled at the behest of the emir; unwilling to condemn the martyrs, yet afraid to challenge the government by approving them, they framed an ambiguous decree, praising those already dead but forbidding any more to step forward. Albar and Eulogius disapproved of the decree, and Flórez infers that Saul did, too, as soon after this he suffered his second imprisonment. There is a difficult passage in the *Indiculus luminosus* which Flórez uses in this connection:

> I marvel that there are some men so petty—perhaps they would better be called not *homines* but the diminutive *homunculi*—who defame their own bishop as accursed, unhesitatingly despise martyrdom, venerating the bishops' decrees against their own bishop which are full of maledictions and curses. And with the same boldness they reverence the bishops' decree against the faith which they lightly think is stuffed with sacrilege and blasphemies against the soldiers of Christ; they pay heed to curses of men uttered by a bishop, and respect human laws with the utmost care; but violate divine sanctions against the enemy of the Church, and condemn those who praise Christ's martyrs. . . . I do not know why these reject their martyr bishop, while they assert the witnesses of Christ and ministers of truth lie under a true condemnation and deserved judgment.[69]

---

[68] *Ibid.*, II, 15.

[69] *Ind. lum.*, n. 19: Miror tamen aliquos invenire praeparvos, forsan non homines, sed vere cum minoratione dicendos homunculos, qui praesulem infamant maledictum, et martyrium aequo animo sufferunt detestatum, venerantes letas episcoporum in praesulem currentes sententias, maledictionibus et detestationibus plenas. Et eodem mentis vigore adversum fidei episcoporum colentes decretum, sacrilegio et blasphemiis, ut leviter putant, in tyrunculos Christi refertum; hominum maledictiones in episcopo adtendentes, et humanas leges summa conservatione venerantes; divinas vero sanctiones contra hostem Ecclesiae temerantes, et damnantes Christi martyres conlaudantes; nec apertis oculis et reserato lumine se juste maledicto vident addictos, dum benedictionem nolentes, Christi contempserunt amicos. Cur enim biothenatum praesulem rennuant nescio, dum testes Christi et veritatis ministros damnationi verae asserant, et congruo subjacere judicio. PL 533A–B. To distinguish praesul from episcopus in the translation, the former is rendered "their own bishop."

Flórez interprets this as meaning that the decision of the episcopal
council was, or at least was by many interpeted as being, not
only against the martyrs but against Saul. And this is likely
enough, since the bishop of Córdoba was a protagonist of the
martyr movement. Flórez goes on to infer a schism in the Church
in Córdoba, those who opposed the martyrs finding in the con-
ciliar decree a justification for open hostility towards the bishop,
and the bishop remaining firm, not to say obstinate, in his position. Thus a gulf opened between Saul and a part of his flock,
and perhaps Saul withdrew into rather soured isolation. At least
this may be inferred from two sentences in Albar's last letter to
Saul.[70] This situation may have grown progressively worse during a number of years following 852. It will be recalled that
Eulogius spoke well of Saul in 857. But at some unknown point
a complicating factor appeared in the person of one whom Saul
termed a false bishop; whether this was some unworthy prelate,[71]
or merely some member of the hierarchy who on his visits to the
capital continued to affirm the decree of 852, and perhaps performed some episcopal functions which Saul refused to perform,
we do not know. In either case Saul could legitimately feel that
any interference in his diocese by another bishop was uncanonical.
Albar received penance from a priest in communion with this
" pseudo-bishop," while Saul had seemingly cut himself off from
communion with this bishop's following and also from those who
opposed the martyrs, and rigidly refused to budge from his in-

---

[70] *Ep.* 13, n. 2: Et non solum unum sed universum gregem nescio quo
consilio morbidum aestimatis, quem non medicinalibus fomentis, sed ravidis
discerpitis dentibus, membraque vestra vestris destruitis manibus. (PL
476B). *Ibid.*, n. 4: Sed miror cur fortissima docens absconditur, et
hominum timore a propriis segregatus per diversa vagatur. (PL 478A).
This last sentence does not mean that Saul was actually in hiding or had
fled from the city; Saul had reminded Albar that he was ready at hand
had Albar wished to see him (Ep. 12, n. 2, PL 475A).

[71] Flórez follows Gomez Bravo (*op. cit.,* I, 153f) in suggesting it may
have been Samuel, Bp. of Elvira, who we know was later an unusual
blackguard (Samson, *Apologeticus,* n. 4 of preface to Bk. II, ES. XI,
379f.); but this is pure hypothesis, and does not seem probable to the
present writer. Baudissin (*op. cit.,* pp. 162f.) accepts the hypothesis and
elaborates it still farther.

transigency until a new council should meet. Hence Albar's charge of rigorism implied in ranking him with the Migentians, Donatists, and Luciferians,[72] all of them rigorist heresies.

This reconstruction does not allay all possible doubts,[73] but it harmonizes with such facts as are known, and gives an intelligible explanation of what was probably the closing episode of Albar's life.[74]

Epistle 10 may well be an epilogue to the story. It was written by one bishop to another, both unnamed. Flórez again follows Gomez Bravo [75] in thinking Saul to be the author. The text is obscure and allusive; but if Saul is the writer, the letter can well be interpreted as having been written after the bishops had again assembled, and the others had brought forward many proofs from the fathers that Saul had adopted too rigid a position; so he had changed his mind and become more moderate. It contains no reference to Albar.

After these letters we have no further information about either Albar or Saul. Saul must have died not later than 862, for in that year his successor, Valentius, was consecrated.[76] It seems unlikely that Albar outlived him. In the very beginning of Valentius' episcopate a new storm broke upon the unhappy Church through the activities of two scandalous bishops, Hostegesis of Malaga, and Samuel of Elvira; both persecuted the Church, and the latter became an apostate to Islam. In 863 Hostegesis dominated a council and forced it to depose Valentius and intrude Stephen. Very prominent in these troublous days was Abbot

---

[72] *Ep.* 13, n. 2, PL 475B.

[73] E.g., why did Albar associate with the "pseudo-bishop" or his party rather than with Saul? If the point that separated the two bishops was their attitude to the martyrs, Albar shared Saul's viewpoint; if the "pseudo-bishop" was Samuel, as Flórez suggests, there is no reason to expect Albar to be more favorable to him than was Saul.

[74] García Villada (*Historia eclesiástica*, III, 106f.) dates Albar's sickness and penance between cc. 11 and 12 of *Mem. SS.*, III, i.e., Sept., 853–July, 854; but he gives neither argument nor reference. Also, he represents Albar as receiving penance from a follower of Bp. Reccafred.

[75] *Op. cit.*, I, 154.

[76] Samson, *Apologet.*, n. 7 of preface to Bk. II, ES, XI, 382.

Samson, whose *Apologeticus* [77] is the source of our information. Had Albar been living amidst these events, we should expect to hear from him; yet there is no hint of them in any of his writings; nor does Samson make any reference to him in the *Apologeticus*.[78]   Since Albar's sickness and penance occurred before Saul's death, and therefore not later than 862 and more probably a year or two earlier, there is reason to suppose Albar died about 861, possibly by a relapse into the same illness in which he had received penance.   For there is no evidence that he died as a martyr.

There is a single document from the following century that lists Albar among the saints.   In 961 Bishop Racemund prepared a calendar for Caliph Hakam II in which he noted the saints' days that were kept by the Mozarabs of Córdoba; here, under November 7, is the statement, *In ipso est festum Albari, in Corduba*.[79] So in spite of his faults, his many virtues led the Christians of Córdoba to keep him in pious memory.   There is a far-off kindly echo of this in the personal devotion of Señor Artiles who speaks of Albar as a saint throughout his recent article on the codex that preserves his writings.[80]

---

[77] ES, XI, 325–516.

[78] Flórez, ES, XI, 31.

[79] The text with notes is published by Férotin, *Liber ordinum*, pp. 486f. Cf. B. de Gaiffier, "Les notices hispaniques dans le martyrologe d'Usuard," *Analecta Bollandiana*, LV (1937), 276.

[80] "El códice visigótico de Alvaro Cordobés," *Rev. bibl. arch. mus.*, IX (1932), 201ff.

PART TWO

THE CORRESPONDENCE WITH JOHN OF SEVILLE [1]

CHAPTER I

The Christian Attitude Toward Rhetoric

Albar took the initiative in this correspondence with John of Seville. Of the six letters, four are by Albar, as each time it needed two letters from him to rouse a reply from John; and at the same time the Cordovan's epistles are much the longer. It is clear that Albar's intention was that this should be a correspondence in the grand manner, one which would not be unremembered. He opens with a paragraph of fanfare on the note that a friendship founded on a common love of the Scriptures and of divine wisdom will endure even after the world perishes; then after stating the occasion of opening this group of letters, he closes the introduction with an epigram. This paragraph, and many others throughout these epistles, show the carefully elaborated style— balanced clauses, prose rime, and cursus—that will be examined later in connection with the *Confessio*.[2] The second letter is a short one aimed to stir John to answer the first; it does not treat the controversies Albar is anxious to carry on, but is a clumsily humorous piece of rhetoric. The fourth is a long epistolary treatise in the manner of Jerome; here Albar's hope of reaching a wider circle than just John betrays itself in his slipping four times into references to his readers.[3]

The two friends had been together and had fallen into a dis-

---

[1] PL 411–461.

[2] On the other hand, the printed text shows many more, and worse, lapses from classical grammar than appear in the *Confessio* or *Vita*.

[3] *Ep.* 4, n. 2: Et ne onerosus multa dicendo fiam legentibus . . . (PL 427C); n. 6: nisi forsitan legentibus scripulum imponere voluisti . . . (PL 429C); n. 18; sed fastidium lectoribus meis dubitavi ingerere (PL 437C); n. 31: et totum hoc recensiri onerosum legentibus vidi (PL 446A).

cussion of various matters. After their meeting was over, Albar had been enough interested to go to his books to find authorities in support of his contentions. Now, well laden with ammunition on two topics, he opens fire by letter.[4] He thinks these citations ought to convince his friend; but if John can prove the authors have a different meaning, Albar is open to conviction, " for I am more anxious to know the truth than to defend falsehood." The first four letters deal with two topics, the place that Christians should give to the study of rhetoric, and a theological problem about the person of Christ. John answered Albar's first letter, but made no reply to the fourth, leaving Albar in possession of the field. The last two letters are not controversial. Albar proposes the problem of how to account for the origin of the human soul and at the same time to preserve the doctrine of the inheritance of original sin; he mentions a number of theories, and the objections to them, and in conclusion asks if John from his reading can throw further light on the matter. John replies, sending a few quotations he has found, and then wanders briefly to other matters before closing. John seems to return Albar's friendship, but not to share his interest in theological problems. We shall treat each of the three topics of discussion separately.

In his first letter Albar touches almost incidentally on the question of the proper Christian attitude toward rhetoric. In its original form, this question was a problem throughout Christian antiquity,[5] and analogous problems exist in all ages. At the beginning, Christians feared straight idolatry; later it was rather the danger to morals and an attraction to heathenism in a more general, secular sense. After the peace of the Church, Christians were no longer debarred from the profession of *grammaticus* or *rhetor* by the necessity of taking part in pagan worship, but there

---

[4] *Ep.* I, n. I: quae vobiscum verbo tenus disputavi, penes me in magnorum virorum volumina desquisivi; et quae de his invenire potui, manu propria ipse in procinctu conscripsi. PL 413B.

[5] Cf. H. Leclercq, " Lettres classiques," *DACL*, VIII, ii, 2885-2942; M. L. W. Laistner, *Thought and Letters in Western Europe, 500-900 A. D.*, pp. 26ff.; P. de Labriolle, *Historie de la littérature latine chrétienne*, 2nd ed., pp. 15ff.

still remained features of the classic education which caused uneasiness. The literature which was studied and admired exalted heroes, morals, and a civilization, much of which Christians were bound to condemn. Heathen society was still a living thing and could exert a real power of attraction upon the minds and feelings even of Christians. At its best, the rhetorical education enshrined the noblest achievements of classic civilization, philosophy as well as art. Yet while this contained much that was good, the Christian could not fail to recognize in it the product of fallen human nature unaided by grace; it contained many errors of thought, many false objectives, and teachings and practices that were definitely immoral; and the literature and education were calculated to form the mind and character of a good pagan, not of a Christian. But rhetorical education was not always at its best; often it went no further than a debased aestheticism, a cultivation of a too-ornate style that was used to say nothing, the product of an over-ripe society. On the other hand, no other educational system was available. So Christians were in a dilemma, and they tried to find some compromise. No one gave unqualified approval to the ordinary classic system, and no one condemned it so completely as actually to prefer illiteracy to studying in the regular schools. The Fathers took various positions, some more liberal, some more exclusive; the Church as a whole adopted no official policy. But all agreed in allowing the liberal arts no independent existence; after being purged of impurities, they were justified, if at all, as a preparatory study to equip the Christian to understand the Scriptures. Among the Latin Fathers the preponderant tendency was toward a severe view. St. Augustine, the greatest of them, had been a *rhetor* before his conversion; and in his earliest writings after his baptism he retained a very liberal attitude toward his former studies. But as he grew older and more experienced he became more strict, perhaps realizing more clearly the dangers to faith and morals from which he had miraculously been rescued. Of the western Fathers it was Jerome who had the most sympathy with classic literature, and throughout his life the Ciceronian in him lived side by side with the Christian. His earlier dream of judgment [6] he smiled off,[7] and later in a letter to the orator Magnus he vindicated the use of profane literature by Christians—provided it was purged, and was used in the interest of the faith.[8] Not even Jerome or Cassiodorus thought of defending profane literature as an end in itself. As we shall see, famous passages of Augustine and Jerome are among those quoted in the present correspondence. Later writers like St. Benedict and St. Gregory the Great, who had a great influence in forming the thought of the earlier Middle Ages, gave even less support to the study of the liberal arts than did St. Augustine in his last years.

Albar opens the discussion by repeating a proposition he had stated in their former conversation: " Holy and apostolic men do not devote themselves to the arrangement of words, but take pleasure in the truth of the meaning; they do not proceed by Donatus' art, but by the simplicity of Christ." Who the " holy and apostolic men " are is not clear until later in the correspondence. Seen in its patristic background, Albar's statement is not extreme; it does not refer to a fundamental education, nor, explicitly, to various branches of higher studies; it concerns only rhetoric in our modern sense, the study and cultivation of a fine style in literary composition; and Albar insists that holy and apostolic men are more concerned with the truth of their statements than with beauty of expression. This statement he had made on the former occasion; now he backs it up with two short quotations from Jerome, in which that Father comments on a sentence of St. Paul, " *Et si imperitus sermone, sed non scientia,*" [9] giving an instance where the Apostle slipped into an error of grammar.[10] With this Albar is content to let the matter rest, apparently being much more concerned with the theological question that he takes up immediately after.

---

[6] Jerome, *Ep.* 22, n. 30, CSEL, 54 :189ff.

[7] *Apolog. contra Rufinum,* I, 30, PL 23 :421f; cf. also *Ibid.,* III, 32, PL 23 :480f.

[8] *Ep.* 70.

[9] II Cor. 11 : 6.

[10] The change from plural to singular in Gal. 6 : 1 : vos qui spirituales estis, huiusmodi instruite in spiritu lenitatis, considerans teipsum, ne et tu tenteris. The loss of the second person singular obscures this in modern English.

When finally he got around to answer, John's balance of interest leaned the other way, and he gives more space to the consideration of rhetoric [11] than of theology. John's enthusiasm in the defense of rhetoric is more evident than the logic of his thought. After repeating Albar's proposition, and noting his citations from Jerome, John takes his cue from the text of St. Paul on which Jerome had commented, " *Etsi imperitus sermone, sed non scientia.*" John hastens to say that St. Paul was *non semper imperitus,* and gives a series of quotations from St. Paul, graduated to show an advance, from " *Macero corpus meum . . . ne forte . . . reprobus inveniar*" to " *Quicumque ergo perfecti sumus.*" [12] However fine these texts may be in themselves, they are wholly beside the point, as Albar clearly shows in his rebuttal, as they deal with Christian virtue and wisdom, not with rhetoric. John had rather weakly asked, *Numquid et peritia non est de virtutibus?*, and this is probably the key to his argument, an effort to escape through the ambiguity of *peritia* and *virtus* from the clear meaning of Albar's proposition onto other ground. However, he was doubly unjustified, for St. Paul's text " *Esti imperitus sermone, sed non scientia*" is also clear in limiting the *imperitia* to literary style. But John was a man of letters rather than a clear thinker.

For the rest, John is content to append a group of seven extracts from the writings of the Fathers, without any amplification of his own. Here also he is unwilling to limit himself to the topic Albar had set for debate, but prefers to take his stand on the wider ground of the use which Christians may be justified in making of profane knowledge. For this purpose the first selection is well chosen; it consists of three short citations from Jerome's letter to Magnus,[13] in which Jerome points out that Moses, Solomon, and St. Paul included quotations from heathen books when they were writing the Sacred Scriptures, and that Juvencus wrote the Gospel story in verse; whereupon Jerome asks

---

[11] *Ep.* 3, nn. 3–5, PL 421–424.

[12] I Cor. 9:27 and Philip 3:10–15. John's text is very different from the Vulgate.

[13] Jerome, *Ep.* 70, nn. 2, 5, CSEL 54:701f, 707.

why he may not adopt a heathen slave girl for her beauty and naturalize her into a true Israelite.[14]

Origen's homilies on Numbers, translated into Latin by Rufinus, furnish the next authorities. The first of these, somewhat garbled at the beginning, is not to the point, for in it Origen is saying that Balaam's prophecy that a star should arise out of Jacob was written down and preserved by the magi of Mesopotamia, and on the basis of this they were able to know the time of our Lord's nativity and go to worship him in Bethlehem.[15] In another homily Origen is again discoursing on Balaam, this time on the text "*sciat scientiam Excelsi,*" [16] and he says this is extraordinarily high praise; then he goes on to assert that all wisdom and knowledge is from God, citing as Scripture examples the workmen on the tabernacle and ark of the covenant (Exod. 31:1–6), and the education of Daniel and the three boys in the learning of Babylonia. John quotes the two Scripture examples, but omits the more apposite argument of Origen that comes between them in the homily, that if the *scientia fabrilis* of the builders of the ark is from God, why not geometry, music, and medicine? [17]

In the midst of the selections from Origen, John introduces two sentences from a work falsely attributed to St. Augustine.[18] In the original text the author disputes against pagans who say that God must have a wife if he has a Son, and draws much of his proof from two books he thinks pagan, Sibylla and Hermes; he mostly quotes Hermes, whose name he usually gives, as he explains, in the Latin form Mercurius. In John's letter the two sentences are given out of their context and, by a slight change of wording, are transformed in meaning, being made to say that the pagan god Mercury is Christ.[19] It is hard to see what John

---

[14] Jerome makes a metaphorical allusion to Deut. 21:10ff.

[15] Origen, *Hom. on Numbers,* 13, n. 7, CB 30:118.

[16] Num. 24:17. The Vulgate wording is different.

[17] Origen, *Hom. on Numbers,* 18, n. 3, CB 30:170ff.

[18] Pseudo-Augustine, *Adversus quinque haereses,* c. 3, PL 42:1103.

[19] John: Beatissimus vero Augustinus ubi contra tres haereses mirabiliter tractavit, de Mercurio dicit: Mercurius, inquit, filius benedicti Dei atque bonae voluntatis, cujus nomen non potest humano ore narrari. Et iterum: Est. Quis? filius inenarrabilis, sermo sapientiae Christus Sanctus. Nonne

had in mind; it is unlikely he took the quotation directly from pseudo-Augustine, for then he could not have garbled the meaning so badly. And since the beginning of the first quotation from Origen is also garbled, and since he fails to use some quite appropriate material in the immediate context in Origen, it is possible that John found the passages from Origen and the pseudo-Augustine already excerpted and assembled in some florilegium, as we shall see he did in other cases.

The next authority he brings forward he claims is Augustine, and the work quoted he cites as "*ubi de tribus Sanguisugis tractavit.*" This I have not succeeded in locating; however the passage is only a paraphrase of Proverbs 1: 2–6. Whether quoted from Scripture or from Augustine, it is in praise of moral wisdom, and has nothing to do with the argument.

One more authority is marshalled for the main thesis, a selection from St. Gregory's *Moralia* [20] where the pope notes that in cursing Simon Magus [21] St. Peter used the optative mode, *sit* instead of *est*. John points out that he was using this art (sc. of Donatus), and then infers that "holy and apostolic men" sometimes spoke simply and sometimes with art, sometimes they

---

(hoc) est, In principio erat Verbum? (PL, 422B–C). In the original the two sentences are many lines apart; in the first the author quotes Hermes-Mercurius (who in turn quotes Scripture), in the second he speaks to him directly: (1) Item alio loco sic dixit: Filius benedicti Dei atque bonae voluntatis, cujus nomen non potest humano ore narrari. Quaerebas, pagane, conjugem Dei? Audi Mercurium: para frontem. . . . (2). Quid tu, Mercuri, ab hominibus dicis nomen Dei Filii narrari non posse? A te narretur, qui non homo sed Deus ab hominibus aestimaris. Loquitur autem ad Filium suum dicens: Est autem. Quis? Filii inenarrabilis sermo sapientiae Sanctus sanctus. Nonne hoc est, In principio erat Verbum? Dic Hermes, sermo iste sapientiae habet matrem? PL, 42:1103. In this chapter the pseudo-Augustine cites Hermes Trismegistos' book entitled *Logos teleios.*

[20] *Moralia,* IV, 1, 2, PL 75:639B. John says it is from the third book. This may be a slip, or it may indicate he used the florilegium from St. Gregory made by his disciple Paterius in which this passage appears in the third part: *Liber de expositione veteris ac novi Testamenti,* pars tertia, lib. V, c. 15, PL 79:1090D.

[21] Pecunia tua tecum sit in perditionem. Acts 8: 20.

offered milk and other times solid food—all according as the Spirit gave them utterance.[22]

In conclusion John adds a point or two of his own. St. Paul uses allegory in the phrase " *In semine tuo quod est Christus;* "[23] while Moses represents God as speaking of Abraham figuratively and hyperbolically when he promised that Abraham's seed should be more numerous than the sands of the seashore (Gen. 22: 17). Though rather pettifogging, these are more to the point than some of John's arguments; yet Albar could well reply that *tropice* and *hyperbolice* were only words invented by learned men to describe a way of speaking that even unlearned men often use.

If in his first letter Albar had passed hurriedly over the matter of rhetoric, in the fourth he goes into it at full length. But first of all, to place the matter in its setting and to show his condemnation of letters is not to be pressed too far, he opens the epistle with the following paragraph, the force of which would be lost in translation:

> Engloge emperie vestrae sumentes eufrasia, imo energiae percurrentes epitoma, jucunda facta est anima, dum vel fere dilecti meruit cognoscere commoda. Unde quia prolixa facundia oratorum more rethoricari est visa, et contra tenuitatis nostrae inscitia magna doctorum usus es flumina, ne iperbatonicis casibus serviam, et quae cupio non expediam, sed involvam; breviter ac succinte defensionis meae ordiam telam.[24]

Of this long letter, paragraphs 4–17 are devoted to rebutting John's arguments and quotations about rhetoric, and paragraphs 18–23 are Albar's positive contribution.[25]

After showing at length that John's opening assembly of texts from St. Paul was wholly irrelevant, Albar counters with very

---

[22] A final quotation from *Moralia,* II, c. 66, n. 90 is added here incidentally, to the effect that only in Christ did the Holy Ghost dwell permanently.

[23] Gal. 3: 16. Vulgate: Et semini tuo, qui est Christus.

[24] PL 427. The opening phrase may be translated: " having received the eloquence of your sweet-tasting skill "; it refers to the receipt of John's letter.

[25] Together they fill PL 428–441.

appropriate verses from the first three chapters of I Corinthians, such as " The wisdom of this world is foolishness with God." John's best patristic authority had been from Jerome's epistle to the orator Magnus; Albar is able somewhat to blunt the force of this by quoting other parts of the same letter [26] where Jerome does not go beyond a utilitarian justification of the use of profane literature when needed to convince pagans. Albar also insists on fulfilling the conditions of Jerome's metaphor—the slave girl must be shaved and cleansed before being adopted; and as an example of how this purgation should be carried out, he quotes from Jerome [27] a statement that the Athenian altar which St. Paul said was dedicated " to the unknown God " really bore a much longer inscription that St. Paul only summarized. In so far as this is not merely captious on Albar's part, it may express an opinion that it is desirable to quote facts, but shorn of all literary expansion. In any event, he insists that only rare necessity induced the Apostle to quote from heathen books; indeed, a careful examination of his epistles will bring to light many mistakes in conjunctions and prepositions, showing he was ignorant of Donatus' art.[28]

John had quoted a sentence of Jerome's letter to Magnus which gave the instance of the Christian poet Juvencus who rewrote the Gospel in classic hexameters. In reply Albar [29] excuses both Juvencus and another poet, Sedulius, on the ground that they were trying to furnish edifying books for those Christians who insisted on reading verses. He does not quote either poet directly, but makes a confused reference to Sedulius, " secundum quod Sedulius in praefatione operis Paschalis Calcidonio prosatice ait." Sedulius wrote the same material in two forms, the verse *Carmen paschale*, and the prose *Opus paschale*, and to each is prefixed a dedicatory letter to Macedonius. There is nothing in the letter introducing the *Opus paschale* that corresponds with Albar's reference. But there is answering material in the letter

---

[26] Jerome, *Ep.* 70, nn. 2, 3, CSEL 54:700ff.

[27] *Commentarium in Epist. ad Titum,* c. 1, PL 26:572f.

[28] PL 432C. This information is in Jerome *Ep.* 121, n. 10, which Albar quotes in n. 22 of this letter to John.

[29] PL 433.

prefixed to the *Carmen paschale*,[30] and also in the opening lines of
the poem [31] and the corresponding part of the *Opus paschale* itself.[32] This looseness, and the mistaken Calcidonius for Macedonius, suggests the possibility that Albar knew Sedulius only
second-hand. In the course of explaining how the Christian poets
were trying to enable the faithful to avoid the *errores* and *sordes*
of Vergil, Albar weaves five phrases from the *Aeneid* into his own
text as examples. It is these quotations from Vergil that led
Traube to assign the present correspondence to a time after
Eulogius' return from Navarre.

Albar repudiates Origen with vigor, and is astonished John
would quote " the old heretic." Presumably he knew Origen only
through the polemics of Jerome and through a letter of Epiphanius
of Salamis, which Albar had a deacon read to Eulogius in Jerome's
translation.[33]

Origen's mention of the craftsmen who constructed the tabernacle and ark leads Albar to break away from quotations for a
moment, and express his own mind more fully.[34] He would not
deny for a moment that their skill, and indeed all *sapientia* and
all *scientia* are given by God to his creatures; as St. James says,
every good and perfect gift comes from the Father of lights.
But can John affirm that Donatus is a perfect gift? On the other
hand Albar does not assert it is wholly bad, and he recalls the
argument to his original proposition that " holy and apostolic men
do not devote themselves to the arrangement of words, but rejoice
in the truth of the meaning; that they proceed by the simplicity
of Christ, not by Donatus' liberal art." Overlooking the possibility
of a simple denial, Albar dares John to affirm the contrary: that
apostolic men do not rejoice in truth and Christ's simplicity, but are
devoted to words and Donatus. Plato, indeed, had located the
sensus of man in the brain, but Christ showed it is in the heart;
and from this it is clear that only the weak need seek help from

---

[30] CSEL 10:5.

[31] Bk. I, lines 17–23, 37–46, *op. cit.*, pp. 16, 18.

[32] *Op cit.*, pp. 176–178.

[33] *Vita,* c. 2, n. 7. Epiphanius' letter is included as *Ep.* 51 among Jerome's
letters, CSEL 54:395ff.

[34] PL 433C–434B.

Donatus, for we who are taught and fostered by Christ have the fulness of *sensus* within, and need not gad about among heathen delusions. Therefore, even when holy and apostolic men seem to be using Donatus, they are really taught by God. Apostles and prophets did not devote themselves to human rules but possessed full *sensus* as a gift from God.

From this argument we can get a fair picture of his mind. He has a certain degree of logical power and some ability to see and keep to a point, more so than the literary John; and he is willing to recognize some degree of good in all forms of knowledge and skill. But he is deeply religious, and has a temperamental bias toward fideism, as we shall see again in the *Confessio*. It seems that the phrase " holy and apostolic men " means primarily the " apostles and prophets," that is, the Biblical writers, so that part of the time he is thinking in the first instance of Biblical inspiration. However, he is also thinking of Christians generally, as in his use of Jerome's letter to Magnus, and of Juvencus and Sedulius, and as when he speaks in the first person plural of those taught and fostered by Christ not needing to seek guidance in heathen delusions. Albar expresses his thought on Biblical inspiration again in paragraphs 13 and 16,[35] that there is not an iota that has not a mystical or allegorical meaning. Again, a little later,[36] he says that every language has its rules by observing which it can convey thought; Hebrew was a language consecrated by God at the very beginning of the world, and its rhetorical rules have no connection with idolatry; hence Albar's effort to " destroy Donatus' art " is in no way an attack on a sacred language.

Albar marshals a greater array of authorities than John, and among them are some of the standard passages of Gregory, Augustine, and Jerome. From Gregory he quotes a sentence from the letter to Leander of Seville which prefaces the *Moralia:* " I hold it entirely improper to constrain the words of the heavenly oracle within the rules of Donatus." [37] In the context, Gregory says he has not worried about observing all the rules of grammar; though

---

[35] PL 435f.

[36] N. 21, PL 439.

[37] Albar, *ibid.*, n. 12, PL 435. Gregory, letter to Leander c. 5, PL 75:516B, MGH, *Epist.*, I, 357.

this may not be so heinous as it sounds, as classic Latin was a
dead language in Gregory's day, and his offenses against classical
grammar may have been of a kind to bring his written text closer
to the spoken language. Gregory's famous letter to Desiderius
of Vienne does not appear in this correspondence,

The last book of St. Augustine's *De doctrina christiana* was
written about 426,[38] and expresses the thoughts of his last years
on the best way to present Christian teaching. From this Albar
gives the following selection:

> The teacher should not be concerned with the eloquence
> but with the clarity of his teaching. An earnest striving
> for this clarity sometimes passes over the more cultivated
> words, and is not concerned with what sounds well, but
> what well expresses and suggests the things it wishes to
> make known. (Here Albar omits two sentences that give
> an opposite quotation from Cicero, without naming him.)
> Good teachers ought to have such a care for teaching
> that, if the only good Latin word available is obscure or
> ambiguous, they speak in a popular way to avoid the
> ambiguity and obscurity; they should speak as the un-
> learned rather than as the learned speak.[39]

In Augustine, this is practical advice to a preacher in a land where
the popular language was Punic rather than Latin, and at a time
when even spoken Latin was changing away from the classical
forms of the static written language. Of course Latin was still
more of a dead language in Albar's time, but he has less excuse
for advocating bad grammar; to write Latin at all was to write
for the educated, and the reasons given by Augustine do not hold
good.

St. Isidore was the great Spanish doctor, and Albar speaks
reverently of him as *noster lumen Isidorus* and *Isidorus sanctis-
simus,* yet it is not often that he quotes from him, and then not
at length. However, here [40] he gives three short selections from
the *Sententiae* [41] which contrast the plain style and rich content

---

[38] Bardenhewer, *Geschichte der altkirchlichen Literatur,* IV, 481.

[39] Albar, *ibid.,* n. 20, PL 438; Augustine, *De doctrina christ.,* IV, 9, 10,
PL 34:99.

[40] *Ep.* 4, n. 21, PL 439.

[41] Isidore, *Sent.,* III, c. 13, nn. 3, 7, 10, PL 83:685f.

of the Scriptures with the ornate but empty writings of the heathen, and Albar underlines the admission that the Scriptures prefer simplicity to the art of Donatus.

A quotation from Cassian [42] is more interesting for its authorship than for any addition to the discussion.

But it was not to be expected that such an admirer of Jerome as Albar should fail to make use of the famous letter to Eustochium. In the nineteenth paragraph Albar quotes at length the well-known passage, " What communication is there between light and darkness? what agreement between Christ and Belial? what has Horace to do with the Psalter, Vergil with the Gospel, or Cicero with St. Paul?", and follows this with an allusion to Jerome's dream of his condemnation at Judgment as a Ciceronian.[43] Albar makes no comments on this, nor from his point of view does he need to.

Still more material lay to hand in Jerome, and Albar quotes from a letter to Pope Damasus several short passages which he interlards with his own comments. From Jerome we have:

> The verses of the poets, worldly wisdom, the pomp of rhetorical style are the food of devils. Such things delight everyone with their suavity, and while they catch the ear by the verses running in sweet modulation, they penetrate the soul and overcome the heart . . . " For if a man sees one who has knowledge reclining at a table in an idol place, will not his conscience, weak as it is, be emboldened to eat idol offerings? And through your knowledge the weak one will perish, the brother for whom Christ died " (I Cor. 8: 10f.). Does not this seem to you to say in other words, Do not read philosophers, orators, and poets, lest you bog down in the reading of them? . . . Today do we not see even the priests of God leave Gospels and prophets to read comedies, to sing bucolic and amatory verses, to cling to Vergil, to make a voluntary crime in themselves of what for schoolboys is a required task.[44]

Thus Albar is not wholly consistent; his main opinion is not extreme, but at times he lets his enthusiasm, or the authors he

---

[42] Albar, *ibid.,* n. 18, PL 437f. Cassian, *Collatio* XIV, 13, CSEL, 13:414.

[43] Albar, *ibid.,* n. 19, PL 438; Jerome, *Ep.* 22, nn. 29f., CSEL 54:188ff.

[44] Albar, n. 22. Jerome, *Ep.* 21, n. 13, CSEL 54:122ff.

quotes, carry him farther. Like Jerome, and most writers of the patristic age, he felt a pull in two directions; his considered opinion at the time of this correspondence was that secular litera-ture and rhetoric were not wholly bad, but were dangerous and unworthy of a Christian. But like many other Christians of those early centuries, he felt throughout his life a strange attraction for an over-elaborated rhetorical style. As has been pointed out, he uses it in these letters, and as we shall see later, he carries it much farther in the *Confessio*. In his few verses he repeatedly pauses to call the reader's attention to the fact that they are constructed on the plan of classical metrics. And in the *Vita*, not only does he adorn his style to the best of his ability, but he praises Eulogius for having read all heathen literature as well as the Christian, and for having revived metrical verse in Spain. In the fourth Epistle he quotes Vergil, and other classic poets in the corre-spondence with Bodo, and in the *Vita*. Yet after all, such quota-tions are few, and we may presume Albar's classical reading was not extensive. Probably not much was available, and it is pos-sible that absence of temptation increased his virtue. Still he was very single-minded, and probably Cicero would have been less of a distraction to him than to his hero, Jerome.[45]

Albar closes the debate with a quotation from Rufinus' transla-tion of Eusebius: Porphyry had ridiculed the Christians for evad-ing the crudities and simplicities of the Pentateuch by means of an unreal figurative interpretation. Albar gives this as a clinch-ing argument that the Scriptures were not written according to Donatus.[46]

The following is a list of the quotations on rhetoric made by Albar and John, in so far as they have been identified.

SOURCES

Ep. 1, n. 2. PL 121:413f.
 Illud enim, ait, quod crebro . . . potest transferre sermone. = Jerome,
  Ep. 121, n. 10, CSEL 56:41.

---

[45] Albar has another long passage on rhetoric, *Ind. lum.*, n. 20, PL 534f., in which he speaks apologetically of his untutored style, and berates the "Donatists" for their empty rhetoric.
[46] Albar, *ibid.*, n. 23, PL 440f. Eusebius, *Ecclesiastical History*, VI, c. 19, n. 4, CB 9, ii, 559.

⁻Qui putant Paulum . . . sensum haberet in tuto. = Jerome, *Comment. in Epist. ad Galatas,* III, 6, PL 26:426C. Albar echoes this again in *Ep.* 4, n. 12.

Ep. 3, n. 3. PL 421f.

Quis enim nesciat et in Moyse . . . Epimenides poetae abusus versiculo est. = Jerome, *Ep.* 70, n. 2, CSEL 54:701.

Quid enim mirum . . . Israelitam facere cupio. = *Ibid.,* n. 5, CSEL, p. 702.

Juvencus presbyter . . . manifestatae sunt et voluntates. = *Ibid.,* p. 707.

N. 4. PL 422f.

Et prophetiae vale amose sacris inserti sunt . . . quasi regem venerati sunt. = Origen, *Hom. in Numeros,* 13, n. 7 (Rufinus' translation), CB 30:118. John gives the opening sentence in garbled form.

1. Mercurius, inquit, filius . . . humano ore narrari. 2. Est. Quis? filius . . . principio· erat Verbum. = Pseudo-Augustine, *Adv. quinque haereses,* c. 3, PL 42:1103. John gives these sentences in garbled form; cf. p. 48 above.

1. Ecce vocavi nominatim . . . scientia ab excelso sit. 2. Quos pueros Nabuchodonosor . . . ab ipso coeperit exordium. = Origen, *Hom. in Numeros,* 18, n. 3, CB 30:170ff.

N. 5. PL 423f.

(Augustinus, ubi de tribus sanguisugis). Scire, inquit, Salomon . . . et aenigmata eorum. Efforts to find this in Augustine were unsuccessful, but it is little more than a paraphrase of Proverbs 1 : 2–6.

Pecunia tua tecum sit . . . de coelo et consumat vos. = Gregory, *Moralia,* IV, 1, 2, PL 75:639B. Albar cites this as "in libro tertio"; this may be a mistake, or it may indicate he took it from Paterius' florilegium from Gregory, *Liber de expositione vet. ac novi testamenti,* pars tertia, lib. V, c. 15, PL 79:1090D. The first part of the *Moralia* was early in Spain, for Gregory himself sent it to Leander of Seville; as to whether the whole work was there in the time of Isidore, cf. Sr. Patrick Jerome Mullins, *Spiritual Life acc. to St. Isidore of Seville,* pp. 57f.

In cunctis namque fidelibus . . . ut volunt habere non possunt. = Gregory, *Moralia,* II, c. 66, n. 90, PL 75:598B. (Also in Paterius, *op. cit.,* p. III, lib. IV, c. 2, PL 79:1073.)

Ep. 4, n. 8. PL 431f.

Quod autem quaeris . . . breviter responsum habeto. = Jerome, *Ep.* 70, n. 2, CSEL 54:700.

Cyprianus, vir eloquentia . . . contraire non poterat. = *Ibid.,* n. 3, p. 703.

(dictum Hieronymi fuit ubi mulieri captivae . . . a Goliath gladio, amputem ipsius impiissimi caput proprio telo) — this is an allusion to *ibid.,* n. 2, p. 702.

Atheniensibus enim dicit: Pertransiens . . . in arae titulo praenotas-
sent. = Jerome, *Comment. in Epist. ad Titum*, c. 1, PL 26:572C.

N. 9. PL 432.

Hoc autem, ut Hieronymus ait . . . opportunitas exigebat. = Jerome,
loc. cit.; this continues the preceding passage.

N. 10. PL 433.

Albar: . . . gentilium serviebat errori dum legerent Virgilii Aeneidos,
et *flerent Didonem* EXTINCTAM, FERROQUE EXTREMO SECUTAM, vel
SPRETAM INJURIAM FORMAE, ET RAPTI GANIMEDIS HONORES, *fallacem*
DONUM MINERVAE, et dolum JUNONIS INIQUAE . . .

Vergil, *Aeneid:*

> VI,　451 Quam Troius heros . . .
> 　　　455 *dimisit lacrimas* dulcique adfatus amorest:
> 　　　"infelix Dido, verus mihi nuntius ergo
> 　　　venerat EXTINCTAM FERROQUE EXTREMA SECUTAM?
>
> I,　　27 iudicium Paridis SPRETAEQUE INIURIA FORMAE
> 　　　et genus invisum ET RAPTI GANYMEDIS HONORES
>
> II,　　31 pars stupet innuptae DONUM *exitiale* MINERVAE
> 　　　et molem mirantur equi.
>
> VIII, 291 ut duros mille labores
> 　　　rege sub Eurystheo fatis JUNONIS INIQUAE
> 　　　pertulerit.

(secundum quod Sedulius in praefatione Operis Paschalis Calcidonio
prosatice ait). The reference is wrong; Albar may refer to the
letter to Macedonius prefixed to *Carmen paschale* (CSEL 10:5),
or to *Carmen paschale*, I, 17–23, 37–46 (CSEL pp. 16, 18), or to
Opus paschale (ibid., pp. 176–178).

N. 11. PL 434.

Nota, ait, quod Deus dederit . . . de Chaldaeorum scientia judicarent.
= Jerome, *Comment. in Daniel.* (on Dan. 1 : 17), PL 25:497.

Discunt autem, ut ait Hieronymus . . . si ignoret dogmata philo-
sophorum. = *Ibid.* (on Dan. 1 : 8).

N. 12. PL 435B.

Absit ut verba tanti oraculi sub verbis perstringam Donati. = Gregory,
Moralia, introductory letter to Leander, c. 5, PL 75:516B; also
MGH, *Epistolae*, I, 357.

Non curare de eloquii rectitudine cum sensum in tuto illam posse
habere. This is an echo of Jerome, *Comment. in Galat.*, as given
under *Ep.* 1, n. 2, above.

N. 13. PL 435C–D.

Nitent quidem, ut magnus. . . . Qui esse vult nucleum, frangit nucem.
= Jerome, *Ep.* 58, n. 9, CSEL 54:538.

Nec sic clausa est . . . nec sic patet, ut vilescat. This precise wording
was not found, but Gregory expresses the same thought. Cf.

Moralia, letter to Leander, c. 4, PL 75:515A; *Hom. in Ezechiel,* Bk. II, Hom. 5, n. 4, PL 76:986C.

Institui animum intendere . . . et velatam mysteriis. = Augustine, *Confessiones,* III, 5, CSEL 33:50.

N. 18. PL 437f.

De hac ipsa, ait . . . potuerunt vel penitus aboleri. = Cassian, *Collatio* XIV, 13, CSEL 13:414.

N. 19. PL 438.

Nec tibi, ait, deserta multorum . . . et calicem daemoniorum. = Jerome, *Ep. 22,* n. 29, CSEL 54:188f. The story of Jerome's dream, to which Albar refers, follows immediately after this passage, *ibid.,* pp. 189ff.

N. 20. PL 438.

1. Non curare, inquit, debet qui docet . . . quod ostendere intendit.
2. Bonis doctoribus tanta docendi cura . . . ut ab indoctis dici solet. Except for the omission of two sentences, these form a continuous passage, = Augustine, *De doctrina christiana,* IV, c. 9, 10, PL 34:99.

N. 21. PL 439.

Gentilium dicta exterius . . . vacua virtutis sapientia manet. = Isidore, *Sententiae,* III, c. 13, n. 3, PL 83:686.

Fastidiosis atque loquacibus . . . comparata videtur indigna. = *Ibid.,* n. 7, col. 687.

Simplicioribus litteris . . . fucus grammaticae artis. = *Ibid.,* n. 10, col. 688.

N. 22. PL 439f.

Daemonum cibus est carmina . . . et pectoris interna devinciunt. = Jerome, *Ep.* 21, n. 13, CSEL 54:122.

Verum, ait, ubi cum summo . . . in virtutum penuria perserverant. = *Ibid.*

Si enim quis viderit . . . ne in eorum lectione requiescas. = *Ibid.,* p. 123.

At nunc, ait, etiam sacerdotes . . . in se facere voluntates. = *Ibid.*

Hoc loco quidem conjunctio . . . ubi repertum fuerit, respondere. = Jerome, *Ep.* 121, n. 10, CSEL 56:49.

N. 23. PL 440f.

Adhaerent, inquit, ineptiis Judaicarum . . . scriptor explicare non valet. = Eusebius, *Eccles. Hist.,* VI, 19, 4, CB 9, ii, 559.

CHAPTER II

CHRISTOLOGY

In his first letter Albar had passed over the question of rhetoric hastily in order to come to a much more important subject. " On that point on which I sharply contradicted you, and was perturbed to hear your opinion, I have gathered here in brief the teaching of the doctors." [1] With this brief introduction and with scarce a word of comment or explanation, Albar appends the series of patristic quotations which constitutes the rest of the letter.[2] Hence we have no explicit statement of the point at issue, yet both writers keep close to the topic. It is the Christological mystery of the relationship of the divine and human natures in the Person of our Lord. In this letter Albar quotes from such authorities as Ambrose, Augustine, Fulgentius, and the Council of Ephesus, and, as may be supposed, the passages are of an unimpeachable orthodoxy. Only the quotation from Vincent is open to question, but when John questions it,[3] Albar tries to give it a satisfactory explanation.[4]

The first three authorities brought forward deal directly with Christ's cry of dereliction from the Cross, and possibly this was the occasion of the dispute when the two friends were together. The rest deal with the more general problem, insisting with varied phrasing on the Catholic doctrine that Jesus Christ is a single, divine Person, the second Person of the Holy Trinity, possessing two complete but unconfused natures, one divine nature which he had from eternity, the other human which he first assumed at the Incarnation; but the human nature belongs to the divine Person,

---

[1] *Ep.* I, n. 3: Item de illo quod acriter refutavi, et pene non aequo animo vos dicentem audivi, quid inde doctores censere hic breviter identidem adnotavi. PL 414B.

[2] *Ep.* I, nn. 3-13, PL 414-418.

[3] *Ep.* 3, n. 7, PL 426B.

[4] *Ep.* 4, n. 29, PL 444ff.

and therefore its dignity and its acts come from a divine and not a human source. Several of the quotations are especially concerned to insist that since the human nature is the possession and instrument of a divine Person, its acts should be attributed directly to him.

As was said earlier, in his reply John was less interested in this theological dispute than in the matter of rhetoric; nonetheless he disputes some of Albar's quotations, and cites some patristic authorities who he thinks are in his support.[5] Except for the first, which will be given separate treatment in a moment, the patristic quotations are all genuine and thoroughly orthodox; they were evidently chosen because they bring out the side of the truth which is complementary to that stressed by Albar, that is, that Christ's human nature does not cease to be complete and unimpaired because of its assumption by the Logos in the Incarnation; in other words, the human nature is not swallowed up by nor blended with the divine nature.

These two truths are very hard to hold in even balance, and through the ages the Church has had to combat many heresies which grew out of giving disproportionate emphasis to the one or the other. One such error aroused widespread controversy about fifty years before John's time—the Adoptianism of Elipandus and Felix.[6] Elipandus was an irascible and rather ignorant metropolitan of Toledo in the closing years of the eighth century. Plunging into a controversy by accident, he tried to express the traditional and somewhat archaic theology which in Spain had continued down from an earlier age. In intention it was entirely orthodox, but it used terminology which had ceased to be safe as subsequent heresies had led to more precise definitions of Catholic doctrine. Thus it held firmly to the truth that our Lord is a single, divine Person in two distinct natures; but it felt free to use the word " adopted " of the relation of the human nature to the divine Person, and to speak of the *assumptus homo*. Elipandus used this manner of speaking, and he and his followers de-

---

[5] *Ep.* 3, nn. 6, 7, PL 424–426.

[6] A good account of Adoptianism is given by E. Amann, *L'Epoque carolingienne,* pp. 129–152. Cf. also J. Tixeront, *Histoire des dogmes,* III, 526–540.

veloped it still farther; in his desire to keep the two natures distinct, he spoke of Christ as being the Son of God by two relationships—by his divine nature he is a natural Son, but in his human nature he is only an adopted son. Taken in its literal sense without explanation, this language expresses the Nestorian heresy condemned at the Council of Ephesus in 431, and it was as a Nestorian that Elipandus was condemned by his opponents. For to speak of Christ as being both a natural Son and an adopted son of God practically implies two personalities, two distinct sons. Elipandus did not mean it so; at times he clearly states his belief in a single, divine Person in two natures. But he made the clumsy mistake of speaking of the impersonal human nature of our Lord in terms that imply personality—words like " son " and " adopted "—and a relationship that is true of the human nature need not be directly true of the divine Person. However, because Toledo was the primatial see of the country, and because his teaching was an outgrowth of Spanish theology, Elipandus had widespread support in Spain. Under his leadership a council of bishops at Seville wrote in his defense to the bishops of the Frankish church,[7] and when the controversy closed some years later with a victory of Elipandus' opponents, Alcuin wrote of twenty thousand having been brought back to the orthodox faith.[8] But traditional ways of thought are not changed quickly, and it may be supposed that the older terminology and the emphasis on our Lord's human nature lingered on. It is in this setting that John of Seville is to be understood.

While most of John's quotations from authorities are unexceptionable, the first raises some problems.[9] John attributes it to Jerome, but I have not succeeded in verifying it; and it is not clear whether the whole of this section is a quotation, or whether some part of it is by John himself. There are places, too, where the text seems corrupt. The opening sentences, however, are clear: " The Son of God is not the son of man. He is the Son of God, he is not the son of man. He is the Only-begotten (*Unigenitus*) of God; but in that he is son of man he is the first-

---

[7] MGH, *Concilia*, II, i, 111–119; PL 101 :1321ff.

[8] *Ep.* 108, PL 100 :329A–B.

[9] *Ep.* 3, n. 6, PL 424.

begotten (*primogenitus*), and is called first-begotten because of
the Only-begotten God who assumed (him), for the Only-begotten
is in him." [10]   A few sentences later: " Only-begotten and first-
begotten are two natures, divine and human, and the diversity of
these natures is shown in the language of the Gospels." [11]   The
passage means to be orthodox, but just as in the case of the
Adoptianists, it uses words in a way that was no longer adequate,
and which by the ninth century smacked strongly of heresy.
Unigenitus, primogenitus, Filius Dei, filius hominis, suum, all
properly refer to a person and not to an impersonal nature, and
so unless carefully explained the first quotation means that there
are two distinct persons in Christ.   However, the second quotation gives the needed explanation, assuring us that the writer by
unigenitus and *primogenitus* means natures and not persons.   Thus
both in its truth and its error this citation strongly suggests the
milieu of Elipandus.

Other quotations, from Augustine, Leo, Jerome, Athanasius,
and Ambrose, follow this, and then John makes two objections to
Albar [12] before closing.   These objections show the same concern
to safeguard the human nature of our Lord.   In both John is
orthodox, and he ends with some clauses of profession of faith:
" True God and true man, born of his mother in time, but eternal
from the Father," and " He put on human nature (*carnem*) but
did not put aside his majesty, true human nature from his mother's
womb, only without sin."   To avoid repetition, the objections
themselves will be treated in connection with Albar's next letter.

Lest the extent of John's theological reading should surprise us,
it will be well to state here what is proved later in the section
on sources, that all his quotations except those from Jerome come
at second hand through the *Hispana,* the great Spanish collection
of canon law.

---

[10] Filius Dei non est filius hominis; Filius Dei est, non est filius hominis.
Unigenitus Dei est; quo vero filius hominis est primogenitus est, et propter
susceptorem suum unigenitum Deum, et primogenitus dicitur, quia in eo
est unigenitus.

[11] Et quia Unigenitus et primogenitus duae naturae sunt, divina et
humana. Nam et diversitas harum naturarum in elocutione Evangeliorum
ostenditur.

[12] *Ep.* 3, n. 7, PL 426.

In his first letter Albar had been willing to rest his case in a series of citations from authorities without adding comment of his own. In his second controversial letter his own argument takes the place of authorities, and few new quotations are added.[13] In orderly fashion he goes over John's authorities and objections in strict sequence.[14] Beginning with the patristic florilegium, he accepts it all, interpreting the selections, including the first one attributed to Jerome, as referring to the distinctness of the two natures. He accuses John of failing to meet the authorities that Albar had lined up against him, but, instead of setting up a straw man to demolish, since Albar is in full accord with the citations John had brought forward. Three times in this section Albar takes occasion to profess the orthodoxy of his faith:

> In what I have said I have been contending for the unity of the Person; I have maintained one Christ in two intelligent natures.[15]

> Again, I freely and firmly profess that there is one Christ in both natures, and one proper Son, not two, as the heretic Elipandus seems to have said.[16]

> I do not say, either that the humanity was changed into the divinity or that the divinity was converted into humanity, or that there was any addition to the simple (divine) nature, nor have I at any time disputed with anyone for such blasphemies; but I truly affirm that God-made-man, Christ the Redeemer, is one and not two distinct sons separated by a diversity of persons, but single, and, through the union of Person, proper and not adopted.[17]

Nothing could be more correct than these statements.

---

[13] *Ep.* 4, nn. 24–34, 36, PL 441–448.

[14] *Ep.* 4, nn. 24–25 = *Ep.* 3, n. 6; *Ep.* 4, nn. 26–32 = *Ep.* 3, n. 7.

[15] *Ep.* 4, n. 24: Nos enim quae diximus pro unione personae certavimus; unumque Christum in duabus naturis intelligentibus bene probavimus. PL 441C.

[16] *Ibid.*: Sed iterum libere et constanter profiteor in utraque natura unum Christum existere, et unum Filium proprium esse, non duos, ut visus est Elipandus haereticus nominasse.

[17] *Ep.* 4, n. 25: Neque enim dicimus aut humanitatem in divinitatem

Albar then comes to the first of John's objections, which revolves around a canon of the Council of Ephesus that Albar had quoted in his first letter:

> Si quis non confitetur carnem Domini vivificatricem esse, et propriam ipsius Verbi Dei Patris, sed velut alterius praeter ipsum conjuncti eidem per dignitatem, aut quasi divinam habitationem habentis, ac non potius, ut diximus, vivificatricem esse, quia facta est propria Verbi cuncta vivificare valentis, anathema sit.[18]

The canon is one of those adopted in condemnation of Nestorianism, and its purpose is to assert that Christ's human nature has no separate human personality, but belongs completely to the divine Person. The only phrase at issue between John and Albar is *propriam ipsius Verbi Dei Patris.* John repeats the canon correctly without objection; then he alters the phrase by omitting *Verbi,* and says: " If you say that it (viz., the human nature) is proper to God the Father—which I am sure the holy fathers (of the Council) did not say—then you seem to follow the Sabellian heresy, holding that the human nature is proper to God the Father and also proper to the Word." [19]   There is nothing in Albar's first letter about the humanity being proper to the Father; perhaps the idea had come up in their conversation. At any rate, in the fourth letter Albar warmly defends this new formula, and it may well be that this is the heart of the dispute between the brothers-in-law.

Albar's rebuttal is confused and confusing; and it is again pos-

---

mutatam, aut divinitatem in carne conversam, nec augmentum eidem simplicissimae naturae, nec de talibus blasphemiis cum quoquam aliquando contendimus; sed veraci persecutione firmamus Deum hominem factum Christum Redemptorem omnium, unum, non duos filios disjunctos et a se personarum diversitate discretos, sed unum et per unionem Personae proprium, non adoptivum. PL 442C.

[18] It is canon 11 of the Council (= Denzinger-Bannwart, n. 123). Albar first quotes it, *Ep.* I, n. 11, PL 417B; John's objection, *Ep.* 3, n. 7, PL 426A; Albar's rebuttal, *Ep.* 4, nn. 26-28, PL 443f.

[19] *Ep.* 3, n. 7: Si enim dicis quia propria est Dei Patris, quod sancti patres minime credo ut ita dixerint, ergo Sabellianam haeresim secutus videberis, qui dicis quia propria est caro Dei Patris, et iterum propria est Verbi. PL 426A.

sible that the text is corrupt in places. One of the roots of confusion is the carelessness with which he moves back and forth
between nature and person, speaking of one in a way that belongs
to the other; another is the way he groups genitives having different relations, and shifts their order. There is a suspicion that
he himself lacks a clear idea of what it is he is trying to say.
He begins with John's conditional rewording of the canon, but
again adds *Verbi* which John had omitted, though in another
word-order.[20] Taken in its exact meaning, Albar's present form
does not change John's meaning,[21] but the addition of *Verbi* makes
it look more like the original canon of the Council, and (was it
by confusion or disingenuousness?) Albar takes it as if it were
the canon, and accuses John of formally rejecting the authority
of the Council of Ephesus. Soon after, Albar undertakes to
restate the meaning of the canon in phrases formed like John's
conditional restatement:

> sanctissimi patres qui dixerunt quod propria est caro
> ipsius Verbi Dei Patris, et propria est Verbi.[22]

What does Albar mean by it? By itself the phrase *propria caro
Verbi Dei Patris* is wholly orthodox, and is the statement of the
Council—that is, assuming that the genitives are taken in this
order: "the human nature is proper to the Word of God the
Father." But the genitives can be taken otherwise, and the
analogy with John's passage, as well as the need to make sense
of Albar's last clause, suggest that the two clauses are in contrast, and mean: "the human nature of the Word is proper to
God the Father, and is (also) proper to the Word." [23] It is hard
to be sure that Albar saw any real difference between the two

---

[20] The Council had said: "carnem . . . propriam ipsius Verbi Dei
Patris"; John's conditional form that he condemned: "Si . . . (caro)
propria est Dei Patris"; now Albar: "Si . . . (caro) propria est Dei
Patris Verbi."

[21] Albar's "God the Father of the Word" = John's "God the Father."

[22] Cf. John: . . . ergo Sabellianam haeresim secutus videberis, qui dicis
quia propria est caro Dei Patris, et iterum propria est Verbi.

[23] Albar uses the genitive and dative after *proprius* indifferently.

ideas; in any event, he held them both, for in the next sentence he says clearly: " it is proper not only to the Word of God the Father, but also to the Father." [24]

Such language as this is dangerous; with careful explanation and in an appropriate context it can be given an orthodox sense. Christ is a single divine Person, and an equal member of the Holy Trinity, and so anything that he possesses has a relationship to the other divine Persons. His human nature, however, is in itself purely a created, finite thing, and in itself is related to the Father only as creature to Creator; its higher relationship is not direct but only through the Son, the divine Person who directly possesses it through his Incarnation. Hence Christ's human nature can be said to be " proper to the Father " only in a secondary, loose sense. Neither the Father nor the Holy Trinity was incarnate. In this same passage Albar once gives the needed explanation: *Propria est caro Patri per proprietatem ejus Verbi.* Nonetheless, as John says, the language is dangerous; and just as John had a tendency to go too far in separating the two natures, Albar had the opposite tendency to merge them.

The lack of precision in his terminology leads him into difficulty. He says in this same paragraph that the human nature together with the divinity is the third Person in the Trinity,[25] whereas nature in itself is not a person. Again, he urges that if one refuses to say that the *caro* is proper to the Father, he seems to affirm that it is " adopted " by the Father. " Adopted " is not the necessary alternative to " proper," and it is an unfortunate choice as it refers only to a person, so even when used with such a word as *caro* it gives a personal connotation. As Albar says, it was precisely this use of " adopted " as applied to our Lord's human nature that was Elipandus' chief error. But Albar's choice of " proper " is equally unfortunate, and, as John says, tends in the direction of Sabellianism, that is, of overlook-

---

[24] *Ep.* 4, n. 26: Propria est non solum Verbi Dei Patris, sed etiam Patri. PL 443B.

[25] *Ep.* 4, n. 26: caro . . . una cum divinitate sua, tertia sit in Trinitate persona. PL 443C.

ing the distinction of the divine Persons in the Holy Trinity.[26]

Albar commits the same faults in meeting John's second objections. At the end of his first letter Albar had quoted a passage of what appears to be a sermon by " our doctor Vincent," a person who is otherwise unknown:

> May the Word of the Father through whom the Father founded the ages, who for us was later silent before the judge, raise (you) up for an eternal reward to be crowned with the saints. May that right hand which made heaven and earth, and which later was falsely judged by Pilate and bound in chains, embrace you in the sight of the saints on Judgment Day. May that face from which Adam fled as he could not bear it in the afternoon in the Garden, and which was spat upon by infidels for the sin of him and his seed, may it show itself to you in tranquillity and peace when it comes to judge the world by fire.[27]

Vincent was carried along by his eloquence. His leading thought is correct, asserting that the man Jesus Christ is also the eternal Son of God. The first of his three benedictions is unexceptionable, as it speaks directly of the Person. The second is transitional, using a conventional metaphor of the arm of God. The third he undoubtedly meant in the same way, but here the metaphor is not conventional, and it leaves itself open to the objection that John made in his reply—that it seemed to imply that our Lord had a human face, and therefore a human body, long before the Incarnation.[28]

Albar began his rebuttal with the correct defence: " He said this, not to affirm that Christ's human nature was established before the ages, but to show there is one Person of the Word and the human nature."[29] Had Albar left the matter there, all would

----

[26] It is interesting to note that in writing to Bodo, Albar had used language like John's: sicut ex Patre est Deus, ita ex matre est servus, unus in utraque natura Dominus Jesus Christus. *Ep.* 18, n. 7, PL 498A.

[27] *Ep.* 1, n. 13, PL 418A.

[28] *Ep.* 3, n. 7, PL 426B–C.

[29] *Ep.* 4, n. 29: Non enim hoc protulit ut carnem Christi conditam ante saecula affirmaret, sed ut unam personam Verbi et carnis ostenderet. PL 444C.

have been well. But perhaps that was too simple a solution for a man loving complication, so again he goes off into a long, confused discussion.

It would seem that he had an idea that in some way our Lord was eternally the God-man, even before the Incarnation. He quotes two sayings of Christ: " No man hath ascended into heaven but he that descended from heaven, the Son of man who is in heaven " (Jn. 3: 13), and, " You shall see the Son of man ascend up where he was before " (Jn. 6: 63). From these he reasons:

> Tell me, where was the Son of man before he took flesh? If in heaven, why then did he take flesh who already had flesh, for he says " Son of man " that he might show that through the union of Person he is from the beginning, and that he was called man. For when he says " Son of man " he shows he is son of Mary.[30]

Again he writes:

> I do not say that the humanity, that is, the body and soul, was corporated from the beginning, but that through (its) indissoluble union with the Word of God, it operated in union with it in the very beginning.[31]

He does not deny that the Incarnation took place in time; but perhaps it is his confusion of person and nature that leads him to think it necessary for the Son's existence before the Incarnation that even then he should in some way be the son of man, and operate as such from all eternity.

> Far be it from me to say that the Son was incarnate before time from some other source, and not from Mary ever Virgin. But be it also far from me and from my

---

[30] *Ep.* 4, n. 29: Dic mihi, ubi erat filius hominis priusquam carnem acciperet? Si in caelo, cur ergo accepit carnem qui jam carnem habebat, quia dicit " Filium hominis," ut eum ostenderet per unionem Personae a principio esse, et eum hominem nominatum fuisse. Nam dum dicit " Filium hominis," ostendit eum filium esse Mariae. PL 444f.

[31] *Ibid.*, n. 31: Dicimus enim non quod humanitas, id est, corpus et anima, ab initio fuerit corporata, sed quia per indissolubilem Verbi Dei conjunctionem uniter in ipso principio extitit operata. PL 445C.

thoughts, that through the union of Person I should assign him a beginning from Mary.[32]

Another aspect of the same confusion of person and nature appears in the same context:

> Tell me . . . whether you call Christ's human nature creator of all according to the union of Person, or openly call it a creature? If you term it a creature only, and not Creator, you prove yourself a transgressor . . .[33]

By "the union of Person," or what is termed *communicatio idiomatum,* our Lord in his human nature is the "Creator of all;" none the less, the human nature itself is created.

Once more, the same confusion crops up in the use Albar makes of a phrase of Cyril of Alexandria. In his first letter, Albar quoted a selection from Beatus of Liebana in which was imbedded a quotation from a letter of Cyril to Nestorius. The phrase in question is:

> Cavemus autem de Christo dicere: propter assumentem veneror assumptum, et propter invisibilem adoro visibilem.[34]

As the context shows, even in the selection given by Beatus and quoted by Albar, Cyril is condemning the Nestorian doctrine of two persons in Christ; but by confusion, Albar understands *assumptum* and *visibilem* as referring to impersonal human nature instead of Nestorius' human person.

---

[32] *Ibid.,* n. 29: Absit enim a nobis, ut incarnatum Filium ante tempora saecularia aliunde, et non de Maria semper Virgine, proferamus. Absit iterum, et procul sit a sensibus nostris, ut per unionem Personae illi a Maria initium demus. PL 445A.

[33] *Ibid.,* n. 30: Velim hic respondeas mihi . . . utrum carnem Christi creatricem omnium secundum unionem Personae dicis, an creaturam aperta voce defendis? Quod si eum (sic) creaturam tantum, et non adstruis Creatorem, te ipsum comprobas transgressorem. PL 445B.

[34] *Ep.* 1, n. 7, PL 416A; *Ep.* 4, n. 34, PL 447A. For the further references, see the section on sources. For Cyril's meaning, cf. Ferdinand A. Stentrup, *Praelectiones dogmaticae,* De Verbo incarnato, (Innsbruck, 1882), pars prior, Vol. II, p. 731.

Still, with all these faults, Albar makes other statements that are correct, and that show that his intention was orthodox though his mind was not clear and his terms ill-defined.

At the end of their letters, both John and Albar make literary allusions to stories of Antisthenes, Diogenes, and Socrates.[35] John would not allow Albar's berating of him to drive him away from his friend, as Diogenes would not let Antisthenes drive him off. Albar counters with a story of how Antisthenes dismissed his disciples in order to become himself a follower of Socrates. However learned such references are in appearance, both come from the same passage of Jerome.

SOURCES

Ep. I, n. 3. PL 414B–C.

Domine, Deus meus, ne discesseris a me. Si a corpore . . . in me transfigurata sunt. = Augustine, *Ennaratio in Psalmum 37,* n. 27, PL 36:411.

N. 4. PL 414f.

Non capiantur quod audit: Quare . . . qui apud Deum semper sum. = Ambrose, *De Incarnationis dominici sacramento liber,* c. 5, n. 38, PL 16:828.

Ergo nec ego erubescam . . . quia vita divinitas est. = Ambrose, *Expositio evangelii secundum Lucam,* lib. X, n. 127, PL 15:1835f. The last sentence given by Albar is not in Ambrose.

N. 5. PL 415.

Cum dicit: Qui me misit . . . et secundum divinitatem propriam. = Heterius and Beatus, *Epist. ad Elipandum,* I, nn. 122f., PL 96:971C–D. The last part of this is again quoted by Albar, *Ep.* 4, n. 24.

N. 6. PL 415.

Ex utero, inquit, matris . . . vivos et mortuos venturus. = Fulgentius of Ruspe, *De fide ad Petrum liber unus,* c. 2, n. 11, PL 65:677B.

N. 7. PL 415f.

Quod si discutere volueris . . . cum propria carne venerandus. = Heterius and Beatus, *op. cit.,* I, nn. 20f., PL 96:906A–B. The latter half of this is a quotation by Heterius and Beatus from Cyril's letter to Nestorius, included in the *Hispana* as a part of the Council of Ephesus, PL 84:154C–D; the same text of Cyril is also in Mansi, *Concilia,* IV, 1075; and Edward Schwartz, *Acta conciliorum oecumenicorum,* T. I, Vol. V, pars altera, p. 239.

N. 8. PL 416.

Idem sibi auctor et opus est . . . cum facit omnipotens docetur. =

---

[35] *Ep.* 3, n. 8, PL 426f.; *Ep.* 4, n. 35, PL 447.

Vigilius of Thapse (who wrote under the name of Augustine), *De unitate Trinitatis ad Optatum liber,* cc. 20, 21, PL 62:348f. (= c. 14, PL 42:1169f.). Albar does not quote a continuous passage, but sentences scattered through a column of Migne; he may have gotten it second hand.

N. 11. PL 417A–B.

Si quis audeat dicere hominem Theophoron . . . vivificare valentis, anathema sit. = Council of Ephesus, canons 5, 6, 7, 11, given in the *Hispana,* PL 84:158f. (= Denzinger-Bannwart, *Enchiridion symbolorum,* nn. 117–119, 123).

Ep. 3, n. 6. PL 425f.

The first two quotations, from Augustine and Leo, are taken from the patristic florilegium appended to the thirteenth canon of the second Council of Seville, and appear in the *Hispana,* PL 84:605f. The sources of this anthology are studied by José Madoz, "El florilegio patrístico del II Concilio de Sevilla (a. 619)," *Miscellanea Isidoriana,* pp. 177–220; he attributes its composition to St. Isidore.

Neque enim illa susceptione . . . Filii natura et una persona. The first half of this (to: ut desisteret esse creatura) = Augustine, *De Trinitate,* I, 7, PL 42:829. According to Madoz, *op. cit.,* p. 209, the rest seems to be a summary of various ideas in the same book of Augustine, made by St. Isidore. The fact that John quotes what is in the *Hispana* but is lacking in *De Trinitate* shows he used the Spanish collection.

Et sicut forma servi . . . nostri generis non reliquit. = Leo, *Ep.* 28, cc. 3, 4. These two sentences, which are close together in the canon of Seville (PL 84:606C), are farther apart in the original (PL 54:765A, 767B).

Dictum est hoc non secundum . . . ipse suae carnis Patrem. = Jerome, *Comment. in evang. Matthaei,* lib. IV (on Mt. 22:41ff.), PL 26:166D. John's quotation is loose.

The remaining quotations in this section, from Athanasius and Ambrose, John has taken from a florilegium that St. Leo attached to his *Ep.* 165; in Leo's works this is printed PL 54:1155ff.; but it also appears among the papal decretals in the *Hispana,* PL 84:731ff. In the original texts of Athanasius and Ambrose the passages are scattered, but in Leo they are assembled into a continuous passage as John gives them, except that in one place John skips eight lines given by Leo. John even quotes Leo's introductions to the several selections.

Sancti Athanasii Alexandrinae urbis . . . et carne sanctae Mariae. (The original text in Athanasius not discovered).

Inde illud quod lectum est . . . Dominus majestatis dicitur crucifixus. = Ambrose, *De fide ad Gratianum*, II, c. 7, n. 58, PL 16:571B.

Servemus, inquit, distinctionis . . . in ea substantia loquebatur. = *Ibid.*, n. 77, PL 16:576B–C.

Sed dum hos redarguimus . . . unius dicere tentaverunt. = Ambrose, *De Incarnationis dominicae sacramento*, c. 6, n. 49, PL 16:831.

Et hi mihi frequenter . . . ex Virgine esse confessi sunt. = *Ibid.*, n. 52, PL 16:831C.

N. 8. PL 426f.

Cum discipulorum Antisthenes . . . possit obsequio separare. = Jerome, *Adversus Jovinianum*, II, 14, PL 23:304C.

Ep. 4, n. 28. PL 443f.

Nothing certain is known of this Basiliscus; Dom Lambert would identify him with a Basiliscus sent by Alfonso II of Asturias to Charlemagne in 798 ("Basiliscus(6)," *DHGE*, VI, 1240). Cf. also Dom De Bruyne, "Un document de la controverse adoptianiste en Espagne vers l'an 800," *RHE*, XXVII (1931), 307ff.

N. 31. PL 445D.

Hoc, ait, fides credat . . . repertum non credat singulare. = Vigilius of Thapse, *De unitate Trinitatis*, c. 10, PL 62:340B (= c. 8, PL 42:1163).

N. 32. PL 446B–C.

Distinctio, unitio, alternatio . . . ita indivisum assignat. This is a loose quotation from Junilius, *De partibus divinae legis*, I, 16, PL 68:22D–23A.

N. 33. PL 446D.

Nestoriani a Nestorio . . . alterum hominis praedicavit. = Isidore, *Etymologiae*, VIII, 5, 64.

N. 35. PL 447C–D.

Hic certe est Antisthenes . . . ego enim jam reperi. = Jerome, *Adv. Jovinianum*, II, 14, PL 23:304B.

In view of the historical background of the discussion between John and Albar, it is interesting to note that their patristic quotations are not those commonly used in the Adoptianist controversy. Only rare overlapping, and then not an exact identity, was revealed by a search through the following important works: Elipandus and Felix (PL 96:859–888); Heterius and Beatus (PL 96:893–1030); Alcuin's writings on the controversy (PL 101: 87–304); and the various documents in MGH, *Concilia*, II, aevi Carolini, i, 111–164.

CHAPTER III

THE LAST TWO LETTERS

The last two letters between the brothers-in-law are of a less strenuous kind. *Epistle 5* is again by Albar, who begins by saying that he had planned not to write until John had replied to his last letter; but his love was hot within him, and so he will not observe the normal order of correspondence, but as he has begun it, he will now bring it to a conclusion.[1] Later in the letter he says he has read many more *floscula doctorum* on the doctrine of the two natures of our Lord, but these he will hold until he receives John's answer to his previous letter.[2]

For the rest, the first part of this letter[3] is rhetorical in two ways. Albar seems to draw a deep breath and then shows what he can do in the way of an ornate style. He employs unusual words—*litterizandi, opplementi, dicacitatem, verbositans, moestificat;* phrases like *solitum inter insolentium, flexuosa catenula et catenatim contentio flexuosa, verbose clamans et clamose verbositans;* cursus, as explained in conjunction with the *Confessio;* and prose rime, which often covers two syllables, and once reaches this climax: *Moritur sapiens, et post mortem virescit; moritur stultus, et post mortem putrescit.*[4] He speaks by indirection; he

---

[1] *Ep.* 5, n. 1: Hactenus silui, et in coepto silentio decreveram permanere, quousque rescripto eloquentiae vestrae aut retunderer aut probarer: sed quia amor internus, aut si commodatius dicitur dilectio, quae caritas aptius in divinis voluminibus nuncupatur, interna obtinens extuat, et extuando modum non servat; inde ordinem litterizandi non servans, atque extraordinario more me totum ipse comatum non nesciens, et primus et medius et novissimus scriptor accedo verbosus; ut qui in initio impuli, et in medio coepta disserui, concludam in finem. PL 448f.

[2] *Ibid.,* n. 6, PL 452C. *Floscula* hints that Albar took the use of anthologies for granted.

[3] *Ibid.,* nn. 1–5, PL 448–452.

[4] *Ibid.,* n. 2, PL 449D.

is sententious; he repeats an idea with all possible variations of phrasing; yet, through the first two paragraphs, he never had less to say. Then he comes again to the value of rhetoric and the liberal arts, but now in a less argumentative way than in the former letters. Quoting liberally from Eucherius, he elaborates on the two senses of Holy Scripture, praising the spiritual meaning which nourishes the wise, and disparaging the literal sense which is patent to the vulgar.[5] The Scriptures contain a truth beyond the reach of pagan sages. Here Albar gives a curious enumeration of the seven liberal arts, with a short derogatory description of each one. The opening description of grammarians is a paraphrase of a famous passage of St. Augustine's *Confessions*.

In principio erat Verbum, et Verbum erat apud Deum, et Deus erat Verbum. Hoc erat in principio apud Deum (Jn. 1: 1). Hoc Plato doctus nescivit, hoc Tullius eloquens ignoravit, hoc fervens Demosthenes numquam penitus indagavit. Aristotelica hoc non continet pineta contorta, Chrysippi hoc non retinent acumina flexuosa. Non Donati ars artis regulis indagata, nec totius *grammaticorum* oliva disciplina. *Geumetrici*, ex terra vocati, terrena et pulverea prosecuti sunt; *rhetorici* verbosi superflui aerem vento repleverunt inani; *dialectici* stricti regulis, et undique syllogismis perplexi, dolosi et callidi, delusores verborum sunt verius quam structores rerum dicendi. *Arithmetici* numerorum causas indagare sunt nisi, sed eorum medullam non potuerunt sentire, quanto magis dicere. *Musici* inflatores vani ventorum flaviles prosecuti sunt auras, et ad veritatem illius musicae artis numquam potuerunt subrigere alas. Jamvero *astrologi* coelotenus voluerunt pennis volare, sed in tantum non potuerunt illuc fanorum ductu conscendere, ut magis terrenam in coelo quam caelestem in terra indiderent rationem. Nam dum arietes et tauros, scorpios et cancros, leones et ursos, capras et pisces in caeli climati locaverunt, quid aliud quam in caelestia sublimarunt? nescientes enim naturam caeli et de eo quod nesciebant temere disputare tenderunt ad inlicita ausum.[6]

---

[5] *Ibid.*, n. 3: et sicut membratim foris hebetioribus lectoribus patescunt, ista prudentioribus invisibilibus spiritale vigore clarescunt. PL 451A.

[6] *Ibid.*, n. 4, PL 451B–D. Laistner, *Thought and Letters*, p. 168, would emend *oliva* to *olida*.

It is likely Albar had some source for this, but it has not come to light.

The vanity of these pretentious earthly studies is in contrast with the divine wisdom which even the simplest Catholic has through the light of faith:

> Hujus argenteae aureaeque columbae speciem saeculares nesciunt litterae, ignorant philosophi, nec vestri potuerunt scire grammatici, sed tantum nostri idiotae et rustici, et manus callosas gerentes ex opere. Unde et noster rusticus cum ficum inseret, invenit quod sophistici nescierunt.[7]

The last half of the letter is devoted to the problem of the origin of the soul. Albar would like some help in solving it. But first he lists [8] the books he already knows that deal with the subject. These are St. Augustine's *Soliloquia* and *De civitate Dei*, Claudian Mamertus' *De statu animae*, Jerome's *Epistle 126*, and also a "De animae natura" and an "In dogma sanctorum patrum," which he ascribes to Jerome but which have eluded identification.

Albar quotes a brief paragraph from Jerome's *Epistle 126* which states five theories of the soul's origin. The fourth of these is the theory of traducianism held by Augustine: that the soul as well as the body of a child is generated by its parents; the fifth, *quae nostra et verior est*, says Jerome, is that each soul is created by God and infused in the body at the time of the child's conception. Following this, Albar gives a long section to quotations from letters of St. Augustine, one of them addressed to Jerome, in which the African doctor less defends traducianism than shows the difficulties of Jerome's creationism, and asks how Jerome would solve the problem.

The heart of St. Augustine's difficulty is the problem of evil. He takes the case of children who die before reaching the age of discretion; they suffer pain, endure sickness, some are tortured by hunger and thirst, some are possessed by unclean spirits; how can it be just for God to permit such things? Or again, and Augustine dwells more on this, take infants who die unbaptized; they have not received supernatural rebirth from Christ and so

---

[7] *Ibid.*, PL 451B.

[8] *Ibid.*, n. 7, PL 453.

are unable to enter heaven; inevitably then, hell must be their eternal lot. In neither case has the child committed any personal sin for which it could deserve punishment; it must be then a punishment for original sin, sin inherited by every descendant of Adam. Now, whatever its inconveniences, the theory of traducianism offers sufficient explanation of how the child can inherit original sin through his parents from the first parents of the race, for both body and soul come to it from its parents, and therefore the soul can come to it in a damaged condition. But, asks Augustine, how can Jerome account for it on the theory of creationism? The Church has no thought of saving only the body by the administration of baptism; it is the soul that is chiefly in view. But if each soul is a fresh creation of God without derivation from human ancestors, how does the soul contract original sin? Can God make it evil from the very beginning? Again, we know that some infants grow into talented adults, others into dull-witted men, and some are little better than animals; how can it be just for God to create souls, infusing one into a gifted body, another into a stupid one, without any merit or fault of their own? Or do the souls choose bodies for themselves? And if so, does the soul that enters a faulty body merely make a mistake, or is it jostled by the crowd of souls rushing to be born, being therein like a man in a theater pushed into a poor seat he did not want?

After giving Augustine's mind on the matter, Albar refers to a passage where Isidore reports the inability of Fulgentius of Ruspe to reach a decision on it. Albar then says that the opinion held by Jerome is now Catholic doctrine, but he feels the force of Augustine's difficulties, and has never seen a solution of them. Certainly Jerome must have written an answer to Augustine's letter, but Albar has never seen one; if by chance John should know of such, or of any other good material on the problem, would he please let Albar know of it. The last long paragraph is only a rhetorical repetition in Albar's own words of the difficulties which had already been stated in the quotations from Augustine.

It may not be without a touch of malice that John begins his last letter: " Since daily we experience the labors of your wisdom and your watchful solicitude for the welfare of the Catholic faith . . ." [9] But loyally, though briefly, he takes up the question Albar had raised. No, he has not heard of any reply by Jerome to Augustine's letter; however he has come across a writing of Ambrose which he herewith sends; he will not quote it complete, but *breviter summatimque,* for a word to the wise is sufficient.[10] This document which he quotes, omitting sentences here and there, forms the backbone of John's letter; [11] however it is not Ambrose, but a pseudo-Ambrosian fragment that argues from various Scriptural texts, and from a text from IV Esdras, that God both forms the body in the womb and creates the soul he infuses into it. This is followed by a passage from Bracharius who takes an uncompromising stand in favor of creationism. John accepts the creationist origin of the soul, and also the fact of original sin; but he admits he cannot solve the problem raised by Augustine.

There was some communication between the brothers-in-law besides the letters preserved in our collection, and in the trivia at the end of the letters questions are sometimes answered that we did not know had been asked. This is the case with the remaining part of John's letter. First, he informs Albar that *maturius* is an adverb, meaning *velocius, citius;* then he copies " that note " on Mahomet for which it seems Albar had asked. It is a brief note, saying that Mahomet, the pseudo-prophet and forerunner of Antichrist, lived in the days of St. Isidore and King Sisebut; that he was lecherous; and that due to the carelessness of the guards, after his death dogs devoured his body; " having ruled for ten years, he was buried in hell." [12]

In conclusion, he asks to borrow a certain book belonging to Eulogius; or if that were impossible, that Albar would copy for

---

[9] *Ep.* 6, n. 1, PL 458A.

[10] John likes this proverb, and embroiders it twice. *Ep.* 3, n. 5: Sed ne nimis fastidiosum sapienti videretur, parva ex multis sufficiant doctis. (PL 423C.) *Ep.* 6, n. 2: Quia sapienti ex multis sapientum dictis sufficere credimus parva. (PL 458C.)

[11] *Ep.* 6, nn. 3–5, PL 458f.

[12] *Ibid.,* n. 9, PL 460.

him the part that says something about the syllables *ba, be, bi, bo, bu,*—which to us is enigmatic. Greetings are sent to *omnem pulchritudinem domus vestrae,* and John expresses the hope to see Albar soon.

SOURCES

Ep. 5, n. 3.　PL 450C.

sumamus columbae illius quae manifestiores visui alas deargentatas habet expositas.　This is a reference to Psalm 67:14, but it is also a reference to Eucherius, *Formularum spiritalis intelligentiae ad Uranium liber unus,* praefatio, PL 50:727.　In the next two paragraphs Albar quotes passages that immediately precede and follow this reference.

N. 4.　PL 451A–B.

Recte itaque procuratum est . . . ipsa divinitas operiebatur. = Eucherius, *loc. cit.*

In principio erat Verbum . . . nec totius grammaticorum oliva disciplina.　This is a free paraphrase of Augustine, *Confessiones,* VII, 9, CSEL 33:154ff.

N. 5.　PL 452A–B.

Nec mirandum quod sermo . . . et margaritas porcis exponeret. = Eucherius, *loc. cit.*

N. 7.　PL 453.

Augustine, *Soliloquia;* Albar used this as a source in his *Confessio.* Printed PL 32:869ff.

Augustine, *De civitate Dei;* Albar says it has many strong things about the strife of body and soul.　This is a theme that runs throughout the work; Bk. 14 is especially devoted to it.

Jerome, " De natura anima."　Albar describes it as a *libellum parvum* maintaining creationism against traducianism.　I have been unable to find such a work.　The chief places where Jerome treats this question seem to be: *Adv. Rufinum,* II, 8; III, 28; *Adv. Joannem Hierosol,* n. 22; *Ep.* 126, n. 1.　There is a spurious work, *Ep.* 37, *seu dialogus sub nomine Hieronymi et Augustini de origine animarum,* PL 30:261ff., into which the compiler has woven pieces from the genuine writings of the two saints; but he explicitly says it is a compilation, so it does not fit Albar's description.

Augustine, *De civitate Dei;* in this second mention Albar says: flatum Dei animam non ex substantia Dei eleganti similitudine comprobavit.　This is a reference to Bk. XIII, c. 24, CSEL 40, i, 658f.; PL 41:402.

Claudian Mamertus.　The references are all to his *De statu animae.* The passage about Hilary is in Bk. II, c. 9, CSEL 11:134f.　The " geometrical formulas " are Bk. I, c. 25.　The assertion that the soul is incorporeal and invisible even to God may refer to Bk. III, c. 12.

Quinque sunt, inquit, opiniones de anima . . . Pater meus usque modo operatur, et ego operor. = Jerome, *Ep.* 126, n. 1, CSEL 56:143.

N. 8. PL 454-456.

All this long section, except for the final passage, is taken from Augustine, *Ep.* 166 (the same letter also appears as *Ep.* 131 in the corpus of Jerome's letters, CSEL 56:202ff.). Augustine, *De libero arbitrio* is printed PL 32:1221ff., and the statements reported by Albar are found in Bk. III, nn. 59, 62; but all that Albar here says of it is said by Augustine himself, *Ep.* 166, c. 3, n. 7, CSEL 44:555f., PL 33:723.

Dic mihi si animae singillatim . . . ille prima uni, ita singulis singulae. = Aug., *Ep.* 166, c. 4, n. 10, CSEL 44:560f.

Sed cum ad poenas ventum est . . . vel faceré vel permittere (three sentences of the original omitted) Deus bonus, Deus justus . . . causa justa reddatur. = *Ibid.,* c. 6, n. 16, CSEL 44:568f.

De ingeniorum vero diversitate . . . corporibus singillatimque factarum. = *Ibid.,* c. 6, n. 17, CSEL pp. 570f.

Beatus quidem Cyprianus . . . non oppugnat, non sit tua. = *Ibid.,* c. 8, nn. 23-25, CSEL pp. 579f.

Scripsi etiam ad sanctum presbyterum Hieronymum . . . in condemnationem trahuntur. = Aug., *Ep.* 169, c. 4, n. 13, CSEL 44:620f.

N. 9. PL 456.

Albar here summarizes what is said of St. Fulgentius' opinion by Isidore, *Differentiae,* II, c. 30, nn. 105-108, PL 83:85f. Isidore in turn had summarized what Fulgentius himself wrote, *De veritate praedesinationis,* III, c. 18, n. 28—c. 20, n. 32, PL 65:666ff.

Orosius vigil in lenio (properly, " ingenio ") : this phrase is from Augustine, *Ep.* 166, n. 2.

Ep. 6, nn. 3-5. PL 458f.

A me exiet spiritus, dicit Dominus . . . ut animam faciat corporibus a se figuratis. = *Altercatio sancti Ambrosii contra eos qui animam non confitentur esse facturam, aut ex traduce esse dicunt,* edited by C. P. Caspari, *Kirchenhistorische anecdota,* pp. 227-229. This pseudo-Ambrosian fragment is made up largely of Scriptural quotations; the abbreviation that John says he performs consists in the omission of some of the quotations; otherwise John gives us practically the whole document. Caspari, *op. cit.,* p. xiii, dates the work to not later than 600 A. D.; it is against traducianism and Priscillianism. Caspari edited the text from a tenth-century Munich MS., three Paris MSS. of the thirteenth and fourteenth centuries, and Flórez' edition of John's letter.

N. 5. PL 459C-D.

Animas hominum non esse ab initio . . . ex utero plenus humana substantia. = *De ecclesiasticis dogmatibus,* c. 14, PL 83:1231 (also PL 42:1216; 58:984B). This is a work commonly attributed to Gennadius of Marseilles, but also printed with the works of Augustine and Isidore. John here attributes it to Bp. Bracharius. Cf. S. Ruiz, "Bracharius," *DHGE,* X, 332; Dom Lambert, "Bachiarius," *DHGE,* VI, 66f. Lambert distinguishes between Bachiarius, a monk of *cir.* 400 A. D. accused of Priscillianism, and who wrote *Professio fidei* (PL 20:1019ff.) and *De lapso* (cf. Joseph Duhr, *Le "De lapso" de Bachiarius,* 1934), and a Bishop Bracharius, probably of Seville in the later seventh century; and he feels this Bracharius may have had a real connection with the composition of *De eccles. dogmatibus* in one or other of its two recensions.

PART THREE

THE CONFESSIO

CHAPTER I

THE LITERARY TRADITION

A. ALBAR'S CONFESSIO

A study of Albar's *Confessio* receives the place of honor in this dissertation. It is one of his shortest prose works,[1] shorter than his *Epistle* 4 to John, but it is one of special interest and one that rewards study. It is given first place in the editions of his works, and in the Cordovan codex it is preceded only by the verses. However, most modern scholars consider it was written in Albar's last years when he had been mellowed by adversity and the approach of death; Baudissin calls it his swansong.[2]

It is a long and elaborate prayer, expressing contrition and asking forgiveness for sin. The editors divide it into four unequal sections, of which the first is the shortest and also the only one that has fairly individual characteristics. It is an address to God, acknowledging his attributes and perfections, first in himself, then in his creation and in his dealings with men. The form is almost wholly a series of clauses beginning *Deus qui, Deus cujus, Deus quem, Tu, A te* and similar forms of direct address; they are not complete sentences but exclamations of praise, each clause adding one thought in worship.

With the second division the connotation of *confessio* changes from praise to the admission of guilt, and so it remains through the rest of the work. Opening with a triple invocation of the

---

[1] PL 121 :397–412.
[2] Flórez, ES XI, 33; Baudissin, *Eulog. und Alvar,* pp. 51f., 55, 164f., 169; García Villada, *Hist. ecles.,* III, 121.

three Persons of the Holy Trinity, the author admits: Too long
have I served the devil; I have furnished him the weapons by
which he overcame me, I freely allowed him to bind me, and
now I find myself helpless in his chains. But, Lord, you are
merciful, help me to escape, for I am your creature. Even Satan
is God's creature; God made him good, and he turned to evil
through his own will; now he wills evil, but his power is strictly
limited—he can act only by God's permission and to the extent
God allows. But I repent; Lord, help me. My sins are enor-
mous, and I weep bitterly over them. You are merciful, but you
cannot abide evil, and I am foul with sin.

The third section continues without a break: Come, snatch me
from Satan, and dwell in my heart; repair the ruin caused by
my numberless sins. Cure me as you cleansed the leper, and
healed the paralytic, and pardoned the adulterous woman. I am
guilty of every kind of sin, even of sins that the devil himself
did not commit. You gave us the Scriptures and sacraments as
medicine; but far from curing me, they only make my case the
worse. The Bible is no help by itself, for your grace is needed
to make it fruitful; a proud and irreligious mind studying it can
only injure itself.

The fourth and final division continues this last thought, then
turns to the praise of God in a passage reminiscent of the Te
Deum, and this changes smoothly into renewed petition for salvation. The figure of a ladder is used, now applied to divine mercy,
now to the Cross, again recalling Jacob's ladder. Before our
human response must come the call of your grace; therefore,
Lord, give me this call. Yet you have already been calling me,
day after day, in the Prophets and in the Gospels. Every cure
is your work; but my sins have blinded me to you, and pride
is the mother of all sins. Yet you are benign to creatures, to
evil in this life as well as to good, though sinners will be condemned at the Judgment. I am little, but have mercy on me as
you did on Zachaeus. Then comes a mosaic of Scripture passages
praying for forgiveness, leading to a final, beautiful prayer for
union with God.

This summary of its contents will show that Albar's work has
little in common with Augustine's *Confessions*. The latter is

fundamentally a prayer of praise of God for his divine providence, especially for his mercies to St. Augustine himself through the course of his life, bringing him from sin and heresy to the true faith and the life of grace. Albar begins on a note of praise, but the rest of the work is basically, and almost exclusively, a prayer for his rescue from his present sinful state. It is not autobiographical, and not a single incident of his life is mentioned. Again, Albar writes as one still in the state of sin, Augustine as one now forgiven and living in friendship and union with God. Nor have I been able to find any clear trace of Albar's having used Augustine's *Confessions* in writing this of his own.

B. THE PSEUDO-ISIDORE

It has generally been said that the *Confessio* was modelled on one by St. Isidore. Nicolas Antonio, followed by Flórez,[3] makes the assertion in this general way. Baudissin[4] is more specific, and says it is based on Isidore's *Oratio pro correptione vitae,* and thinks this is what Antonio meant by Isidore's " Confessio." That this *Oratio* lies behind Albar's *Confessio* is now commonly accepted, though the better scholars no longer attribute it to Isidore.[5]

The *Oratio* is the last of a group of three interrelated pieces which have received some careful study in modern times. These are: *Exhortatio poenitendi, Lamentum poenitentiae,* and *Oratio pro correptione vitae.*[6] In some of the manuscripts and in an early edition of St. Isidore's works these pieces appear as pendants to Isidore's *Synonyma.* Arévalo[7] without being fully certain, inclines to think them authentic, but in Migne's reprint of Arévalo's

---

[3] *Bibl. hisp. vet.,* first ed. I, 351; second ed. I, 478. ES, XI, 33.

[4] *Eulog. und Alvar,* p. 165; "Alvar," Herzog's *Realencyklopädie.*

[5] Ebert, *Gesch. Lit. Mittelalters,* II, 309; Tonna-Barthet, "Alvare de Cordoue," *DHGE,* II, 856f.; C. Gutiérrez, "Alvaro (Paul) de Cordoue," *Dict. de spiritualité,* I, 410.

[6] The text of these three pieces is printed PL 83:1251–1274. The first two, being in verse, have been re-edited, by Wilhelm Meyer, *Abh. d. bayerisch. Akad.,* XVII (1886), 431–449 (reprinted in his *Gesammelte Abhandlungen,* II, 183–200); and again by Karl Strecker, MGH, *Poetae Latini,* IV, ii, 760ff.

[7] *Isidoriana,* c. 81, PL 81:582ff.

edition they are relegated to an appendix. Meyer and Strecker are confident they are not by Isidore, but by some later imitator who is not so mercilessly thorough in his use of Isidore's "synonymous style," and whose verse construction shows relationships with some Lombard inscriptions which in their opinion would suggest a date early in the eighth century; they can not be later than about 800 A. D. as they still survive in three ninth-century manuscripts. Strecker assigns their composition to Spain. Manitius [8] and Raby [9] accept this anonymous authorship; Bardenhewer [10] merely records the statements of Arévalo, Meyer, and Strecker, without giving any opinion of his own.

First is the *Exhortatio poenitendi cum consolatione misericordiae Dei ad animam futura iudicia formidantem.* It is an address to a sinner in 176 rhythmical hexameters. Why are you disturbed by storms of sorrow? Do not grieve over worldly trifles and loss of position and the hardships of prison, but over the ruin of the soul and the fear of hell. These last you can avoid by giving up sin and by turning your heart from the world to Christ. The world has cast you off and mocked you; yet this comes to you not from man's hand but from God's, for you have offended him and he gives you this as a kind warning to correct your sins. Examine your conscience and weep for your sins, for crimes are expiated only by penance and punishment. Fear Judgment and Hell, repent, "punish your sin" and live (line 47). Those who in this life conquer sin need have no fear of hell, for God is merciful and quick to forgive the penitent. But true repentance, and the only kind effective, is not only to be sorry for the past but to avoid sin thereafter. Turn to the Lord, confess to him, have compunction, and say "I have sinned" (1.84); prostrate on the ground, pray with many tears. Hate what you formerly loved, and so you will heal your wounds and will return to God's favor. Though you are guilty of sin of every kind, pray with full confidence to God who cleanses all who repent. No one need fear Judgment Day if beforehand he has turned from sin to righteousness. Paul and Matthew, Cyprian and

---

[8] *Gesch. christ. lat. Poesie*, pp. 416ff.; *Gesch. lat. Lit. Mittelalters*, I, 188ff.
[9] *Christian Latin Poetry*, p. 127.
[10] *Gesch. altkirchl. Lit.*, V, 416.

Augustine are examples of sinners who became saints; in the Old Testament are the city of Nineve, Manasses, David, Achab; and again, Peter, and the publican, and the woman taken in adultery. But those who like Judas and Solomon turn from good to evil, go to hell. It may even be that God has a tenderer love for those who turn to him from a sinful life, than for those who never wandered astray. So do not despair; reform your life; and read with sighs and sing with weeping the poem that next follows.

The *Lamentum poenitentiae* which is thus introduced is an alphabetical poem of 113 stanzas of three lines each, in trochaic tetrameter catalectic. In it the sinner himself speaks, lamenting his sins and asking God for pardon. For years he has suffered from both sin and tribulation; if the suffering is needed for expiation, he is willing to undergo it, though may God administer it mercifully (nn. 14, 15). It is better to suffer in this life than to be given to the endless pains of hell. Stanzas 18–44 treat the Last Judgment, somewhat in the style of the later *Dies irae.* The writer then admits, my sins are so great that even hell is hardly enough for them. I am straitened on every side, and my soul finds no rest from fear, and there is no place where I can go and escape from you (n. 50). Therefore I must take up the weapons of a penitent—sackcloth and weeping. Hear my prayers, have mercy on me and heal my wounds; lift me from the filth of my sins and make me clean. You are merciful, and gladly are placated by the confession of the humble. I shall gladly endure punishment in this world, but preserve me from eternal damnation. I have sinned like the Prodigal Son, but now I turn back to you. Punish me, but do not destroy me. Raise me like Lazarus from the dead.

> Miseratione tua fac justum ex impio,
> Fulgidum de tenebrosum, nitentem ex horrido,
> Innocentem ex iniquo, viventem ex mortuo (n. 87).

I am your creature, the work of your hands. No sin is too great for forgiveness, and often in the Gospel you promised pardon to those who repent, therefore I trust in you. I have sinned; receive back your runaway slave. Soften the heart of the king who has been so hostile to me; and do you, Lord, give me your

grace and save me forever. The *Lamentum* is long, and has no
very clear structural development; rather it repeats certain leading thoughts over and over again, which is perhaps more psychologically true than artistically satisfying.

The last of this group is the prose *Oratio pro correptione vitae,
flenda semper peccata*. This is far the longest of the three, and
in Migne's edition is divided into forty-three sections for convenience of reference. The author makes it clear [11] that he intended the penitent to use this prayer as a continuation of the
Lamentum. O God of mercies, the whole work of our conversion
and perfection is a product of your grace. You have drawn me
out of the world's snares and the net of sins. You have given
me confidence to ask for what is necessary for me, and it is your
grace that prevents me from being silent (nn. 1–3). You moved
me to bewail my sins in the *Lamentum poenitentiae*, and now I
wish to do penance, gladly bearing tribulation and hardship as
a means of expiating my faults.[12] Praise and glory be to you,
O Lord, who give us temporal afflictions for our sins to save us
from eternal loss (n. 9). Then follow nn. 10–15 which still
remain nominally in the form of prayer addressed to God, but
which are rather thoughts for meditation—the nature and qualities
of *poenitentia*, that we cannot sufficiently mourn for our sins, and
that Judgment is to be feared. With the latter part of n. 15 the
attitude of prayer becomes more definite again, and the author
bewails his sinfulness. Paragraphs 16 and 17 point to Christ as
our only help, and become an eloquent praise of our Lord, addressed to the Father, and ending with a reminiscence of a full
doxology. Paragraphs 18 and 19 are a trustful prayer to Jesus,
expressing contrition and being confident of mercy if he does
penance. Paragraphs 21–25 are a catena of Scripture passages,

---

[11] Paragraph 4: Idcirco consurgens ad te *lamentationem clamoribus*
prece multifaria pietatis tuae pulsans auditus, *per alphabetum quod praemisi,
singulas ejus litteras* rigans flumine lacrymarum.

[12] Do nn. 5–8 refer to canonical penance? They would be appropriate
to it, but are too elusive to be clear, and may just as well refer only to a
pious life with self-denial and patience. N. 10 explicitly mentions both
public penance and private contrition. Nn. 18, 41, 42 are on private contrition.

all but the last two being from the Old Testament, in which God promises mercy to the repentant. This leads again to an affective prayer for fidelity, and then again for contrition, the author accusing himself of a catalog of all sins (nn. 27–28). Then more paragraphs of contrition; about n. 35 this begins to shade into petition for virtues, and from 37 to 41 this prayer for future good life wholly displaces sorrow for the past. This portion is made of short clauses for well-defined qualities that give it a didactic character like that of some of St. Thomas Aquinas' prayers. In conclusion, he rejoices that by God's grace he has done penance and received forgiveness (n. 42), and mingles praise with a final petition for mercy.

C. ST. ISIDORE'S SYNONYMA

Both the manuscript tradition and modern editions point to a relationship between this group of three works and St. Isidore, especially his *Synonyma*.[13] The theological and psychological tone accord with St. Isidore in general, and his *Synonyma* is a work of the same fundamental type, though differing in two matters of style. Isidore divided his work into two parts, only the first of which concerns us here, as the second book gives moral and ascetical rules for the virtuous life that the converted sinner is to live for the future, and for this there is no counterpart in Albar's *Confessio*.

The first of Isidore's special features in this work is the use of what is sometimes called the " synonymous style." Starting with the love of many words common among the earlier writers of the Peninsula, and which is clearly evident in the Mozarabic Liturgy, for some reason Isidore conceived the idea of creating a new literary style formed by a three- or four-fold repetition of each word, or phrase, or clause, using as many synonyms as possible. This trick of style is pursued rigorously to the end, and is so disconcerting to a modern reader that he finds it difficult to follow the thought; Bardenhewer [14] goes so far as to list it as

---

[13] Text printed PL 83:825ff. Cf. Sr. Patrick Jerome Mullins, *Spiritual Life acc. to St. Isidore*, p. 79, n. I.

[14] *Gesch. d. altkirchl. Lit.*, V., 404f. It is lexicographical, like a schoolboy exercise based on a dictionary of synonyms; an especially bad example is n. 23.

a grammatical writing instead of the ascetic work that it is. Yet however distracting is this "style," Isidore's mind was clear and logical; and the reader will have no difficulty in understanding it, if he will pause to notice the one or two thoughts contained in each small paragraph. In thus stripping the husk of style from the kernel of thought he will discover a well-planned and intelligent spiritual writing.[15] The other noteworthy point of rhetoric is that the *Synonyma* is in the form of a dialogue between a sinful man and his *ratio* or conscience.

Man begins by complaining of his afflictions. I have injured no one, but all men persecute me. All flee from me, hate me. False charges are brought against me; legal justice is corrupted by bribes, and I am driven into exile while my property is confiscated and I am forced to beg alms. I am consumed with misery; why was I born? death would be better and would end my misery. After a short dialogue, *Ratio* reminds him that all men suffer hardship, and if others bear it, so can you. Sorrow like all else in this world is transitory, and tribulations are necessary if we are to enter the kingdom of God. They do not destroy you but cleanse you from sin and prepare you for salvation. Acknowledge your sin, and that your sufferings are less than you deserve; if you do not profit from them now, you will suffer both here and in hell. Nothing can happen to you without God's permission; our own sins supply the weapons used against us. Examine your conscience, and repent that you are guilty of all sins. Calamity has no other cause but your sin. The sinner admits this is true, but objects that, though he fell into sin by his own free will, now his bad habits have forged chains which are too strong for him to break (nn. 43–45). *Ratio* urges him to use his whole strength in struggling to break sinful habits; hell is hotter than lust; remember the Judgment and that death approaches, and the time of its coming is unsure; do not let it catch you unaware. Can I hope for mercy? Indeed you can; *confessio* heals, justifies, and gains forgiveness. Do not despair, for no sin is too great for pardon. May God give you strength to bewail your sins.

---

[15] Göller gives a favorable opinion and a good abstract of it, *Römische Quartalschrift*, XXXVII (1929), 271ff.

The sinner then begins to lament for his guilt (nn. 57–74). Alas, among so many sins, which shall I weep for first? I am the worst of sinners, and hell hardly suffices for me. I dread the day of doom; help me, God, before death catches me and I am burned in hell. Woe to the day I sinned, woe to the abominable day I was born into this world! Wail for me, heaven and earth; and pray for me, all good men! There is no sin I have not committed, but do not cast me off, my Redeemer. How many sinners before me you have pardoned; now I repent; hear me, O God. No one is without sin before thee, the very heavens are unclean in thy sight; as for me, I am abominable, rottenness, a worm, dwelling in the dust. Remember, Lord, that I am but dust and ashes, and the day of death approaches; cleanse me before I die. Now *Ratio* gives absolution in the deprecative form,[16] and warns not to fall back into the old faults, for penitence is vain that is defiled by new sin; do not give up the good life which you have now undertaken, and persevere in *confessio* and *penitentia*. So ends the first book which brings the sinner to repentance and forgiveness; as was said before, Isidore, great practical moralist that he was, proceeds in the second book to give advice and rules to guide and protect the convert in the moral responsibilities and duties of the Christian life.[17]

D. CONFESSIO BEATI ISIDORI

In addition to these more formal works, there are certain other writings which in whole or in part belong to the same type. First, there is a poem of thirty-six hexameter lines bearing the title *Confessio beati Isidori*. This survives in a Visigothic manuscript

---

[16] N. 75: (I am moved by your tears and compunction) . . . Deus tibi veniam tribuat, Deus tibi culpas tuas parcendo ignoscat. Peccata tua Deus a te suspendat, peccata tua laxando dimittat, criminum tuorum maculas abluat, ab omni te mali labe detergat, liberet te ab imminenti peccato. PL 83:844C.

[17] The late Dom Wilmart writes, in connection with a thirteenth-century prayerbook of the Italian Carthusians, that Isidore's *Synonyma* exercized a considerable influence in the field of prayers composed and collected for private use apart from liturgical offices.—*Ephemerides liturgicae*, XLIX (1935), 40, note 5.

of the ninth century [18] that contains an anthology of Spanish
poetry. Here, among verses of Sedulius, Eugenius of Toledo,
Cato, and others, tucked away on folio 24 is this *Confessio*
ascribed to Isidore. It would seem that De Rossi is the only one
who has printed it.[19] On a small scale this is a similar lament
for sin. Let me now pour forth my weeping for the ruin I have
caused myself by sin. For I am guilty of all sins, and have not
feared to pollute Christ's altars by touching them with my defiled
body. Now I am pale and woebegone; sleep does not visit me;
I take no pleasure in days and years, in food and drink; nothing
gives me joy. Only death pleases me, as my misdeeds stand
before my eyes. Now, O Christ, stretch forth your right arm to
save a wretch sinking in the deep, for pardon is easy for you.

E. VERSES OF ST. EUGENIUS

St. Eugenius II, Metropolitan of Toledo 646–657 A. D.,[20] was
the leading poet of the Visigoths, and was also esteemed by his
contemporaries as a liturgical writer. When St. Braulio was
anxious to honor the memory of St. Emilian, and wrote a *vita*
of him, he turned to Eugenius for the composition of a Mass for
the feast. Among his surviving verses [21] there is one, *De brevitate
hujus vitae,*[22] that has a general similarity to the type we are
considering. I am burdened with the mass of my sins, and wet
my cheeks with tears and beat my breast. The world is tottering
to ruin; happy times are past and evil days draw near. The end
of life is pressing on, and the messenger of death knocks at the
gate. Why do you lust for the false joys of earth? While you
are hunting these little trifling gains you are losing the supreme
gifts. After death what solace will you have? You can take
nothing with you; no kindred nor friends will console you, but

---

[18] Paris, Bibl. Nat., lat. 8093. De Rossi quotes L. Delisle as assigning
the codex to the eighth century, but García Villada (*Paleografía española,*
I, 117) and Millares Carlo (*Paleografía española,* I, 467) both place it in
the ninth. Vollmer also describes the MS (MGH, *Auct. Ant.,* XIV, p. xix).

[19] *Inscriptiones christianae urbis Romae,* II, 292, note 2.

[20] Cf. Lynch, *St. Braulio,* pp. 56ff. Raby, *Christian Latin Poetry,* p. 127,
calls him Eugenius III, and has a poor opinion of his poetry.

[21] Edited by Vollmer, MGH, *Auct. Ant.,* XIV, 231ff.

[22] Carmen V., *op. cit.,* pp. 235f.

everything you have dearly loved will leave you. So bewail your sins, wash away guilt with tears, mournfully confess to Christ the sins of your heart. O God who art unending good and always willing to hear prayer, behold me weeping from the bottom of my heart, and break the bonds of my sins. Father, do not give me over to the flames of hell. Punish me here as I deserve; let there be peace after my passing. O mortal men, pour forth your tears with me, give food to the poor, and pray Christ pardon; perchance he will restrain his anger and grant mercy.

It will be noticed that, though not a true dialogue, this little piece has something of that effect, as the writer now stands at a distance and addresses himself, and now in his own person prays to the Lord. It has certain features of its own, especially that it is written for an aging man who sees a natural death approaching, and now bestirs himself to prepare for eternity. But it contains in brief compass the essential elements of the writings already described—a general admission of sinfulness, an effort to arouse contrition and tears, and a prayer to God for forgiveness.

Another of Eugenius' poems, *Lamentum de adventu propriae senectutis,* gives evidence of the same frame of mind. After speaking of old age, death, and judgment, it concludes [23] with a passage again confessing guilt for all kinds of sins, fear of death and judgment, and a prayer for forgiveness before it is too late.[24]

F. VERECUNDUS' DE SATISFACTIONE POENITENTIAE

Passing now from Spain to Africa, two more poets can be added to the group. Verecundus was Bishop of Junca, in the modern Tunisia, who opposed Justinian in the struggle over the Three Chapters, and was in consequence taken to Constantinople. He fled from there to Chalcedon, where he died about 552 A. D.[25] A poem

---

[23] Carmen, XIV, lines 59–80, *op. cit.,* pp. 244f.

[24] A few other brief passages in the same spirit are: Carmen I, lines 17f.

> Da, Pater altitonans, undosum fletibus imbrem,
> quo valeam lacrimis culparum solvere moles.

and Carmina XVI–XIX, which are short epitaphs for himself.

[25] Bardenhewer, *op. cit.,* V, 324ff.; Schanz-Hosius-Krüger, *Gesch. d. römisch. Lit.,* IV, ii, 394ff.

of his survives in two manuscripts, one of them the "Azagra"[26] that preserves Albar's *Vita Eulogii*. Cardinal Pitra edited it, along with the *Exhortatio poenitendi* which he erroneously ascribed to Verecundus.[27] Meyer and Strecker, who re-edited the *Exhortatio*, are severe in their criticism of Pitra's bad editing of that poem; perhaps his edition of the genuine Verecundus is no better, but it has not had the benefit of the care of other scholars. The *De satisfactione poenitentiae* is a poem in 212 hexameters,[28] but only the first 141 lines directly concern us now. Like the other writings we have gathered here, it is a tearful lament for sinfulness and for general, unspecified tribulations caused by his sins. Life is swiftly passing and death draws near; so, with his only hope in God's mercy, he will spend his remaining time in prayers and tears. May your mercy heal me, for the punishment I have deserved, if given in full, would never end. But I am the work of your hands, so do not destroy me. Do not let me fall to Satan. My sorrow has worn me down till I am only skin and bones, and my tongue cleaves to my dry throat. This is followed by lines 123–141 which are a verse paraphrase of the third chapter of Job in which that patriarch curses his day. The rest of the poem is eschatological, describing the burning up of everything in the world at the Last Day; it is rather powerfully done, but has no relation with Albar's writings.

G. DRACONTIUS' DE LAUDIBUS DEI

Blossius Aemilius Dracontius[29] was an African layman who flourished in the last decade of the fifth century. A Catholic of native family, he was a rhetorician and lawyer who fell into the displeasure of the Arian Vandal King Gunthamund (484–496

---

[26] Toledo, 14.22 — Madrid, Bibl. Nac. 10029.

[27] *Spicilegium Solesmense*, IV, 138ff.

[28] Pitra printed only 205 lines; Meyer, in connection with his edition of the *Exhortatio* and *Lamentum,* printed the last seven lines from the Berlin transcript of the Azagra codex, Abhandlungen d. bayerisch. Akad., XVII (1886), 431, note 1.

[29] Cf. Bardenhewer, *op. cit.,* IV, 658ff.; Schanz-Hosius-Krüger, *op. cit.,* IV, ii, 58ff. His works are edited by F. Vollmer, MGH, *Auct. Ant.,* XIV, 22ff., where Eugenius' versions of the *Satisfactio* and *De laudibus Dei* are printed on pages facing, the original text of Dracontius.

A. D.) for the writing of a poem in honor of some other ruler, presumably the Byzantine emperor Zeno. He was imprisoned, and both he and his family were harshly treated. In jail he wrote two poems with the hope of winning his release. First was the *Satisfactio*, which is a confession of guilt and prayer for pardon. But in spite of both the title and the theme, it is not in our tradition, for it is addressed to King Gunthamund, not to God; apologizes for a political offence, not a religious sin; and at times is almost playful in tone; and its purpose is to obtain not the cleansing of conscience, but release from prison. It was not successful in its purpose, and Dracontius next wrote a much longer and more religious work on the theme of God's goodness, the *De laudibus Dei*.

The first book, among other things, describes the Creation, and the fall of Adam and Eve; the second, God's maintenance of the world and the coming of Christ; the third encourages us to love and trust God completely in return, and Dracontius avows that mankind is a sinful and ungrateful race and he himself the worst sinner; he complains of his misfortunes, asks divine aid now and restoration of his fortune, and that he may go to heaven at his death.

It is in the third book, after a passage on the mercy and goodness of God, that there comes a section to our purpose.[30] How can we hope to obtain our desire, the poet asks, when we wilfully despise God's commandments? Mankind is a sinful race, and I am the worst sinner of all. If I had as many tongues as hairs I should tell all my faults. But it is enough to say I am guilty of every crime. I merely harm myself if I try to hide my sins from you, so I confess my numberless offences. The deluge of my sins beats against me and the floods of them drown me. Lord, where is your former mercy? Forget not me, but my misdeeds. I am straitened on every side—bound in chains, in want, despoiled of most of my possessions, clothed in rags; kindred, acquaintance, and former friends drop away from me, and also my servants and clients. You have punished me as an offender, now have mercy on me a penitent. I repeat my sins, spare me, for

---

[30] Lines 562–691.

I cannot endure so many misfortunes. You have taught us to forgive one another, so do you forgive me. My life is short; I am broken by so many evils on every side. You forgave Nineve when it repented on Jonas' preaching, and you forgave the thief on the cross. I too am sorry for what I did, and pour forth my tears, and lift up my manacled hands in supplication. Behold the horror of my prison, the tortures and the hunger and want that I suffer, and contrast these with my former station of high honor, wealth, and influence. Now grant me pardon and put an end to my tribulations—break off my chains, and relieve my hunger and thirst. Pity me, for long imprisonment wears me down. May these sufferings be profitable to me. Lift me up as I lie prostrate. May the king's favor return, and like Job, may I regain what I have lost. From here Dracontius moves farther away from Albar, developing Ezekiel's vision of the valley of dry bones as a figure of his return to his former condition; and in conclusion he prays for years of health, happiness, and prosperity on earth, to be followed by a pleasant eternity in heaven.

Like some other Christian poets of the late Empire, Dracontius was widely read for a few centuries, to be forgotten in the later Middle Ages and modern times. Vollmer [31] brings together evidence for his use by later authors through the Carolingian period. Spain seems to have been the center of diffusion of all recensions of the *De laudibus Dei*.[32] Yet Vollmer believes that Isidore and Eugenius, not only used only a part, but knew only an incomplete text containing but a portion of the first book.[33] At the command of King Chindaswinth, Eugenius of Toledo made a new and "improved" version of both the *Satisfactio* and the *De laudibus Dei,* in which he used considerable freedom in altering the original text. His recension of the *De laudibus Dei* includes only the part of the first book that deals with the Creation, and therefore it bears the changed title *Hexaemeron.* Eugenius' text is contained in the same Azagra codex which preserves Albar's *Vita Eulogii* and the poem of Verecundus; and also in Paris Bibl. Nat. lat. 8093 which includes the *Oratio*

---

[31] *Op. cit.,* pp. viii–x.

[32] *Ibid.,* p. xxvii.

[33] *Ibid.,* pp. xviif,

beati Isidori. But Eugenius' version does not include the third book of the *De laudibus Dei,* wherein appears the passage with which we are now concerned. Could Albar have known a fuller text than was known to Isidore and Eugenius? Two facts suggest that it is possible. Since the surviving manuscripts of the original text of Dracontius go back to a Spanish exemplar at a date not later than the beginning of the seventh century,[34] it is possible that at least one exemplar of the full text lingered on till Albar's time. Again, Paris 8093 contains besides Eugenius' version, another little thirty-five line cento based upon the first book of the *De laudibus Dei;* and although it is drawn from the same part as Eugenius' *Hexaemeron,* Vollmer thinks its readings show a knowledge of the original text of Dracontius; the Latinity is bad, and Vollmer dates its composition in the ninth century with a reference to Albar's equally bad verse.[35]

H. POINTS OF COMPARISON AND CONTRAST

We can divide these writings into groups. First is the group of the three major books, Albar's *Confessio,* Isidore's *Synonyma,* and the pseudo-Isidorian triad of *Exhortatio, Lamentum,* and *Oratio.* These stand apart not only by their much greater length and elaboration of treatment, but, as we hope to suggest, in their purpose. Two others, Dracontius and Eugenius, are rather clearly personal in their origin and viewpoint. It will be remembered that Dracontius wrote the *De laudibus Dei* in prison; and with some hope that it might obtain his release. It is true that it differs from his earlier poem in being directed primarily to God; but as his offence was political, though he repents sins and prays God for forgiveness, the goal of his prayer is to gain relief from the hardships of prison life and the restoration of his fortune and honors.

> erige prostratum, vindex, adtolle iacentem
> et repara adflictum tali sub clade malorum.
> quae per me cecidit, per te spes nostra resurgat.

---

[34] I.e., just before Isidore. Vollmer, *loc. cit.* For the reasons for Eugenius' version, cf. Manitius, *Gesch. d. latein. Lit. d. Mittalalters,* I, 195.
[35] *Ibid.,* pp. xxii—xxiv.

munera percipiam domini redeunte favore
quicquid amara dies quaecumque (et) tempora dempsit.
lucida redde, precor, qui tempora subtrahis Job
aspera, restituens quicquid malus hostis ademit.[36]

Eugenius' two poems are both lyrics, addressed to himself, and
express his personal feeling. The short *Confessio beati Isidori*,
and the poem of Verecundus perhaps may be considered as coming between the two other groups, lacking the elaborate development of the first, and the clear personal references of the second;
they are literary compositions with affinities with the major group.

Each one of these writings has its distinct, individual characteristics, and no one is a mere imitation of another; yet they have
a family resemblance. It is entirely possible that Albar had read
them all, as all come to us through Spanish manuscripts. On the
other hand, there is nothing to prove that they represent more
than a general, loose tradition, with others of the type that have
escaped the present writer's notice.[37] The common theme which
has brought them together here is prayer to God of contrition for
sinfulness and the request for pardon. In some of the works
this is the leading, or even the only thought, while in Dracontius
and Eugenius it holds second place. Yet even in these latter two
it is a key element. It is only in Dracontius that there might be
some suspicion of the author's religious sincerity, since it might
be thought that his compunction was a means to obtain temporal
blessings. However it would probably be fairer to him to judge
him sincere, but not of so high a spiritual development as to be
willing to resign himself to afflictions if such were God's will.
It is to be noted that his African successor, Verecundus, who
died a confessor for the faith, says not a word about temporal
sufferings in his poem.

----

[36] Lines 675ff. There is another passage to the same effect at the very
end of the poem.

[37] The prayers with which Albar opens the *Indiculus luminosus* (PL
513–515) and Idlefonsus the *De virginitate perpetua Sanctae Mariae* (PL
96:53–55) speak a similar language, but have no direct relationship with
the *Confessio*.

CHAPTER II

The Nature and Purpose of the Confessio

In the preceding chapter we worked our way backward from the ninth century to the fifth through a series of writings which, if not complete, seem at least to represent the development of something of a tradition; and this tradition will help us understand the purpose of Albar's *Confessio*. The main theme of these writings is sorrow for sin; but before coming to this, we should examine another common element, complaint of temporal tribulations, which is transformed as the tradition progresses.

A. TEMPORAL AFFLICTIONS LEADING TO CONTRITION

In Dracontius, the afflictions are specific and concrete enough, for he writes from prison of his disgrace and punishment by King Gunthamund. I am straitened on every side, he says; chains bind me, torments master me, want consumes me; I have become the laughing stock of my son-in-law, and a grief to all. Most of my property has been taken away; my hair is uncut, and I am clothed in rags. Friend and stranger, kinsmen and clients run away, taking no pity on my ruin (lines 597–607). Kneeling and holding out my hands, I raise up my clanking chains to you; look on the horror of my prison, the tortures, the beatings, the terrible hunger! From what a height have I fallen, who used to be wealthy and honored, and able to dispense favors to clients (lines 649–661). And later, he prays that he may regain the king's favor (line 678).

In the sinner's complaint which opens the *Synonyma* St. Isidore introduces the same theme. It will be remembered that the sinner begins by complaining of his manifold misfortunes, and that only gradually is *ratio* able to bring him to see that these external calamities are due to his own sins. He laments (I, 6–17) that though he has never harmed anyone, evils pursue him on every

99

side; men rage against me, he says, and seek to destroy me. No
one deigns to offer help or comfort, unless it be with the deceitful
purpose of injuring me. Avarice has corrupted the law courts
so that evil is rampant and innocence has no hope of protection.
Groundlessly they accuse me of crimes and bring false witness,
and no attempt is made to investigate their truth; my accusers
are my judges and condemn me. All hate me, cast me forth,
and seek my destruction. I am driven into exile after being
despoiled of my goods; I have to labor as a slave, to ask public
alms as a beggar, and no one is willing to show me any mercy.
My body is loaded with chains, and tortures are inflicted on me;
they invent new refinements of cruelty, and now my flesh is
rotting from its wounds. It will be noted that this differs from
Dracontius in more ways than one; there is no reason for thinking it describes a situation in which Isidore ever really found
himself. The whole passage lacks a personal ring, and while the
colors are high, it is generalized and conventionalized, a part of
the dramatic *mise en scène,* which is forgotten in the latter part
of the book.

The pseudo-Isidore continues the same tradition. In the *Exhortatio* there are a few passing allusions. " Do not grieve for
the trifles you have lost, or for the fall from honor, but bewail
the ruin of the soul " (lines 5, 6). " Do not bother about the
hardships of prison that will come to an end, but avoid the unending miseries of Avernus " (lines 9, 10). " The world has cast
you off, buffeted you, proscribed you, derided you " (line 17).

In the *Lamentum* there are similar allusions, but so softened
and blended into the general griefs which sin has forced God to
inflict on the guilty man that they seem to be metaphorical only.
" Merciful God, look upon the griefs I endure; take away the
afflictions and withhold the scourge; do not break me in your
anger. . . . You have laid the hand of punishment heavily upon
me, breaking my flesh with the harsh vengeance of the lash, with
slaughter, iron, filth, plague, and the darkness of prison " (nn. 7,
9). And near the end, the author begs God that the king's wrath
against him may cease (n. 106).

The *Oratio* continues references of the same kind. You have
taught me this in the solitude of my confinement (n. 20) ; may

my penitence be fruitful to me, producing joy from grief, bringing indulgence out of indigence (*ex indigentia indulgentiam afferens*) and rest from labor, and thus by the strait path of prison's afflictions may you lead me to the entrance of life, and by the bond of an iron chain may you cause me to receive the release from sins (n. 27). Save me in this place of peril where my body lies confined with iron chains, beaten with scourges, wearied with punishments, worn out with sorrows, abandoned without human care, separated from companions, walled in with square stones, justly consigned to stenches and the dunghill, and in darkness and in shadow exposed to long and fatal miseries (n. 31). O Lord, graciously lend your aid where human aid is lacking, and help me in my loneliness. Do not be a stranger to me in the days of need, and do not abandon me in the time of tribulation (n. 32). Be the lifegiver and the life of both my body and soul, the healer and health of all my infirmities until, pacified by your inspiration, the indignation of him who is afflicting me may grow quiet, for yours is the power to bend the heart of princes (n. 33).[1] As it is not known who the author of these three pieces was, we cannot know whether these references to imprisonment are based on actual events of his life.[2] It is possible that they are not; for the references are incidental, and the author's main purpose is religious, and he would have the precedent of St. Isidore's *Synonyma* for using such details as fictitious dramatic coloring.

Albar still uses some of this language: *equuleum, gladium gutturi meo, in mortis deflendam ruinam deveni, gaudet hostis*

---

[1] *Lamentum*, 106, 1 reads: Tolle furorem perennem ab animo principis. Meyer's note on this queries whether the princeps here is the devil, or whether the poet is in the same straits as Dracontius. Strecker, *op. cit.*, p. 782, refers to Meyer's note, and doubts it could mean Satan since not even God can remove Satan's unending fury. We may compare the line with Dracontius, *De laudibus*, III, 678: munera percipiam domini redeunte favore, where the *dominus* is the Vandal king. May we not suppose that the pseudo-Isidore may be referring to a human ruler, continuing a literary tradition, even though it did not literally fit his circumstances?

[2] Manitius guesses from the text that the author was an ecclesiastic exiled by a civil ruler; *Gesch. d. latein. Lit. d. Mittelalters*, I, 190; *Gesch. d. christ. lat. Poesie*, p. 419.

meus, disrumpe vincula perplexionum (PL 400f.). But now it is a matter of only an occasional phrase and not of a description, and the meaning has clearly changed; it refers no longer to human enemies and the king's prison, but to Albar's sins and the slavery to the devil to which they have subjected him.[3] There is no reference to temporal afflictions, and this portion of the tradition has been completely spiritualized.[4]

In connection with this general theme there are a few phrases common to two or more of the authors.

1. Dracontius, *De laudibus Dei*, III,
    tristis et extenso *prostratus corpore* plango. line 620.
    en *genibus curvis* palmas extendo supinas. line 649.
  Verecundus, *De Satisfactione*,
    *deflexo*que, *genu* contractus verticem poples
    contenat, et genibus connectant brachia frontem. . . . lines 29f.
    stratus humi, valido gemitu praecordia rumpe . . . line 32.
    sit tibi detritus *prostrato corpore* vultus. line 34.
  Pseudo-Isidore, *Exhortatio*,
    curva cordis genua prostratus corpore terrae   line 86.

2. I am straitened on every side:
  Dracontius, *De laudibus*, III, 597
    . . . gravor undique pressus.
  Pseudo-Isidore, *Lamentum*, 50, 1.
    Arctor undique pressuris, conprimor angustiis.
  Albar, *Confessio*, PL 402B.
    . . . ea quae me indique premunt . . .

3. I should like to die; why was I born?
  Verecundus, *De satisfactione*, lines 123–141 are a paraphrase of the third chapter of Job in which the patriarch curses his day.
  Isidore, *Synonyma*, I, 19, 64, 65.
    Cur infelix natus sum? cur in hanc miseram vitam projectus sum? . . . Utinam velocius egrederer a saeculo quam sum

---

[3] Cf.: Et inde est quod prolongatam captivitatem (sc. to the devil) sentiens doleo, PL 401B. Nowhere in the *Confessio* does Albar allude to his quarrel with Bishop Saul, or to his penance and excommunication, which is an argument against dating the *Confessio* at the very end of his life.

[4] Isidore's *Synonyma* is transitional; beginning with worldly tribulations, *ratio* convinces the soul that afflictions are due to its sins, so that the burden shifts to repentance.

ingressus? . . . Vivendi enim mihi taedium est, moriendi
votum, sola mihi mors placet. O mors, quam dulcis es
miseris! PL 83:832B.

Vae diem illum quando peccavi! vae diem illum quando trans-
gressus sum! . . . utinam non illuxisset mihi! . . . o dies
abominanda . . . quae me in hoc saeculum protulit . . . PL
83:841f.

Melius mihi fuerat non esse ortum, melius non fuisse genitum
. . . quam aeternos perpeti cruciatus . . . PL 83:842.

Confessio beati Isidori, line 27.

mors sola oblectat miserum, mors sola merentem (i.e., moeren-
tem).

Pseudo-Isidore, *Lamentum,* 60, 1.

Ac per hoc opto misellus, nec fuissem genitus.

B. CONTRITION FOR SIN

We now come to the theme that underlies the whole series,
contrition for sins. The summaries that have already been given
are sufficient to show this in a general way. In Dracontius, the
passage concerned is fairly brief and somewhat incidental—a
means of regaining God's favors: humanity is a sinful race, and
Dracontius admits being the worst sinner, guilty of every sin.
It is idle to try to hide sins from God, and so he confesses his
numberless offences, and with tears asks God for forgiveness
and restoration to his former condition. Verecundus created what
is almost a *tour de force:* for 122 lines he expresses the deepest
and most heartfelt contrition with scarcely a passing hint at what
he is sorry for; here and there a single word like *peccatum* or
reatus slips in, but that is all; for the rest, he rings the changes
on his grief with a surprising lack of monotony. Almost exclusive expression is given to the subjective feelings of the soul,
and none to the objective sins committed.

The major Spanish writings of our series form a group apart.
Dracontius' main interest was clearly personal to himself. Verecundus seems to have composed a religious poem, sincere no
doubt, but essentially a work of art, a late product of the Chris-
tianized schools of rhetoric. The Spaniards, however, were
composing definitely spiritual works, books of devotion—they
might even be called prayer books. Since this is not the conception of Albar's *Confessio* held by previous writers, it will be the

leading purpose of this section to advance reasons for thinking
so. If this view is correct, it means that the *Confessio* cannot be
thought of as autobiographical, except in the broad sense that
Albar's personality is deeply impressed on all his writings.

1. *Background of the Sacrament of Penance*

The background is the penitential discipline of the early
Church,[5] in which the Church's power to forgive sins was exercised in a public and solemn way, very different from what we
are accustomed to today. Baptism cleanses the soul of all
previous sin and constitutes a man in the new, supernatural Christian life; so an adult convert may by it receive forgiveness for
a whole course of sins in his earlier pagan life. But baptism can
be received only once; and once a Christian, a man was expected
to live a life worthy of his new vocation. There are of course
the little, daily faults which no one can be expected wholly to
avoid; but every Christian very definitely was expected to avoid
any sin after baptism which was so grievous that it would prevent
his entering heaven. Still, some did sin grievously; and for them
the Church was willing to use its power of forgiveness once more,
in Penance, but only once more.[6]

Penance, as then administered, was a very rigorous discipline,
meant to be both a severe punishment for a heinous offence, and
a protection of the weak brother against any future repetition
of his sin. Those who confessed themselves, or could be judicially
proved to be, guilty of grievous sin were brought to the bishop
who assigned them a time during which penitential exercises were

---

[5] For a general account of penance cf. Amann, "Pénitence—sacrament,"
DTC, XII, i, esp. cols. 749–948; Poschmann, *Die abendländ. Kirchenbusse.*
For recent literature, and a special attention to Visigothic Spain, Sr.
Patrick Jerome Mullins, *op. cit.,* pp. 89ff. The rites of the Mozarabic
liturgy are in *Liber ordinum,* ed. Férotin, cols. 80–86 (for conversi), 86–93
(for the sick), 94–100, 200–205, 351–358 (for public penitents).

[6] Cf. St. Ambrose, *De poenitentia,* II, c. 10, n. 95: Merito reprehenduntur
qui saepius agendam poenitentiam putant; quia luxuriantur in Christo.
Nam si vere agerent poenitentiam, iterandam postea non putarent; quia
sicut unum baptisma, ita una poenitentia, quae tamen publice agitur; nam
quotidiani nos debet poenitere peccati: sed haec delictorum leviorum, illa
graviorum. PL 16:520A–B.

to be performed, and with accompanying prayer placed them in the special class of penitents. In the West the length of the penance was not normally so great as in the East, and by the end of the patristic period seems to have usually been only the duration of Lent. Sackcloth, ashes, and often tonsure were imposed at the beginning of the period; and during it the penitent was debarred from Communion, was placed in a special part of the Church, and had to leave with the catechumens. Prayers, almsgiving, and severe fasting, the wearing of a distinctive garb, continence, and inability to carry on business or social life were the most prominent elements of the discipline. When the assigned penance was completed,[7] the bishop by another solemn ceremony reconciled the penitent to the Church and so restored him to Communion. But the reconciled penitent could not return to the ordinary laity; many obligations remained with him for life. He could neither marry nor be admitted to the clergy; public office was forbidden him, and he was to live like a monk in the world, until death. In part, these lifelong consequences were meant to protect him from any relapse into serious sin, for in Spain a relapse after having once received penance was regarded as an irremediable disaster, and the lapsed penitent could only resign himself to the mercy of God.

Canonical penance did not make forgiveness available for all sins, and other means had to be found. In many cases this other means was a special emphasis on compunction. First, all members of the clergy were debarred from canonical penance to avoid giving scandal; their grave sins, if brought to light, entailed their deposition; but otherwise they had only compunction available.[8] Again, canonical penance was intended for very grave sins only; the daily venial sins had no regular provision other than compunction; and since some late theologians like St. Caesarius of Arles, St. Gregory, and St. Isidore taught that in practise if

---

[7] Commonly on Holy Thursday in the early Roman rite, but Good Friday in the Mozarabic; cf. the rite of reconciliation, *Lib. ordinum,* cols. 200–205, and Férotin's note, col. 96, note 1.

[8] It will be remembered that in the seventh century and later it was largely the clergy who could read Latin, the language in which Isidore's *Synonyma,* the pseudo-Isidore, and Albar's *Confessio* are written.

not in theory a sufficient accumulation of venial sins might imperil salvation as truly as mortal sin,[9] compunction was a matter of serious concern for everyone.

The severity and the non-repeatable character of canonical penance, though well meant, gave rise to further problems. Many Christians who needed it postponed receiving the sacrament until their deathbed, so that, like Extreme Unction, it came to be thought of as a preparation for death. Like others of the Fathers, St. Isidore protested against this procrastination,[10] but it became the general practice none the less.[11] This meant that the mass of Christians went all their life long without any sacramental means of forgiveness for the accumulation of their sins, some of them doubtless being guilty of mortal sin and therefore possibly guilty of sacrilegious communions in addition. So for the general body of the faithful compunction was throughout life the only means of cleansing the soul, until perhaps they received Penance on their deathbed.[12] There was still one more group to whom compunction was a matter of life and death—those who having once received penance had fallen again into mortal sin; to them under this ancient regime the Church offered no further sacramental help; all it would do was urge them to contrition and remind them of the infinite mercy of God.[13]

There was indeed another system of "private penance" which

---

[9] Amann, *op. cit.*, col. 832.

[10] *Sententiae*, II, 13, 15; *De eccles. officiis*, II, 17, 9.

[11] Poschmann, *op. cit.*, p. 92.

[12] Cf. Sr. Patrick Jerome Mullins, *op. cit.*, pp. 101–103. She believes that the Good Friday service of "indulgentia" (*Lib. ordinum*, cols. 200ff.), originally meant for the reconciliation of canonical penitents, came to be directed to the whole congregation; that it was regarded as a climax of personal Lenten efforts toward contrition, satisfaction and amendment, and a preparation for the reception of Holy Communion on Easter. The people do not receive formal reconciliation, but apparently it was thought God at this time forgave informally those who were truly contrite. Amann, *op. cit.*, col. 836, suggests that something of the kind is the background of the Lenten sermons of SS. Leo, Caesarius of Arles, and Gregory, in which they try to stir the people to compunction, prayer, fasting and alms-giving.

[13] In this connection there is an interesting passage in Augustine, *Ep.* 153, c. 3, n. 7, CSEL 44:401–404, PL 33:655f.

was developed out of the older system by Irish monks and spread by them in the sixth century to England and the Continent. This rectified some of the shortcomings of canonical penance, and was much closer to the confession known to modern Catholics. Likely enough it was this form of penance of Celtic origin whose appearance in Spain roused the famous denunciation of the Third Council of Toledo in 589 A. D.[14] Thereafter the Visigothic councils continued to legislate in terms of classical canonical penance.[15] Through the seventh century the Spanish Church was not only conservative but was well organized and able to keep a firmer control over the practise of its members than was the case elsewhere in the West. Even so, Amann thinks that in spite of the resistance of the councils, private penance of the Celtic type probably continued to spread quietly in Spain.[16]

The Moslem conquest of most of the Peninsula in 711 not only entirely changed the organization of church and state, but cut down the amount of records that were written and that have survived. And in contrast with the Visigothic period, what documents there are have not been searched for the light they might throw on penance. Le Bras says that before writing the history of penitentials in Spain, it will be necessary to make a new search of Spanish libraries.[17] Meanwhile we have only scattered facts, mostly from northern Spain.

The first of these come from Theodulf, whom Charlemagne made Bishop of Orleans.[18] He repeatedly alludes to his Gothic origin, and while his birthplace is uncertain, he is thought to have come from northern Spain. He went to the Frankish empire where the Insular penitential system held a monopoly of the field,[19] and where the English Alcuin was its enthusiastic ad-

---

[14] Sr. Patrick Jerome Mullins, *op. cit.*, pp. 90f., gives text and references.

[15] Amann, *op. cit.*, cols. 847f.; Mullins, *op. cit.*, pp. 100f.

[16] *Op. cit.*, col. 853.

[17] G. Le Bras, "Hist. des collections canoniques," *Revue historique de droit*, 1931, p. 130.

[18] O. D. Watkins, *History of Penance*, II, 693ff.; Göller, "Das spanische-westgotische Busswesen," *Römische Quartalschrift*, XXXVII (1929), 308ff.

[19] Poschmann, *op. cit.*, p. 92; Amann, *op. cit.*, cols. 862ff.

vocate. Theodulf issued two sets of regulations for the clergy of his diocese which, without being controversial, express his views on penance.[20] These are a compromise between the two systems. He prefers the older system, but does not deny the efficacy of private penance; however, if the latter is to be used, it must include a detailed and complete confession, and the penalties inflicted must be based on Scripture and the canons of the Fathers; the penitential books he passes by in complete silence. Some scholars are inclined to believe that in some ways Theodulf furnished material that was later used in the movement of reform which was initiated in the synods of 813.[21] This greater conservatism of Theodulf, and his desire to keep the canons of the Fathers, would seem to be the result of Spanish training, if the assumption that Spain was still conservative is correct.[22]

On the other hand, two penitentials of the Insular type, both written in Spain, still survive, and it is possible that the desired search of Spanish libraries may disclose more. Both of these are contemporary with Theodulf himself. The first of them is the *Paenitentiale Vigilanum* or *Albeldense*,[23] so-called because it is preserved in the famous codex (Escorial d. I. 2) made by the priest Vigila in the abbey of St. Martin of Albelda. Though of Spanish provenance, as is frequently the case in this literature, there is not much that is original in its contents; the material is almost wholly drawn from two well-known Insular families of penitentials. But in the present connection, that makes it all the more interesting. The other is the *Paenitentiale Silense*,[24] which is preserved in a manuscript from the monastery of Silos now in the British Museum. This contains most of the Celtic material of the *Albeldense,* but with a notable addition of canons drawn

---

[20] Theodulf, *Capitula ad presbyteros parochiae suae,* nn. 29, 30, PL 105:200ff.; *Capitulare ad eosdem, ibid.,* 211f.

[21] Watkins, *loc. cit.;* Amann, *op. cit.,* col. 872.

[22] So at least Watkins, *op. cit.,* p. 693; Amann, *op. cit.,* col. 882.

[23] Le Bras, *op. cit.,* pp. 116–118; Fournier and Le Bras, *Hist. des collections canoniques en Occident,* I, 87; McNeill and Gamer, *Medieval Handbooks of Penance,* p. 291 gives a selection in translation.

[24] Le Bras, *op. cit.,* pp. 118–129; Fournier and Le Bras, *loc. cit.;* McNeill and Gamer, *op. cit.,* pp. 285–290.

from the *Hispana* collection of councils. Apart from these two, no other penitential from early Spain is known.[25]

With only these two penitentials yet brought to light, it is hard to determine the extent that Insular private penance permeated Spain. Le Bras is of the opinion that Spain did not take much to these books. This would not necessarily mean that private penance was not in use: that would be possible as today, by leaving the determination of penalties to custom and to the discretion of each priest; the penitential merely marks a transition stage in which the effort was made to form a fixed tariff of penalties for all conceivable sins, which all priests (who used that particular penitential) would be expected to follow. Yet the relative absence of penitentials at the time they were in general use in northern countries may well be an indication that frequent, reiterated private penance was not common south of the Pyrenees. Perhaps the old canonical penance in its vestigial, deathbed form still remained the only form of the sacrament commonly known.

These indications come to us from the free, Christian Spain of the north. If that part of the country remained relatively uninfluenced by the Celtic system which had conquered the lands north of the Pyrenees, it may be presumed that the Mozarabs, still more separated from Christendom, were still more untouched. Two pieces of evidence tend to corroborate the presumption.

A Mozarab council was held at Córdoba in 839 to take action against some local heretics it calls Acephali or Cassiani, and its acts are fortunately preserved for us in the Codex Samuelis. The first page is badly damaged and in part undecipherable; here, after a lacuna, comes the fragmentary clause ". . . esse institutum a Sanctis Patribus ut nullus ordinetur clericus absolutus," which seems to refer to the old rule that a man who had received canonical penance was not allowed subsequently to enter the clergy. Again, a few pages later, the same heretics are condemned for refusing to receive penance from Catholic clergy: if they go on a journey, they remain excommunicate until they can return to their own sacrilegious *sacerdos;* and they are warned not to

---

[25] Le Bras, *op. cit.,* p. 130. McNeill and Gamer, *op. cit.,* pp. 360ff. gives a selection from a penitential of the fifteenth century, but this belongs to a different world.

receive penance from Catholics even at death.[26] From these references some hints may be drawn. In both cases it is evident that some sort of penance was in ordinary use; and this was not merely received at the approach of death, for the heretics are reproved for remaining excommunicate during a distant journey. The excommunication in question was not likely a mere disciplinary action, like the general excommunication of heretics by the Church, since the heretics looked forward to being released from it[27] by their own heretical clergy; penance is explicitly mentioned in the next sentence. But is it public or private penance that is in view? The first reference to the old rule that a penitent could not be ordained points in the direction of canonical penance, though the damaged state of the text makes certainty impossible. The first sentence of the second passage would seem to imply that the excommunicated person could, if he wished, be restored to communion before setting out on his journey. This would be possible under some circumstances with canonical penance,[28] but it would seem more normal with private penance which was easily available at any time of the year. However, rather strongly against the Celtic form of the sacrament is the fact that the traveller in question is already excommunicate, and must await another visit to his *sacerdos* to be restored to communion; thus the penance here in view (if we may assume that it was penance) was a form that consisted of two parts separated by a period during which the penitent was excommunicated. This was the case with canonical, but not with Insular penance. So the probability is that in the acts of this council we can see the earlier form of the sacrament still surviving.

---

[26] Quid pejus qui ab ipsis peregre proficiscens excomunicatus manet, donec ad suum sacrilegum sacerdotem reddeat. Quinimmo etiam ab extrema die vitae terminum a Catholicis ne poenitentiam accipiant admonuntur. Sane de talibus lethale virus cancri venena sauciant, atque damnabilis doctrina.—ES, XV, pages unnumbered, but this at top of fifth page of text.

[27] Therefore they recognized it as binding in conscience, as they would not have done a ban of them by the Catholic Church as heretics.

[28] Good Friday was the liturgical day for the solemn reconciliation of penitents in the Mozarabic rite; cf. *Lib. ordinum,* cols. 200ff. But another service of reconciliation was provided (cols. 96-100) that could be used at other times of year, whenever the imposed penance was completed.

Another piece of evidence is the episode of Albar's closing years, when he received canonical penance in danger of death.[29] Here is a perfectly clear case of the old order still being in use. Since at the time of reception actual death was not imminent, the rubric [30] was observed that reconciliation should not follow immediately. So as Albar convalesced, he found himself excommunicated like one who received the sacrament in ordinary health. Reconciliation now depended on the bishop, whereas in private penance a simple priest would have sufficed.

Thus what evidence we have gives us no clue of the practise of private penance; the old discipline appears to be in full force in Andalucia in the middle of the ninth century.

The series of writings we are considering have a few passages on penance that are adequately clear. Thus the *Oratio* contains an explicit statement on canonical penance, the only one in the series: " Penance is to be done according to the quality of the faults; for as slight sins are removed by secret prayer, so grave ones are remitted before the Church through penance and satisfaction." [31]

But the penitence which the user of the *Oratio* is arousing is of another kind, the direct dealing of the soul with God. Close to the end there is a passage (nn. 41, 42) in which the soul sums up what it has done in these prayers; four times the statement is repeated, *" egi poenitentiam coram te "* : " Lord, I have recognized the sound of your calling, and accusing myself I was converted, and I have done penance before you, as this day shows. . . . For after you converted me, I did penance; and after you showed it to me, I struck my thigh, I was confused and blushed . . . for in your mercy my soul arose from the dead and came

---

[29] See pp. 32ff. above.

[30] *Lib. ordinum,* col. 91.

[31] *Oratio,* n. 10: Ipsa autem poenitentia juxta qualitatem delictorum agenda est; nam sicut levia peccata occulta oratione delentur, ita gravia coram Ecclesia per poenitentiam et satisfactionem remittuntur. The sentence sounds Isidorian, and is sandwiched in between two lengthy quotations, one from the *Etymologiae,* one from the *Sententiae;* but I have failed to find this particular sentence in Isidore.

to life again. . . . Wherefore I am become a man of good·hope, for you have preserved me until the time of conversion, in which considering my sins I was contrite, and did penance before you. . . . Let the confession of my mouth be pleasing to you, and instead of the offerings of gifts which I do not offer you by hand, I submit as a sacrifice to you this weeping of my contrite heart." Here the author represents his contrition as the *poenitentia,* the only *poenitentia,* he has done; and for this he speaks of his sins having been remitted, without any reference to ecclesiastical penance, either public or private. But we can perhaps go even farther than this. In the first passage quoted (n. 10) he said that canonical penance was needed for grave sins; now he writes that by his personal contrition " in your mercy my soul arose from the dead and came to life again." This language ought to mean that he has been forgiven grave sins, for it is only by grave sins (which we therefore call mortal) that the Christian loses his supernatural life. Possibly it may be thought that the author is now using words with devotional abandon rather than with theological precision. But we have the fact that sacramental penance was generally left until the approach of death; and that, if mortal sins committed earlier in life were to be forgiven before the last moment, it would have to be by compunction. And when we notice the kinds of sins the author mentions here and there in his three works, and continually he speaks of their extreme gravity, we can hardly avoid concluding that he expects contrition (perhaps with the *votum* of the sacrament on the deathbed) to cleanse the soul from grave sins during life.

In a beautiful prayer to our Lord, the author attributes to him directly the power of " binding and loosing," without any reference to his delegation of authority to the Church: " thine is the power of putting to death and of freeing, of binding and loosing; I have yielded my soul to be bound in the toils of many crimes . . . Lord, now loosen the chains about my neck " (n. 18). It is not that the author denies the delegation to the Church—he once speaks explicitly of canonical penance—rather he does not think of it; sacramental penance is received, like Extreme Unction, on the deathbed; through the long years of life when the sins are being committed the delegated power is not used, and the sinner in the interim relies on our Lord's forgiving directly upon seeing his compunction.

A stanza in the *Lamentum* (n. 63) implies the same doctrine: "Kind Father, pardon what I admit and confess; I declare my sin and do not hide it; accept my admission and grant indulgence."[32]

These passages from the pseudo-Isidore, representing the late Visigothic or early Mozarab period, harmonize well with the other evidence. There is no hint of private penance such as the Third Council of Toledo condemned in 589, whether Celtic or otherwise. There is one explicit statement about canonical penance, which takes for granted that it is normal; for the rest it is exclusively a matter of private compunction operating apart from the sacrament. Spain was conservative, public penance survived as a shadow of its former self—on its own deathbed; the new form had not yet been accepted, and meanwhile they were making shift to get along without the sacrament as best they could.

2. *Compunction and Tears*

There is no forgiveness of sin under any system without compunction. But the frequent repetition of private penance has an advantage over the older system in that a sorrow for sin that is a little less than perfect can be helped along by the sacramental action. When this was lacking, it was doubly important to make sure that souls were wholly contrite. So we are not surprised to see how large a place compunction holds in the teaching of the great Spanish doctor, St. Isidore, whom we may take as expressing the mind of the Spanish Church.[33] To him compunction of heart is not just one of the necessary virtues which are given each its place in an orderly synthesis of doctrine; " it is the central theme of his spiritual teaching." He has little to say about the ordinances of canonical penance and reconciliation; his

---

[32] Benigne Pater, ignosce, quod agnoscens fateor,
Pronuntio malum meum, non, vindex, operio;
Excipe professionem et da indulgentiam.

NB. that *indulgentia,* shouted scores or hundreds of times by the congregation, was the climax of the reconciliation liturgy on Good Friday.

[33] St. Patrick Jerome Mullins, *op. cit.,* pp. 96-111.

emphasis is on the interior dispositions of soul—genuine sorrow even to tears, self-inflicted punishment, whole hearted effort to avoid relapse into sin, and a life-long remorse coupled with a humble and loving confidence in God. His writings continually urge it on others, and sometimes there break through them rays of his own deep spirit of contrition. At the approach of death he solemnly received public penance himself in the presence of his clergy and people.

In the book of *Sentences* Isidore describes the process of conversion as beginning with a weeping for sin, and proceeding to the desire for heaven; first we purge with tears the faults we have committed, and then with a clean soul we may contemplate what we seek.[34] We are reminded that public tears were formerly more esteemed than today. "Compunction," says Isidore following Gregory, "is humility with tears."[35] Tears are but a sign of compunction of heart, but it was a sign that was taken seriously, and which plays a notable part in Albar's *Confessio* and its related literature.

Weeping for sin occurs constantly in Isidore, and it will not be amiss to bring together a few passages from the *Sententiae*. "The bitterness of penance causes the soul to examine its deeds with care, and to recall with weeping God's gifts which it despised. Nothing is worse than to recognize guilt without bewailing it."[36] "He does penance worthily who weeps for his guilt as a lawful satisfaction, that is, condemning and mourning what he has done, being the more profuse in his grieving as he was more headlong in sinning."[37] "The servant of God ought to have such a remembrance of sin that he is continually confessing with tears what he has done."[38] On the other hand, unfortunately, there are "many who relentlessly shed tears but do not cease from sinning. Some receive tears to penance and do not have the effect of penance, for by their inconstancy of mind, now they

---

[34] *Sententiae,* II, 8, 2,

[35] *Ibid.,* II, 12, 1: Compunctio cordis est humilitas mentis cum lacrymis, exoriens de recordatione peccati et timore judicii.

[36] *Ibid.,* II, 13, 4.

[37] *Ibid.,* II, 13, 6.

[38] *Ibid.,* II, 24, 3.

pour out tears at the recollection of sin, but again as old habit revives they again commit the acts they were bewailing." [39] " Never pray without groaning, for the recollection of sin begets sorrow. . . . Therefore when we stand before God we ought to sigh and weep." [40] In another work St. Isidore writes of three ways in which sin is forgiven: after mentioning baptism and martyrdom he says that the third is " the fruitful compunction of penance," " for in God's sight the tears of penitents are like baptism." [41]

The pseudo-Isidore is also an advocate of tears and explicitly mentions their power to wash away sin. " What do admitted crimes need but lamenting, and what does the wound of misdeeds require but the medicine of weeping? "[42] " There is no evil that cannot be wiped out by tears." [43] And in a thoroughly Isidorian passage: " It is certain that all guilt is removed by weeping, if the evil character is reformed and the old sins are not repeated. . . . And since by the satisfaction of weeping the fallen soul is again raised up and by this laver it receives the dignity of its former brightness, it behooves me to increase my weeping and to shed plenteous tears for my oft repeated iniquities." [44] And again farther on: " Loosen the reins of my eyes, and let my eyelids pour forth waters in a broad stream, that the guilt of all my crimes may be washed away by the torrent of tears, and let them run without hindrance down my face until all the foulness of iniquity is cleansed away." [45]

The general effect of Albar's *Confessio* is one of deep grief, but when we come to look closely, we are surprised how infrequently appear the group of words that circle about the idea of

---

[39] *Ibid.*, II, 16, 2.

[40] *Ibid.*, III, 7, 5.

[41] *De ecclesiasticis officiis*, II, 17, 6. St. Ildefonsus echoes Isidore on the three means of forgiveness, " The third is the overflowing of tears which is done to the remission of sins—laboriously accomplished indeed, but through the loving-kindness of the Redeemer sure to obtain mercy," *De cognitione baptismi*, c. 120, PL 96:160f.

[42] *Exhortatio poenitendi*, lines 38f.

[43] *Lamentum poenitentiae*, 95, 1.

[44] *Oratio pro correptione vitae*, n. 13.

[45] *Ibid.*, n. 26.

crying and tears. It seems like a desert after Verecundus and
Isidore and the *Lamentum.* Albar expresses his sorrow in other
ways. But difference in wording does not mean a difference in
doctrine; he, too, believes that penitent tears wash away guilt
from the soul. "Whence it comes about that where I ought to
flood myself with tears and to cleanse myself wholly with continual weeping, by daily belying my desire I do nothing but
double the sum of my guilt." [46] "What has restored others to
health I am terrified to find has injured me—not that the medicine was impotent, but that I have not properly wept for my
uncurable disease; for if I had shed a sufficient flood of tears, I
should not now have to seek a remedy elsewhere." [47]

3. *The Synonyma and the pseudo-Isidore's Works as Prayer-books*

In spite of the fact that some modern readers have failed to
see it, St. Isidore very clearly had a religious purpose in writing
his *Synonyma;* it was a purpose very close to his heart—to aid
a sinful soul to arouse the spirit of compunction. It might be a
little hard to say whether he intended it primarily for his own
use or for that of others. To us it may seem impersonal and
generalized like a schoolbook; but like St. Thomas Aquinas, St.
Isidore was so thoroughly a teacher that even his devotional
writings and prayers might well unconsciously fall into a didactic
form. But in substance, "synonymous style" apart, it would be
most suitable for general use—a devotional book to be prayer-
fully read, and then serve as a model for the further meditation
of those seeking to rise to a better level of Christian life. As the
sketch already given above has shown, there is a logical development leading a soul from mere complaints about temporal mis-
fortune to a realization of his own sin and then to a heartfelt
sorrow for it, to contrition and forgiveness, and then to advice
for the living of a virtuous Christian life. It is well designed to
be the " Serious Call to a Devout and Holy Life " or " Introduction to the Devout Life " of the seventh century.

---

[46] *Conf.*, n. 2, PL 402C.
[47] *Ibid.*, n. 3, PL 406A.

The same is true of the pseudo-Isidore. The sequence of three pieces loosely parallels the development of the *Synonyma*. The dialogue is simplified, the *Exhortatio* bringing together into one speech all the reasonings and encouragement of Isidore's *ratio,* bringing the soul from agitated complaints about temporal calamity to compunction for sin. At the end it urges the converted reader to use the next piece, the *Lamentum,* as the vehicle of his penitent grief.

> Sequentia vero carmina constructa lamentis
> Suspirando lectita, nonnumquam plorando decanta. lines 171f.

The *Lamentum* is essentially the expression of the tears so much emphasized by Isidore; there are other elements like the long passage on the Last Judgment, but they are used only as further motives of sorrow. The *Oratio* begins after the sins have already been forgiven,[48] for the author does not share our modern readiness to forget about our old sins as quickly as absolution has been received. Like the older Christians [49] he continues to recall in humility and sorrow his former evil life, the need for making satisfaction for it, and a holy fear of his own discovered weakness which could easily, if unguarded, lead him to relapse. So sorrow and tears still form a notable part of this long prayer to be used after absolution. But other elements are brought in, some giving reassurance of God's mercy, some being direct praise and thanksgiving to God for his loving-kindness; and then there are parts that look to the future. It will be remembered that the last half of the *Synonyma* gives moral advice for the leading of a true Christian life; only a part of this concluding *Oratio* of the pseudo-

---

[48] Cf. n. 2: Tu enim abstraxisti me de laqueis mundi, et eduxisti me de retiaculo peccatorum.

[49] He quotes twice, first in part, then in its entirety (nn. 9, 10), Isidore's etymology of *poenitentia:* Poenitentia appellata, quasi punitentia, eo quod ipse homo in se poenitendo puniat quod male admisit. Nam nihil aliud agunt, quos veraciter poenitet, nisi ut id quod male fecerunt, inpunitum esse non sinant. Eo quippe modo sibi non parcentibus ille parcit, cuius altum justumque iudicium nullus contemptor evadit; *Etymologiae,* VI, 19, 71. Cf. also Isidore, *Sententiae,* II, 13, 2: Magna jam justitiae pars est, seipsum nosse hominem, quod pravus est, ut ex eo divinae virtuti subdatur humilius, ex quo suam infirmitatem agnoscit.

Isidore deals with this, but it is none the less very decidedly present, paragraphs 35–41 consisting largely of prayer for a long list of virtues in crisp, precise phrases. This is clearly meant to be studied as well as prayed, for a continuous rapid reading of such a long catalogue of short phrases, each introducing a new thought, would leave the reader thoroughly confused. It is meant for meditation rather than simple petition. It is evident that the pseudo-Isidore is following in the same path as the *Synonyma,* leading a soul to contrition, and thereby to absolution without recourse to the sacrament of Penance, and ending with encouragement and direction for an improvement of life. Much of the *Oratio* has the same didactic tone as Isidore, only part of it being due to the extensive excerpts from the great doctor.[50]

4. *The Particular Sins Lamented in These Works*

In books designed to arouse contrition it is important to see in what way the conscience is examined and how the sins are confessed. Are they mentioned merely in globo, or are they specified in considerable detail? If the latter, do they cover, at least representatively, the whole field of possible sins, or are they only a certain group of sins which may be those particular sins that some real individual has actually committed? Of the documents which are being considered, all but Verecundus accuse themselves of sin in a more than perfunctory manner.

Dracontius leads the procession of penitents. "We are a wicked race deserving no kindness, and of them I am the first and worse than a sinner. When shall I confess all my wickedness, the guilt of heart and body? Even if I had an iron throat, and as many mouths as teeth, and as many tongues as hairs on my head, I could not tell the full number; but it is enough to say that I am guilty of every crime. What your commandments forbid, that I confess I have committed; and what you shudder

---

[50] Cf. *Oratio,* n. 10, quoting, *Etymol.,* VI, 19, 71–73; *Oratio,* n. 11 quoting *Sententiae,* II, 13, 18. Cf. also *Oratio,* n. 15: "peccavi nequiter, deliqui crudeliter, erravi vehementer, corrui fortiter," with *Synonyma,* I, 65: peccavi enim crudeliter, lapsus sum fortiter, cecidi graviter, corrui miserabiliter."

at, I cannot deny I have done." [51] " Therefore I confess with
pitiable mind the full guilt and great evil, sprung from no single
crime; for all my wickedness surpasses the number of the sands
of the beach, and our evils are more than the waters of the sea.
I think the flood did not punish so great sins as I bear, oppressed
by the burden of wrongdoing. The rivers of crime take hold of
me and storms shatter me, and the torrent of sin rolls like a
wave over me. The streams of sins have drowned me in their
waves; the waves, the terrible horror of the waters, have come
up even to my soul." [52] This confession is at the same time
strong, universal, and thoroughly vague. Of course, elsewhere
Dracontius makes mention of his offence to the Vandal king; but
his confession of sins committed against God does not specify a
single fault. This kind of confession may indeed help arouse
compunction as a general hatred of sin, but it is of no use in
helping a struggling soul to examine his conscience for the past
nor to correct his faults in the future.

Two of the short poems have brief references. Thus St.
Eugenius of Toledo says: " I have oppressed, robbed, denuded,
committed crimes, I have been deaf to the voice of the poor, I
have corrupted my own body with a lewd wound." [53] This is
concise and, if a little poetical in phrasing, mentions injustice to
the poor and unchastity. The little *Confessio beati Isidori* is
rather in the style of Dracontius: " And now whatever evil desire
is able to produce, all the crimes that drown a burdened life, these
I confess I performed in demented fury." [54]

In the *Synonyma* there are three passages which use both
motifs. In the first [55] *ratio* is accusing man: You sin daily, by
pride, anger, envy, jealousy. Whom have you not torn to shreds?
Whom have you not disparaged? To whom have you not boasted
about infamy? False, inconstant, unfaithful, avaricious, stubborn,
sterile, inhuman, fruitless; there is no mercy in you, you have
fallen into the lusts of the world; you are fired with an earthly

---

[51] *De laudibus Dei,* III, 365–374.

[52] *Ibid.,* lines 582–591.

[53] *Carmen,* XIV, 61ff.

[54] *Conf. b. Isid.,* lines 16ff.

[55] *Synonyma,* I, 35 –37.

love; you hoard perishable things, the thirst of your greed knows
no satiety.   Daily you involve yourself in new sins, you increase
the old with new crimes, nor do you ever sate the flame of lewd
concupiscence.   You poor wretch!   Are you not ashamed to be
splashed over with many lusts?   Lustful corrupter, luxurious
adulterer, are you going to remain this way in concupiscence, will
you continue so in your shame?   Alas, how long will you go
astray?   Farther on (nn. 58f.) the sinner is now praying: Give
me bitter wailing, for I have fallen worse than the others.   I have
sunk lower than all.   I have surpassed the guilt of all the wicked
by my sin, the torments of hell are scarcely enough for my misdeeds.   There is no sin greater than mine.   I am worse than all
sinners.   And again, a few paragraphs later (nn. 65f.): I have
sinned cruelly, I have lapsed terribly (*fortiter*), I have fallen
grievously; there is no sin with which I am not stained.   There
is no vicious disease of which I have not caught the contagion.
Ignominious, infamous, overwhelmed with all shame, times without end I have given myself to filth.   I have promised to live
well and never kept the promise.   I have always gone back to
my sin, always have I repeated my derelictions.   In destroying
myself I have defiled others; by my depraved habits I have turned
many to iniquity. . . . In these passages Isidore combines the two
methods; the accusations cover in a general way the whole field
of possible sins—of all of which the soul is said to be guilty;
and a good many are mentioned by name, with a few being given
special attention, unchastity receiving the greatest emphasis.

The pseudo-Isidore follows the tradition.   When he urges repentance in the *Exhortatio* he assumes the reader is guilty of all
sins: "Although you are a sinner, impious, malignant, iniquitous,
long since polluted with every kind of crime, ask God for pardon
with undoubting faith, for he purges all penitents from every sin"
(lines 102ff.).   The *Lamentum* throughout its whole length is a
repeated expression of sorrow for sins, all sins—of all of which
the reader or speaker is guilty; but it never becomes specific.
Perhaps stanzas 48 and 49 are the most to the point: "The very
pains of hell will scarcely suffice for the measure of my sins and
the accumulation of my crimes, for no wretch has done such and
so great evils.   I sigh with fear for what I wickedly did; I am

smitten with the wound of the worst sins; I think it will be hard
to be saved from such great evils." The *Oratio* develops the
subject at greater length. First comes a long passage (nn. 27f.)
in which he confesses himself supremely sinful in general: " Behold, Lord, now is the time of confession, and the days of remission are at hand in which the promised pardon is given to those
seeking it; what more should I confess to you, when I do not
deny that I am worse than all the wicked, who are righteous in
comparison with me? For there was lacking no heinous sin, no
vicious misdeed with which I did not defile myself: headlong to
lust, bold in impudence, constantly given to luxury, shameless in
fornication, every day piling crime upon crime, I have not ceased
joining even worse things to those already bad; harsh in will,
perverse in mind, indecent in morals, polluted in heart, blas-
phemous in lips, wrathful and abusive. Wherefore I am now
confused, and blush to raise my eyes, knowing I am unworthy
to see the starry skies. . . . As I trust in you, give me forgiveness to salvation and the remedy of indulgence, that being merciful
you may destroy all the villainy of my sins, and not hold against
me the sins of my youth and ignorance committed in an age that
is treacherous, rude, wanton, vain and foolish, prone to evil and
very slothful to good, swift to death but mulish to manage in
leading to life . . ." Later, in the section that deals with the
good life to be led in the future, the long list of virtues to be
practised is introduced by a few lines of sins to be avoided:
" Cut away the old rottenness of cupidity and avarice, of vanity
and arrogance, of anger and impatience, and of other vices; trim
off what is superfluous, cut off what is indecent, depress pride,
cut back the poisonous and fruitless, that the bitterness of the
evil tree may be changed to produce good juices " (n. 34).

It is in a very similar way that Albar describes his sins in the
Confessio. Like the others he is deeply repentant, but he scarcely
tells us for what. " I must bear witness against myself, that I
never put an end to my iniquities." [56] " Behold, Lord, I fall every
hour both in act and in thought." [57] " If I should try to enumerate

---

[56] PL 402D.
[57] PL 404D.

all the grave faults into which I have fallen and in which I still lie, my confession would never come to an end." [58] " I pass over those grave ones that send a soul to the unending fire of hell; I shall speak of those that seem slight to men who know not how to weigh in a true balance. . . . For when under your gaze I turn the eyes of my mind upon myself I find there nothing light, nothing that is not grave. For what is more serious than lust, what more burdensome than fraud, what more weighty than vain boasting, what worse than murder, what more evil than false witness, more unjust than despoiling the unfortunate, what more wicked than to refuse to the harm of others to tell what one knows? Yet, as you know, who are the searcher of hearts, all these things and others which I lack words to tell have I committed, partly in act and partly in volition; yes, wretch that I am, I have done in action everything that even the devil could not do. If we think of concupiscence, even now I fight against myself through various kinds of allurements. If of frauds, my conscience is witness that even until today I pursue them in body and in mind. If of violence, I am the murderer of my soul not merely figuratively but literally. If of false witness, often up to this hour I set no limit to my tongue in perjury. If of swelling pride, I have no equal in it. If of envy, at every moment I am burning with envy at the good fortune of my brethren. If of injustice, I exult like an unbridled horse over falsehood. If of covetousness, out of greediness even in my dreams I seek mountains of gold. Finally, if I have even a trifling good thought, immediately I yield to the gnawing worm of vainglory." [59]

Thus it is seen that in this respect Albar's book is much like its predecessors. None of them is at all like the Insular penitentials in their thorough cataloguing of all kinds of sins, nor like more modern examinations of conscience. Both of these latter belong where the emphasis is on integrity of confession, and so their aim is to help the penitent or confessor to discover all individual sins as completely as possible. But this group of Spanish writings grows from a religious setting where compunction—intense

---

[58] PL 403C.
[59] PL 405A–C.

sorrow for the past, and good intentions for the future—is given most prominence; contrition of course must cover all the sins committed, but it can do that effectively in a general way without listing each individual lapse. Another important point is the difference of immediate purpose of the two types of list: the Celtic penitential and the modern examination are both concerned with bringing sins to the tribunal of the sacrament; but if we are right in our theory of the Spanish group, they were to be used privately at times when the sacrament of penance was not being approached; in fact, they were a temporary substitute for the sacrament, and in this case there would be no need for minute analysis, but only for an effective, all inclusive contrition.

CHAPTER III

Sources of the Confessio

A. PARALLELS WITHIN THE GROUP

I. Parallels between Albar and His Predecessors

We now come to a patient examination of some detailed similarities between Albar's *Confessio* and the penitential writings of his predecessors which we have been studying. We begin with a passage that is unusually rich in parallels, and so will indicate his manner of working. In form it is an expansion of a stanza of the *Lamentum*.[1]

I. . . . ' peccatorem semper revocasti: sed ubi justitiam tuam cogito, et examen judicii tui mente pertracto, illico ut cera *liquefactus tabesco*. Numquid justitia tua injustitiam probat? aut veritas tua mendaces coronat? aut sanctitas tua iniquos remunerat? ut me iniquum, impium, et mendacem, impunitum evadere credam? Absit. Imo sine dubitatione firmissime credam, me similes mei odio detestare, vel ulciscere summo. Neque enim *tenebrae communitatem fruuntur lucis;* nec foetor suavitatem boni gerit odoris. Quod si juxta te nemo habitat mente malignus, nec ad te pertinget nisi corde et corpore sanctus; quid de me dicam ego *foetidissimus hircus,* quem adsiduitas iniqua ut crudelis et acerrima domina ad perpetranda quasi violenter adtrahit scelera?

Cf. *Lamentum,* n. 17, 3: Cujus pavore *tabesco, liquesco* formidine.
Ibid., n. 13, 1, 2: Abominabilis erit coram te iniquitas,
Nullus enim inmundorum tibi sociabitur;

Cf. II Cor. 6: 14. Quae enim participatio justitiae cum iniquitate? Aut quae *societas luci ad tenebras?*
Cf. I Pet. 4: 18.

Lamentum, n. 31, 3: Quomodo tunc *fetens hircus* mundis jungar ovibus?

---

[1] Albar, *Confessio,* n. 2, PL 121:403A–B. *Lamentum,* n. 31.

Most of the passage is an elaboration of the first two lines of the stanza of the *Lamentum;* midway he weaves in a verse of Scripture, and ends with an unmistakable proof of influence in the *fetens hircus,* which Albar characteristically multiplies to the superlative. In the *Lamentum* the reference to the goat comes in naturally in a forthright treatment of the Last Judgment and the Scriptural metaphor of the sheep and the goats. Albar, too, is here referring to the Last Judgment, but with more self-conscious ornament and indirect allusion, which brings us upon his superlatively stinking goat with a shock.[2]

The theme of these lines of Albar is the fear of Judgment Day, but he touches rather lightly upon it. The *Lamentum,* from which he took one stanza to embroider, develops the theme at great length until it becomes the largest episode in the poem. And others of the works use the fear of Judgment and hell as a motive for repentance. The *Synonyma* uses it rather briefly: " I fear Judgment Day, the day of darkness and cloudiness, a day bitter and hard. . . . Help me, my God, before I die, before death prevents me, before hell clutches me. . . . If the just man will hardly be saved, where will a wicked man like me be? . . . Woe to the day I committed sin! "[3] There is here no verbal similarity between the *Synonyma* and the *Confessio;* we may notice, however, that Isidore employs the Scriptural thought: if the just are hardly saved, what will become of the sinner?[4]

In the *Oratio* the same ideas enter briefly: (n. 15) " But who will be unconcerned about your judgment, when before your tribunal not even the righteousness of the just is secure? If an account must be rendered even for an idle word, how shall I be safe who have committed the leading sins? My mind had no

---

[2] This forceful self-depreciation is a part of the tradition; cf. Eugenius, *Carmen* XIV, 59f.: quid faciet ergo vermis, putredo, favilla . . . and Isidore, *Synonyma,* I, 71: coeli non sunt mundi in conspectu tuo; quanto magis ego abominabilis, et putredo, et filius hominis, vermis, qui hausi quasi gurges peccatum. . . . As Jerome was a favorite with Albar, we may add here his *Ep. 73,* n. 4: quanto magis nos vermiculi et pulices solam debemus scientiam inscientiae confiteri . . .

[3] *Synonyma,* I, 62ff.

[4] I Peter 4: 18; cf. Proverbs 11: 31.

security in view of your judgment, and my conscience no peace
in view of my sins. Therefore my contrition is great as the sea,
because my wound is very great." [5] Eugenius makes a passing
allusion:

> quid faciat ergo vermis, putredo, favilla,
>   si Christi faciem corda beata pavent? [6]

This thought is contained, not too conspicuous because of the
embroidery, in the last part of the quotation from Albar, " Quod
si juxta te . . . ."

We also see in this selection from Albar a Pauline turn of
style that is a favorite with Albar; it is to ask a rhetorical question, and follow it with the answer " Absit." The *Oratio* uses
the turn once, in n. 29.

The phrase " nisi corde et corpore sanctus " has not been identified. It may be a reminiscence of II Thess. 3: 5, Dominus autem
dirigat corda et corpora nostra in caritate Dei . . . , or of Juvenal's mens sana in corpore sano. This particular phrase of
Juvenal was used twice by Dracontius, *De laudibus Dei*, III, 626,
745; and the works of Juvenal were among those volumes brought
from Navarre by Eulogius (*Vita*, n. 9).

II.   Towards the end of the *Confessio* Albar remembers that
in this life God gives his blessings to both good and evil men,
but that after death each is rewarded according to his works;
then he recalls that we sometimes receive afflictions also here on
earth.   Of the just he says: " Here often he tests the just with
sufferings, whom there he introduces to the heavenly mansions
and crowns." [7]   It is an idea common in this tradition, that God
uses trials in this world to try and to cleanse our souls.   A few
lines later Albar adds: " For here it is I seek cleansing, here I
ask mercy, here I beg the pardon of sins, because I know there
is no meritorious confession in hell."

The truth is a favorite with the pseudo-Isidore. In the *Lamen-*

---

[5] Cf. Lamentation of Jeremias 2: 13.
[6] *Carmen* XIV, 59f.
[7] *Confessio*, n. 4, PL 410C.

tum we have: " I beseech you, after the discipline, grant me mercy " (n. 11, 2). " As a remedy for the evils of eternal judgment, it is better to be struck now with a temporary scourge than to be given unending tortures in the future. Please use now the stings of the goads of torments by which the old putrid guilt is done away; let healthy life at last take the place of so great a sickness. Apply what you will me to suffer for my crimes, but not in anger, that it may be endurable, and that after my punishment you may again be gentle " (nn. 13–15). " Wear down my flesh for its sin as much as it pleases you, for I shall gladly accept temporal wounds; my only prayer is that you should not in wrath impose eternal ones. Afflict me here with sorrows, burden me with griefs, purge me now with scourging, so as not to have to punish me in the future; let the soul be redeemed by the punishment of the guilty flesh " (nn. 69f.). " But if you sentence me to be still loaded with afflictions, be severe to me, chastise and reprove me as you do those you love, but in mercy to cleanse, not to destroy me " (n. 76). " I confidently believe that, not wishing to destroy me, you subjected me to scourges which would bring me to my senses, that by hating sin I might return to grace " (n. 98). In the *Oratio* the same idea is developed at still greater length (nn. 6–9, 34), but the quotation of only two or three sentences will be sufficient: " Why should I take amiss the suffering by which the soul is rescued from eternal destruction and restored to eternal salvation? " (n. 8). " To thee, O Lord, be praise and glory, who both strike and heal, wound and cure. You give a passing sorrow, and after a little you refresh with eternal joy, for you are just and kind: just, for you never spare the guilty; but kind also, for you do not refuse mercy to the penitent " (n. 9).

St. Isidore found comfort in the same thought: " The perverseness of evils does not kill but teaches you. . . . . If here we are worn down with scourges, we shall be found purged at the Judgment. Here God always wounds those he is preparing for eternal salvation. . . . Therefore do not murmur nor blaspheme. . . . He who patiently bears adversity quickly appeases God. If you wish to be cleansed, when being punished accuse yourself and praise God's justice. . . . If you have been converted, correction is what you suffer, for stripes absolve the convert from sins." [8]

Dracontius also: "May such stripes be of profit to me, may the fierce pain avail for forgiveness; it will help to remember when you are kindly indulgent and change this pain into joys." [9] "You have punished the prodigal, now have mercy on the repentant." [10]

And Eugenius: "Father, do not consign me to the fire of hell where the flame continually burns the members without limit; here inflict what we deserve: let there be peace after our passing." [11]

III. Near the beginning of the *Confessio,* in a passage later to be studied as a whole, there is a clause: "You are the invincible right hand of those who ask your aid." [12] Though the fundamental idea is Scriptural, this is probably not without an allusion to another element common to the tradition—"stretch forth thy right hand to help me."

Pseudo-Isidore, *Lamentum,*
　　Jam non possum sustinere, *da dextram et eripe.* 8, 3.
　　Porrige nunc manum tuam et succurre misero. 83, 3.
　　Fessum de pulvere leva, tibi reconcilia. 108, 2.
Confessio beati Isidori,
　　Subleva iacentem miserum *tua dextera* Christe. line 32.
Verecundus, *De satisfactione,*
　　Cerne, precor, mitis, *manibusque attolle jacentem.* line 117.
Dracontius, *De laudibus Dei,* III, 675,
　　Erige prostratum, vindex, adtolle iacentem.
Isidore, *Synonyma,* I, 72,
　　operi manuum tuarum porrige dexteram
Job 14: 15
　　operi manuum tuarum porriges dexteram.

IV. Twice Albar speaks of his sins being "ulcers" which require medical treatment. "You who see the ulcers of souls,

---

[8] *Synonyma,* I, 28–31.
[9] *De laudibus Dei,* III, 672ff.
[10] *Ibid.,* line 610.
[11] *Carmen* V, 25ff.
[12] PL 399C.

do yourself compound a special dressing for them." [13] " For since the very medicine with which you cure our ulcers produces in me wounds and not healing . . ." [14] The pseudo-Isidore also twice uses the metaphor. " I beg you, apply a remedy to the bad wounds, binding up the flowing ulcers of vices, restoring the corrupt to permanent health." [15] " You have come to my help from afar, providing the remedy of my cure, for you have given my soul, scored by an awful ulcer, to be healed with the medications of this penance." [16]

In this same connection there is another, and this a verbal parallel. Close to the end Albar writes:

Quod si me non dignum levi *medicamine* vides, et *ferro,* imo *cauterio,* mundandum cognoscis; exerce in servum cauterio medicinam, cui hostis magnam infixit plagam.[17]

Cf. pseudo-Isidore, *Oratio poenitentiae,* n. 7,

Si enim noxium exterius cernerem in corpore vulnus, aut aliquem intrinsecus sentirem viscerum dolorem, ocius omnino ad *medicum* currerem, secandam cum doloribus *ferro* traderem carnem, et ignito cremandam *cauterio.*

V. Near the beginning of the second section Albar uses the fact that we are God's handiwork, his creatures, as a basis of appeal to him for help. " Lord God, kind and merciful, look upon your works . . . because it is in no way right to leave the works of your hands under the dominion of the hateful enemy— that, formed by you, I should be a slave of the devil; that, created by you, I should be the feeding ground of the plunderer." [18]

Compare this with the *Lamentum:* " Bring me medicine, for I am a creature of your making, your moulding " (n. 55, 3). " Snatch your workmanship from the devil's hands; be mindful of the thing you have made, and be placable. Your hands have

---

[13] PL 404A.
[14] PL 405D.
[15] *Lamentum,* n. 56.
[16] *Oratio,* n. 6.
[17] PL 411C.
[18] PL 400C-D.

made me, your fingers formed me, outlining my body member by member in my mother's womb, the body created by your power in which you have enclosed a soul. Lord, do not give your handiwork to the ruin of death " (nn. 88–90). The author of this is in turn echoing Psalm 138.

And with Verecundus: " I beg you, turn a kind face toward me, cleansing my wounds, that your handiwork may not perish in complete ruin " (lines 91f.).

VI. Albar: Subveni, Domine, perdito vago et profugo. . . . (PL 412A)
  Esto dux itineris servulo, via regia erroneo profugo . . . (PL 407C)
  Genesis 4: 12, Vagus et profugus eris super terram. (Spoken to Cain)
  Pseudo-Isidore, *Lamentum*, 103, 1: Recipe, Domine pater, fuga lapsum servulum.
  Augustine, *Soliloquia*, I, 1, n. 5: Recipe, oro, fugitivum tuum, Domine, clementissime pater: jamjam satis poenas dederim, satis inimicis tuis, quos sub pedibus habes, servierim, satis fuerim fallaciarum ludibrium. Accipe me ab istis fugientem famulum tuum. . . . (PL 32:872)

" Via regia," which occurs in the second quotation from Albar, appears only once in Scripture (Num. 21: 22), and then in a purely literal sense. St. Eulogius uses it figuratively: Ne respiciatis retro, nec primam fidem irritam faciatis, nec, manum super aratrum tenentes, ab itinere regio in devium declinetis . . . (*Documentum martyriale*, n. 12, PL 115:827B). And St. Isidore: Qui viam regiam, hoc est, Christum, deserit, etsi videat veritatem, a longe videt . . . (*Sententiae*, I, 17, 6).

VII. Albar: *Restaura*, Domine, *ruinam* corporis mei, et mentis meae vigorem redintegra . . . (PL 403C)
  per inobedientiam mandatorum tuorum in mortis deflendam *ruinam* deveni. (PL 401A)
  Pseudo-Isidore, *Oratio*,
   et ut in brevi concludam, omnis *ruinae* haec est *reparatio*. (n. 8)
   Numquid non hoc modo *reparabis* casus *ruinae* meae? (n. 20)

VIII. Three Scriptural examples are used to illustrate the return to the life of grace after the death of sin.

(a). Lazarus.

Albar: Dic mihi, Domine: Lazare veni foras, et statim licet
ligatus jaceam, licet putrefactus quatriduanus jam foeteam,
ad vocem tuam et solutionem et odorem cum vita pariter
capiam. (PL 411C)

Lamentum, Karpe moras, visita me, immo veni, libera,
" Surge " dicito captivo, " prodi foras! " misero,
Releva carcere trusum, pande iam abconditum. (n. 82)

Solve Christe vincla pedum, ligamenta criminum,

Resera limen obstrusum tenebrosi carceris,
Redde iam luci sepultum, peregrinum patriae. (n. 105)

Oratio poenitentiae, n. 8 speaks of the other Lazarus, the character in the parable of the rich man.

(b). The prodigal son. Cf. Luke 15:11ff.

Albar: Domine Deus, pie et misericors, respice super opera tua,
et illo pietatis vigore quo prodigum recipis filium, me quoque
protege miserum, quia opera manuum tuarum in dominio
iniquissimi hostis relinquere fas est (n)ullo modo . . . (PL
400C–D)

Lamentum, Errasse me dudum plango profanus et prodigus,
Meretricio amore bona perdens patria,
Hinc ad te vilis, egenus et percussus remeo.

Ecce me indignum loco filiorum clamito,
Quod paternitatis tuae renuens ad monita
Vagus perquaquam defluxi, cucurri per avia.

Feci malum miser ego in insipientia,
Provocavi te ad iram diris facinoribus,
Quibus rite consternatus magno luctu conteror.

Fletibus tamen revertor confitendo poenitens:
Aufer indignationem culpae factus inmemor
Et paterna pietate sume, precor, errulum. (nn. 72–75)

Jerome, *Ep.* 2: Ego sum ille prodigus filius, qui omni, quam
mihi pater crediderat, portione profusa necdum me ad
genitoris genua submisi necdum coepi prioris a me luxuriae
blandimenta depellere. Et quia paululum non tam desivi a
vitiis, quam coepi velle desinere, nunc me novis diabolus
retibus ligat, nunc nova impedimenta proponens maria undique circumdat et undique pontum, nunc in medio consti-
tutus elemento nec regredi volo nec progredi possum. CSEL,
54:11, 12.

(c). The woman taken in adultery. Cf. John 8 :2ff.

Albar: et adultera mox inlaesa evasit, dum et praeterita et sequentia peccata a te sibi dimissa percepit. (PL 404C)

Exhortatio: there is just a passing allusion to her in line 133.

IX. Albar: Sed iam diu est, Domine, quod dominium ejus a me rejicere malui; quod merito exigente non valui, quia quasi ex potestate vindicat subditum, quem a nativitatis exordio diro vinculo tenuit captum. . . . Quemque sibi numquam deprehendit repugnantem, nunc catenis insolubilibus ligat gementem. (PL 400C)

Oratio: Quaero portum evasionis, et nequaquam reperio quomodo regredi (possim) de pedica deceptionis Satanae; illaqueavit pedes meos, et nullo modo praevaleo. (n. 15)

X. Albar: et ab eorum (sc. delictorum) inlecebra me tota mente cupio retrahere, sed vinculorum praeditione connexus, quod promitto nequeo adimplere. (PL 402C)

Isidore, Synonyma, I, 66: Ut bene viverem ultro promisi, quod pollicitus sum numquam servavi.

XI. Albar: Ecce enim leprosi illius vocem adsumpsi, quia pejor ut ille me sentio addictum pesti. Dico namque: Si vis, Domine, potes me mundare. Dic verbo, et curabor ab isto morbo lethale. (PL 404B)

Mt. 8: 2, Et ecce leprosus veniens, adorabat eum dicens: Domine, si vis, potes me mundare.

Oratio: sed noli a me avertere faciem tuam, quia si vis potes me mundare. (n. 18)

XII. Albar: Sed numquid abbreviata est manus tua, ut salvare nequeas? aut auris tua adgravata est ut non exaudias? Absit. (PL 404B)

Isaias 59: 1, Ecce non est abbreviata manus Domini ut salvare nequeat, neque aggravata est auris eius ut non exaudiat.

Lamentum, 66, 1: Brevis non est manus tua ut praestare nequeat.

XIII. Albar: Aspice Domine, et me haerentem in vepribus vide, et respiciendo vincula mea disrumpe. (PL 406A)

Genesis 22: 13, Levavit Abraham oculos suos, viditque post tergum arietem inter vepres haerentem cornibus, quem assumens obtulit holocaustum pro filio.

Oratio: quatenus novum tibi hominem ex inutili vetustate, cunctis vitiorum vepribus concrematis, poenitentiae caminus restituat . . . (n. 41)

Verecundus, *De satisfactione:* Crucifixusque premor peccati vepribus . . . (line 53)

XIV. Albar: Tu enim es, Domine, qui scalam nobis crucem tuam
dedisti, quam et nobis tollere humeribus, et te sequere pura
mente jussisti. (PL 408A)
Luke 9: 23, Si quis vult post me venire, abneget semetipsum,
et tollat crucem suam quotidie, et sequatur me.
Oratio: ut memetipsum abnegans sequar te cum cruce mea,
perdere pro te promptus animam meam, ut per te inveniam
illam. (n. 41)

XV. The last page of the *Confessio* has a vague general resemblance to *Oratio* n. 36, but they avoid close contact in detail;
the nearest parallel is:

Albar: perducas me ad te, qui vera tutatio es. (PL 412A)
Oratio: Trahe me post te, et duc quocumque placet. (n. 36)

XVI. Albar: Exue me meis, et induar tuis. Exime totum me a
me ut totus restituar tibi. (PL 412B)
Oratio: Exue me foeditate omnium vitiorum, et indue dignitatem cunctorum virtutum. (n. 34)
Augustine, *Soliloquia,* I, 1, n. 3: Deus qui nos eo quod non
est exuis, et eo quod est induis. (PL 32:871)

XVII. We now come to a passage with wider relationships.

Albar: et in tam innumerabiles formas dividitur (sc. iniquitas
mea), ut *ex una superbia matre multae robustiores filiae*
quotidie oriantur. Et quas dinumerare, nec perpendere queo;
quomodo destruere valebo? Certe enim *ex superbia omnis
iniquitas captat principium,* quia omne quod agitur *vitium
ex contemptu mandatorum tuorum habet exordium.* (PL
409C–D)

  1. *Oratio:* Mater et regina septem principalium vitiorum
  superbia non ingrediatur, nec requiescat in domicilio cordis
  mei, neque soboles eius mihi adhaereat. (The author then
  gives the same list of seven deadly sins as that in Isidore,
  Differentiae, II, 161.)
  Isidore, *Sententiae,* II, 37, 8: Principalium septem vitiorum
  regina et mater superbia est, eademque septem principalia
  multa de se parturiunt vitia.
  Gregory, *Moralia,* XXXI, c. 45: Ipsa namque vitiorum
  regina superbia cum devictum plene cor ceperit . . . (PL
  76:620D)
  Ibid., XXIII, c. 13: Humilitatem namque, quae magistra
  est omnium materque virtutum . . . (PL 76:265B)

2. · Ecclus. 10: 15, Quoniam initium omnis peccati est superbia.

3. Isidore, *Sententiae,* II, 38, 2: Omnis peccans superbus est,
eo quod faciendo vetita contemptui habeat divina praecepta.
Recte ergo " initium omnis peccati superbia," quia nisi
praecesserit mandatorum Dei inobedientia, transgressionis
non sequitur culpa.

XVIII.   Towards the end, (PL 411f.), Albar uses a rhetorical
device four times, a double imperative separated by a vocative.
The *Oratio* uses the same device but employing different words.
Each of Albar's petitions has sources of its own.

A. Albar
1. Miserere Domine miserere, et veniam tribue te oranti.
   Ps. 56: 2, Miserere mei Deus, miserere mei.
   Ps. 122: 3, Miserere nostri, Domine, miserere nostri.

2. Exaudi Domine exaudi, et iniquitates meas tu dimitte.
   III Kings 18: 37, Exaudi me Domine, exaudi me.
   III Kings 8: 36, Exaudi eos in caelo, et dimitte peccata ser-
   vorum tuorum.
   Augustine, *Soliloquia,* I, 1, n. 4: Exaudi, exaudi, exaudi me
   Domine.

3. Parce Deus, parce, et scelera mea tu pius dimitte.
   Joel 2: 17, Parce Domine, parce populo tuo, et ne des heredi-
   tatem . . .
   Oratio, n. 31: Iam miserere mei, placare, et revertere, parce
   animae meae, parce peccatis meis.
   Lamentum, 8, 2: Vilis factus consummavi; parce mihi de-
   precor.
   Exhortatio, line 85: Dic " peccavi nimium," " parce mise-
   rere! " proclama.
   Eugenius, *Carmen* V, 29: Pauperi praebete victum, " parce "
   Christo dicite.
   Carmen XIV, 77: Parce, precor, animae pulsanti, parce
   petenti.

4. Peccavi Domine peccavi, et iniquitates meas ego agnosco.
   (cf. Ps. 50: 5)
   Lamentum, 100, 1: Peccavi tibi, peccavi et deliqui nequiter.
   Isidore, *Synonyma,* I, 71: Peccavi Deus, miserere mei; peccavi, Deus, propitiare mihi.
   Oratio Manassae:[19] Peccavi Domine peccavi, et iniquitates
   meas ego agnosco.

---

[19] The *Prayer of Manasses,* an apocryphal addition to the Old Testa-

B. *Oratio.*
1. Solve, Domine, solve jam vincula colli mei. (n. 18)
2. Deliqui, Domine, deliqui multum, et hanc ob causam . . .(n. 19)
3. Parce animae meae, parce peccatis meis. (n. 31)
4. Proba me, Domine, proba me in camino humiliationis. (n. 33. cf. Isaias 48: 10)

2. *Parallels among Other Members of Group, but not in Albar*

I. Old age a motive of compunction.

Eugenius, *Carmen* V, 7–9:
Eugeni miselle plora: langor instat inprobus,
vita transit, finis urguet, ira pendit caelitus,
ianuam pulsat ut intret mortis ecce nuntius.
Verecundus, *De satisfactione,* lines 59–62:
Ecce breves anni vitae pereuntis abibunt,
ingrediorque viam numquam rediturus per illam.
Spiritus in vacuas meus attenuabitur auras,
nec mihi iam superest praeter ferale sepulchrum.
Dracontius, *De laudibus Dei,* III, 624:
Addo quod et vita brevis est, mors longa moratur.
Isidore, *Synonyma,* I, 49,
(The time of death is uncertain; do not be caught unaware.)

---

ment, is a short penitential prayer of only two paragraphs. It was used in two places in the Mozarabic liturgy. The last paragraph alone, which contains the sentence quoted above, forms the "lectio libri Paralipomenon" in the *Ordo de Missa unius penitentis (Liber ordinum,* col. 351). The complete text, though with a wording considerably different from that in modern Biblical editions, was one of the canticles for Lent in the Breviary (*The Mozarabic Psalter,* ed. Gilson, pp. 153f., and PL 86:858f.). In this canticle form, the sentence in question not only appears in its place in the text, but also is used as the antiphon for the whole canticle, and so would be all the more familiar. In the liturgical version, this is the only duplicated petition, but in the modern text of the Vulgate there are two others: 1) multiplicatae sunt iniquitates meae Domine, multiplicatae sunt iniquitates meae, 2) remitte mihi Domine, remitte mihi. Besides these, there are other phrases which find echoes in our group of potential writings: 1) super numerum arenae maris abundaverunt iniquitates meae (cf. Dracontius, III, 584f.; Verecundus, 57f.); 2) percurvatus multis vinculis ferreis ad non erigendum caput; 3) quoniam irritavi furorem tuum, et feci malum coram te. Manasses as a person is used as an example of a penitent forgiven in *Exhortatio,* lines 124ff.

II. Penance implies a reform of life. Of course this is taken for granted by Albar as by all Christians, but he does not state it explicitly.

> Isidore, *Synonyma,* I, 76f.; II complete.
> Isidore, *De eccles. officiis,* II, 17, 7.
> *Exhortatio,* lines 66–72, 150–169.
> *Oratio,* nn. 13, 34–41.

III. Why do you waste yourself on false joys?

> *Exhortatio,* line 5: Non ablatas resculas mundi facesque
> suspires.
> *Ibid.,* line 77: Et sequi vanissima respue, contempne, rescusa.
> Eugenius, *Carmen* V, 10–12.
> Cur, inique, concupiscis falsa mundi gaudia?
> Cur caduca non relinquis, curris ad perennia?
> Dum petis tantilla lucra, dona perdes maxima.

IV. Dracontius, *De laudibus Dei,* III, 647: et lacrimis maduere
> genae . . .
> Eugenius, *Carmen* V, 3: lacrimis ora madescant . . .
> *Confessio b. Isidori,* line 2: Reple genas lacrimis magnisque
> gemitibus ora.
> Ovid, *Ars Amatoria,* III, 378: lacrimis . . . madere genas

V. I am a creature of dust and ashes.

> Isidore, *Synonyma,* I, 72: Memorare Domine quae sit mea
> substantia, memento quia terra sum, memento quia pulvis
> et cinis sum, operi manuum tuarum porrige dexteram.
> *Oratio,* n. 30: Num dolebis contra me in perpetuum . . . cum
> sim ego creatura ex terra et cinere corruptibilis et mor-
> talis . . . ?

VI. God rejoices more over the penitent than over many who need no repenance (Luke 15: 7). This is a favorite theme with the pseudo-Isidore.

> *Exhortatio,* lines 150–164.
> *Lamentum,* n. 93.
> *Oratio,* n. 43.
> *Liber ordinum, Missa de penitentibus,* " Post nomina," (col.
> 357): Domine Deus omnipotens, qui plus gaudes super

unum penitentem quam super nonaginta et novem iustos non indigentes penitentia . . .

VII. *Exhotatio,* line 74: Et peccasse poenite et iam peccare desiste.
   Oratio, n. 18: . . . noli contemnere poenitentiam, Domine, poenitet me errasse.
   Dracontius, *De laudibus Dei,* III, 611: poenitet en peccasse nimis, iam parce flagello.
   Ibid., line 644: . . . me poenitet ante quod egi.

VIII. Ninive an example of penitents forgiven.

   Dracontius, *op. cit.,* III, 633–640.
   Exhortatio, lines 122f.

IX. Where shall I flee from God?
   Verecundus, *op. cit.,* lines 54f.
   Lamentum, nn. 51–53.
   Psalm 138: 7ff.

X. Isidore, *Synonyma,* I, 1: Anima mea in angustiis est, spiritus meus aestuat, cor meum fluctuat . . .
   Exhortatio, line 1: Quur fluctuas anima merorem quassata procellis?
   Lamentum, 50, 2: Fluctuat mens in merore, cor natat in lacrimis.
   cf. Verecundus *op. cit.,* lines 17f.: Cur, anima inflelix, sontes te evolvere curas
   Anxius instigat dolor?

In content and in general point of view the pseudo-Isidore is very Isidorian. The fact that he here adopts the opening words of the *Synonyma* to form the first line of his own trilogy, and again uses it in his second piece, is a strong indication that he was consciously producing a work of the same nature as the *Synonyma.*

XI. *Lamentum,* 104, 3: Sed quem viventem fatigas, refice post obitum.
   Eugenius, *Carmen* V, 27: Hic repende quod meremur, sit quies post transitum.

XII. *Oratio,* n. 20: ab omni morte criminum per te reviviscere, et omni colluvione peccatorum . . .

Ibid., n. 34. hic ab omni vitiorum colluvione deterge . . .
Isidore, *Sententiae*, II, 37, 1: Tunc se viri sancti veracius a
vitiorum colluvione detergunt . . .

XIII. I am the worst sinner.

> *Oratio,* n. 29: Semper corrui in deterius, et de malis in pejora
> defluxi . . . haec etiam causa fecit te in hunc mundum
> descendere, ut peccatores salvos faceres, quorum prin-
> cipalior ego sum . . . (Cf. I Tim. 1: 15)
> Isidore, *Synonyma*, I, 59: Non est peccatum super peccatum
> meum, non est iniquitas super iniquitatem meam, nequiorem
> me cunctis peccatoribus penso. Comparatione mea nullus
> iniquus est . . .
> Dracontius, *op. cit.*, III, 565f.: gens scelerata sumus, nil de
> pietate merentes,
> quorum primus ego plus quam peccator habendus.

These parallels and similarities are sufficient, it would seem, to
place it beyond a doubt that there was some kind of continuous
tradition in this literature. Not that each writer necessarily had
all his predecessors directly before him, nor that all wrote with
precisely the same purpose; but that there was a literature of
repentance which displays not only a similar point of view, but
the use of no inconsiderable body of material in common. They
share a certain theology, certain motives and examples, certain
references and phrases.

Beyond this, there is no doubt that Albar directly knew and
used the pseudo-Isidore, especially the *Lamentum* and *Oratio;*
the *Exhortatio* is shorter and would naturally offer less material,
since its purpose is preparatory, to arouse compunction, whereas
Albar begins with compunction already in full flood. That he
also used the *Synonyma* is probable, but it is less thoroughly
proved, no doubt partly because the " synonymous style " does not
invite quotation. Again, it might not at first be realized how
short the first book of the *Synonyma* is in substance; it is divided
into seventy-eight brief paragraphs, some containing only a single
thought, but in most cases two; if these are stripped of the
padding of repetition with which St. Isidore is here experiment-
ing, the real body would be reduced to rather slender dimensions.
It cannot be proved from his text that Albar used any of the other

writings we have been concerned with. He may well have known some; but when there is a parallel passage, either the wording is sufficiently divergent, or there is a possible common source such as Scripture, to leave the matter uncertain.

And it is not likely to be questioned that in the main Albar intended to write a book in the general tradition of the *Synonyma* and the pseudo-Isidore. Doubtless like every author, he also had motives and coloring of his own; but even so, it was not written only for his own eyes and heart.

B. PATRISTIC SOURCES AND PARALLELS FOR ALBAR

1. *St. Augustine's Soliloquia*

Unlike the correspondence with John, in the *Confessio* Albar is not given to verbal quoting; even in citing Scripture he usually weaves the text into his own composition. He uses the Fathers for doctrine rather than for quarries of precise quotations, so it is seldom we can catch him with incriminating proof of direct employment of them. And as much of St. Augustine was adopted, diluted, and preserved by St. Gregory and St. Isidore, we often cannot be sure where it was that Albar picked up the thoughts.

However there is one work we can be certain Albar knew at first hand, Augustine's *Soliloquia*.[1] This is a dialogue between Augustine and reason on semi-philosophical subjects. For the most part it is fairly rapid dialogue, as in Isidore's *Synonyma*, not long speeches as in Boethius' *Consolation of Philosophy*. Most of the first chapter[2] is an introductory prayer of invocation, and it is this that Albar has used. It will be remembered that it was said above that the *Confessio* has been divided by editors into four unequal portions, the first being the shortest and also the most distinctive. Its distinctiveness is due to the influence of the invocation introducing Augustine's *Soliloquia*.

In form the invocation consists almost entirely of a long series of short clauses, like exclamations, addressed to God, each one

---

[1] The *Soliloquia* was written at Cassiciacum, in the fall of 386, along with three other dialogues whose aim was to set out clearly some points of Christian philosophy. Augustine was baptized on April 24/25, 387.

[2] *Soliloquia*, I, 1, nn. 2–5, PL 32:869ff.

mentioning some single divine attribute or work. Until the conclusion, they are almost wholly worship and praise, with little
petition; they contemplate God's glory and goodness, and do not
consider the author's sinfulness. In fact, the whole work is one
of Christian philosophy, and is in no way a part of our penitential
literature. It is this influence that makes the first division of
Albar's *Confessio* stand apart from the rest of that book and
from the type to which it belongs. The following quotations are
chosen to show the different forms the clauses take.

2. . . . Deus qui paucis ad id quod vere est refugientibus,
ostendis malum nihil esse. Deus per quem universitas
etiam cum sinistra parte perfecta est . . . Deus quem
amat omne quod potest amare, sive sciens, sive nesciens.
Deus in quo sunt omnia, cui tamen universae creaturae
nec turpitudo turpis est, nec malitia nocet, nec error
errat . . .

3. Te invoco, Deus veritas, in quo et a quo et per quem
vera sunt, quae vera sunt omnia. Deus sapientia, in quo
et a quo et per quem sapiunt, quae sapiunt omnia. Deus
vera et summa vita, in quo et a quo et per quem vivunt,
quae vere summeque vivunt omnia . . . Deus a quo
averti, cadere; in quem converti, resurgere; in quo
manere, consistere est . . . Deus a quo admonemur ut
vigilemus. Deus per quem a malis bona separamus . . .

4. Quidquid a me dictum est, unus Deus tu, tu veni mihi
in auxilium; una aeterna vera substantia, ubi nulla dis-
crepantia, nulla confusio, nulla transitio, nulla indigentia,
nulla mors . . . Deus cujus legibus in aevo stantibus,
motus instabilis rerum mutabilium perturbatus esse non
sinitur, frenisque circumeuntium saeculorum semper ad
similitudinem stabilitatis revocatur . . . Deus a quo
manant usque ad nos omnia bona, a quo coercentur a
nobis omnia mala. Deus supra quem nihil, extra quem
nihil, sine quo nihil est . . .

5. Jam te solum amo, te solum sequor, te solum quaero,
tibi soli servire paratus sum . . . Jube quaeso atque
impera quidquid vis, sed sana et aperi aures meas,
quibus voces tuas audiam . . . Expelle a me insaniam,
ut recognoscam te . . . Ad te mihi redeundum esse
sentio: pateat mihi pulsanti janua tua; quomodo ad te
perveniatur doce me . . .

In general form, the first division of the *Confessio* is the same as the *Soliloquia*. It, too, is an invocation of God, composed in large measure of a series of exclamatory clauses, many of which follow one another without the formation of a complete sentence. These are the opening lines:

> Excelse Deus, ineffabilis, invisibilis, a quo bonum, et per quem fit quodcumque claret honestum, quem digne rogare valet, et quem omnis sermo, licet indigne, rogare, audet: sine quo nihil est, et absque quo impietas omnis procedit . . . Deus qui Adae progeniem sola bonitate ex parte restauras, et eam partem quam perire sinis ob parentelem (sic) vitium juste condemnas: Deus qui ipsis notitiam dedisti fidei quos credituros ante mundi initium nosti: Deus qui licet multa occulta, tamen juste fecisti quae facta sunt omnia: Deus sine cujus nutu nullus sermo procedit; et contra quem plerumque ipse sermo datus agere praesumit: Deus quem nemo nescit, et quem nullus plene ut es ipse cognoscit: Deus cujus magnitudo incomprehensibilis, cujus gloria inaestimabilis, cujus jussio fortis, cujus dispositio justa, cujus judicia vera, cujus clementia super opera sua extenta . . . Tua ab initio creaturam singulari misericordia foves, potentiali virtute regis, ineffabili consilio vel potestate disponis. Deus qui contritorum non despicis preces, nec deprecantium te vero corde spernis clamores . . .

Besides the similarity of general structure, there is a similarity in some of the details. Many clauses of both authors begin with *Deus qui, Qui, Deus quem, Tu.* Albar sometimes uses the phrase *a quo et per quem* which is an abbreviation of Augustine's *in quo et a quo et per quem.* These locutions form a part of the pattern of the two works. Again Albar writes: *Deus quem nemo nisi corde adtingit purgatus,* while Augustine has: *quem nemo invenit nisi purgatus.*

A few other reminiscences are scattered through the later parts of the *Confessio.*

> Albar: Satis est Domine quod hucusque diabolo militavi: quod hostis orbis servitium sponte implevi: quod inimico famulatum iniquitatis opere praebui; quod insidianti mihi obsequens fui; quod latentes insidias ejus licet intelligerem non devitavi. (PL 400B)

Augustine: Recipe, oro, fugitivum tuum, Domine clementissime pater: jamjam satis poenas dederim, satis inimicis
tuis, quos sub pedibus habes, servierim, satis fuerim fallaciarum ludibrium.   (n. 5)

Much later, where Albar is developing a metaphorical meaning
from the conversation between our Lord and the woman of
Samaria (John 4: 7ff.), he writes:

Et vere Domine qui te vero corde sitit, haustum vitae
non morientis a te digniter sumit: nec aliquando sitire
novit cujus mens tui fontis poculum haurit.   (PL 408D)

The wording is based on the Gospel where *aqua viva, sitire
haurire* are repeated, but it undergoes characteristic elaboration,
and the word *haustum* is his own.   Cf. Augustine's,

Deus per quem sitimus potum, quo hausto numquam
sitiamus. (n. 3)

Already mentioned above:

(1). Albar: Exaudi Domine exaudi
     Soliloquia: Exaudi, exaudi, exaudi me, Deus meus.
(2). Albar: Exue me meis, et induar tuis.   Exime totum me a
     me, ut totus restituar tibi.
     Soliloquia: Deus qui nos eo quod non est exuis, et eo quod
     est induis.

The parallelism between Albar and Augustine extends to the
thought as well as the form.   It may even be said that in these
two works Albar is more Augustinian than Augustine himself.
The *Soliloquia* is an early work composed on the eve of his conversion; it is Christian, but also it is the work of one who is
much influenced by the spirit of Greek philosophy.   The body of
the dialogue deals with how to come to knowledge of God and
of the soul, the nature of truth and falsehood, and proof for
the immortality of the soul.   The invocation is primarily a prayer
of praise of God for those things that would especially interest
a philosopher—God the First Cause and Last End, eternal, perfect, true, beautiful, his greatness in creation, his natural support

and guidance of men. Grace and revealed truths are included, but take a secondary place. It has the soaring, remote, impersonal, intellectual tone that is a beauty of Platonism. But it has little of the sense of personal struggle, suffering and sin that are the characteristics of the *Confessio*, and that are more prominent in the later writings of Augustine himself.

The opening section of the *Confessio* then is a hybrid of the two spirits. Some of Albar's adoration of the divine attributes appears in the specimen already given. But in larger measure, while maintaining the attitude of praise, he makes a substitution of the truths for which he praises God: it is for God's mastery over evil, for the mystery of predestination, for his merciful dealings with men.

> Deus qui mala omnia odis, eaque occulto consilio, utique justo, plerumque permittis: Deus qui sicut malum, quod nihil est, odis; ita bonum quod aliquid est amas . . . Deus qui partim operis tui aeternitate consolidas nullo merito praecidente, partim juste mortalitate corrumpis nullo peccato patescente . . . Tu divitia pauperum, Tu consolatio tribulantium, To erector humilium . . .

As a result, there is not too sharp a break between the introductory division and the rest of the book. Albar is either artist enough or lucky enough to use the *Soliloquia* to enrich his own work without letting it become a distracting influence.

2. Other Patristic Parallels, Mostly of Thought

Except for the *Soliloquia* it has been impossible to prove any case of direct use of a Father; in this book Albar followed too independent a manner of writing. His ideas are naturally not all original, but he makes them his own, weaving them into his own text. But the ideas themselves are interesting, so many of the parallels now to be presented are of thought rather than word. In looking for the sources from which Albar drew his doctrine, it will be wise to look first to St. Isidore; for though it is certain that Albar knew some of the works of Augustine, Gregory, and Jerome, it may be supposed that the complete writings of Isidore were more readily available in Spain, and that his selection and synthesis of earlier material was often used instead of going back again to his predecessors.

I. Albar: Deus qui sine qualitate es bonus, sine quantitate magnus, sine situ praesens, sine effusione formae ubique diffusus: Deus qui corporalis non es, et per incircumscriptam substantiam ubique es. Qui sursum residendo regis, deorsum continendo ades, extra circumdas, infra et omnia penetrans. (PL 397f.)

Isidore, *De ordine creaturarum*, c. 1, n. 2: (una Divinitas . . . et Trinitas) . . . in qua nihil inferius, nihil superius, nihil anterius, nihil posterius, in natura Divinitatis esse credendum est; nihil serviens, nihil subjectum, nihil loco comprehensibile, nihil temporaneum, nihil infirmum, nihil crescens, nihil ad sexum habitumque pertinens, nihil corporeum sentiri fas est; sed est unus Deus sine initio sempiternus, sine loco ubique totus, sine sui mutatione omnia mutabilia disponens creaturarum; tempora praeterita, praesentia, futura pariter cernens; cui nihil est praeteritum, nihil restat, sed cuncta praesentia sunt. Cui nihil displicet quod bonum est, nihil placet quod malum est; a quo nihil naturaliter malum creatum est, quod per se nihil nisi creati boni vitium est. Bonus ergo sine qualitate, magnus sine quantitate, aeternus sine tempore, praecipuus sine situ, qui omnibus creaturis infunditur, cum non sit illi locus; quem nulla capit creatura, nulla comprehendit intelligentia. (PL 83:915).

Augustine, *De Trinitate*, V, 1, 2: sic intelligamus Deum, si possumus, quantum possumus, sine qualitate bonum, sine quantitate magnum, sine indigentia creatorem, sine situ praesidentem, sine habitu omnia continentem, sine loco ubique totum, sine tempore sempiternum, sine ulla sui mutatione mutabilia facientem, nihilque patientem. (PL 42:912).

Isidore, *Sententiae*, I, 2, n. 3: Immensitas divinae magnitudinis ita est, ut intelligamus eum intra omnia sed non inclusum, extra omnia sed non exclusum. Et ideo interiorem ut non contineat, ideo exteriorem ut incircumscripta magnitudinis suae immensitate omnia concludat.

Taio, *Sententiae*, I, 2 (= Gregory, *Homil. in Ezech.*, II, Hom. 5, n. 11, PL 76:991): Deus omnipotens ipse est interior et exterior, ipse inferior et superior: regendo superior, portando inferior; replendo interior, circumdando exterior. Sicque est intus ut extra sit, sic circumdat ut penetret; sic praesidet ut portet, sic portat ut praesideat. (PL 80:733C)

Mozarabic liturgy, Inlatio, Missa in octavo Dominico de quotidiano: Dignum et justum est . . . cuius divinitatis inmensitas sic inmutabiliter circumplectitur omnia, ut in singulis creaturis permaneat tota et in omnibus habitet universa. Non minoratur in minimis, non augetur in magnis. Non concluditur tempore, non adstringitur quantitate: non initio cepta, non termino finienda. A quo totus homo creatus est ad iustitiam sine peccato, et reparatus est post ruinam sacrificio eiusdem Christi mundissimo. Per . . . (*Lib. sacramentorum*, n. 1375, cols. 624f. The same as PL 85:649f.)[3]

In this passage Isidore would be a sufficient source for the general thought, but the word order of some of Albar's phrases is closer to that of Augustine: (1) Albar: sine qualitate bonus, sine quantitate magnus; Augustine: sine qualitate bonum, sine quantitate magnum; Isidore: bonus sine qualitate, magnus sine quantitate. (2). Albar: sine situ praesens; Augustine: sine situ presidentem; Isidore: praecipuus sine situ. The lines quoted from Taio-Gregory are sufficient to account for the last sentence given from Albar.

II. Albar: Deus qui mala omnia odis, eaque occulto consilio, utique justo, plerumque permittis. (PL 398C)

---

[3] This grouping of the divine attributes, which would seem less peculiar in theology, is rather unexpected in the liturgy. However, other examples are known, e.g.: the Mozarabic Illatio of the Third Sunday of Advent (*Lib. sacramentorum*, n. 23, col. 17 = PL 85:129A); the Gallican Contestatio of the Third Mass of Mone (PL 138:868A); and a Contestatio preserved in a Bobbio codex (PL 138:883B–C). This last is especially noteworthy, and Cagin (*Te Deum ou Illatio?*, p. 392f.) shows how it is based on the ten categories of Aristotle. It will be recalled that these latter are: substance, quantity, quality, relation, place, time, position, state, action, and affection or passive action (Aristotle, *Categories*, c. 4). The Bobbio Contestatio reads: *sine qualitate bonum, sine quantitate magnum, sine situ praesentem, sine habitu omnia continentem, sine loco ubique totum, sine tempore sempiternum, sine ulla sui mutatione mutabilia facientem, nihili patientem.* In hac ergo natura tibi Patri Spirituique tuo suoque conformis et consubstantialis unigenitus, abiectionem pulveris nostri, celsitudinem tuae maiestatis. The italicized words are exactly those of Augustine, *De Trinitate*, as cited above, with the omission of one phrase of Augustine.

Isidore, *Sententiae,* I, 3, 2: Dei secreta judicia non posse sensu penetrari, vel angelico vel humano (constat). Et ideo quia occulta, sed justa sunt, tantumdem venerari ea opus est, et timere, non discutere.

Augustine, *Ep.* 204, n. 2: Sed quoniam Deus occulta satis dispositione sed tamen justa nonnullos eorum poenis praedestinavit extremis . . . (CSEL 57:318; PL 33:939)

III. Albar: Deus qui sicut malum, quod nihil est, odis; ita bonum, quod aliquid est, amas; qui non naturam mali, quae nulla est, sed eos qui malum faciunt damnas . . . (PL 398f.)

That evil is not a substance but only a deordination is ordinary Christian doctrine; it is a commonplace in Augustine, and cf. Isidore, *Sententiae,* I, c. 9, and Taio, *Sententiae,* I, 15 (PL 80:748)

IV. Albar: Deus qui partim operis tui aeternitate consolidas nullo merito praecedente; partim juste mortalitate corrumpis nullo peccato patescente: Deus qui creaturam illam quam primam dignitate seu fortitudine vel decore esse voluisti, vitio suo corruptam ad inferiora dilapsam, ut esset quod creata est justitia exigente noluisti: Deus qui sicut nulla extante bonitate humanum genus creasti, ita nullo praecedente merito nos ratione creaturis aliis praetulisti. (PL 399A)

The rather cryptic middle part of the passage refers to Lucifer, and may be compared with Isidore, *Sententiae,* I, 10, 5: Primatum habuisse inter angelos diabolum, ex qua fiducia cecidit, ita ut sine reparatione labaretur.

In this passage Albar grasps the thorny question of predestination with both hands. The Augustinian phrase *nullo merito praecedente* is a favorite of his, and appears with modifications of wording three times here and twice again later in the *Confessio.* Albar here fully affirms absolute double predestination—absolute, in that it is without any regard of God's foreknowledge of the future merits and demerits of souls; and double, being predestination of some to hell as of others to heaven. In this he undoubtedly intended to follow that part of St. Augustine's teaching that is represented in such statements as the following:

Ep. 204, n. 2: Sed quoniam Deus occulta satis dispositione
sed tamen justa nonnullos eorum poenis praedestinavit
extremis . . . (CSEL 57:318; PL 33:939)

Enchiridion, c. 100: (Deus) bene utens et malis, tamquam
summe bonus, ad eorum damnationem quos juste praedestinavit ad poenam, et ad eorum salutem quos benigne
praedestinavit ad gratiam. (PL 40:279)

De perfectione justitiae hominis, c. 13: . . . in eo genere
hominum quod praedestinatum est ad interitum. (PL
44:308)

De anima et ejus origine, IV, c. 11, n. 16: . . . qui est et
illis, quos praedestinavit ad aeternam mortem, justissimus
supplicii retributor. (PL 44:533)

There is some discussion whether such statements give an adequate or fair expression to Augustine's thought when studied in
its whole context.[4] Certainly not all his disciples and followers
accepted it; St. Prosper of Aquitaine and St. Fulgentius of Ruspe
clearly reject predestination to damnation, and the Second Council
of Orange (529 A. D.) explicitly condemned it.[5] St. Isidore does
not seem to be consistent. In the first of the following citations
he holds the view of Augustine just given; in the second, he
weakens a little in regard to the reprobate, substituting *permittat*
for *faciat;* and in the third he copies Gregory in a similar modifica-
tion:

Differentiae, II, 118f.: Quidam enim gratissimae misericordiae ejus praevenientis dono salvantur, effecti vasa
misericordiae; quidam vero reprobi habiti, ad poenam
praedestinati, damnantur, effecti vasa irae. Quod exemplum de Esau et Jacob . . . Sicut per prophetam idem
Deus loquitur dicens: Jacob delexi, Esau autem odio
habui. Unde consequens est nullis praevenientibus meritis
conferri gratiam, sed sola vocatione divina. Neque
quemquam salvari sive damnari, eligi vel reprobari, nisi
ex proposito praedestinantis Dei, qui justus est in repro-
batis, misericors in electis. (PL 83:88B–C)

Sententiae, II, 6, 1: Gemina est praedestinatio, sive electorum ad requiem, sive reproborum ad mortem. Utraque

---

[4] Cf. Saint-Martin, "Prédestination . . . ," *DTC,* XII, 2856.

[5] Aliquos vero ad malum divina potestate praedestinatos esse, non solum
non credimus, sed etiam si sunt qui tantum mali credere velint, cum omni
detestatione illis anathema dicimus.—Denzinger-Bannwart, n. 200.

divino agitur judicio, ut semper electos superna et in-
teriora sequi faciat, semperque reprobos ut infimis et
exterioribus delectentur deserendo permittat.

Differentiae, II, 117: Nemo autem Deum meritis antecedit,
ut tenere eum quasi debitorem possit. Sed miro modo
aequus omnibus conditor alios praedestinando praeelegit,
alios in suis moribus pravis justo judicio derelinquit.
(Cf. Gregory, *Moralia,* XXXIII, c. 21, n. 38, PL 76:699B)

Taio of Zaragoza, who arranged material from Augustine and
Gregory into an orderly book on theology, flatly denies predestination of the reprobate:

Sententiae, I, 35, 1f.: Deus non omne quod praescit praedestinat. Mala enim tantum praescit, bona vero et praescit
et praedestinat . . . (Tenenda est inconcusse haec regula,)
omnes peccatores in malis propriis antequam essent in
mundo, praescitos esse tantum, non praedestinatos;
poenam autem eis esse praedestinatam secundum quod
praesciti sunt. (PL 80:765f.)

But if, like Augustine, Albar sometimes speaks of outright
predestination to damnation, also like Augustine, he elsewhere
writes of the other half of the mystery, God's love for all men,
and of our duty to lead a virtuous life:

Scio enim quia omnes velis facere salvos; sed huic tuae
sanctissimae voluntati illi qui pereunt se praebent in-
dignos: secundum opera enim nostra aut devoramur a
bestia, aut detrudamur gehenna. (PL 404A. This is
the reading of the printed text, but it must be corrupt;
Albar clearly means to contrast heaven and hell, not to
refer twice to hell.)

V. Albar: Deus qui massam perditioni deditam juste perimis,
et massam regni misericorditer sola bonitate qua affluis
eligis. (PL 399A)

Both the thought and the words are thoroughly Augustinian,
cf. *Enchiridion,* 95, 98f., 112. The phrase *massa damnata* and
its variants is common in Augustine, e.g., *Sermo* 27, c. 12, PL
39:177; Taio uses it thrice in an Augustinian passage, *Sententiae,*
I, 35, PL 80:765B–C. The word *massa* is much less often used
in a good sense, but cf. Augustine:

Ennarratio in Ps. 47, n. 10: Non solum illi multi erunt qui stabunt ad sinistram, sed et ibi erit plenitudo massae ad dexteram constitutae. (PL 36:540)

The Mozarabic liturgy uses it in both senses:

Inlatio in Adsumptione BVM: Qui enim ab initio massam faciens fortiter electorum. (*Lib. sacramentorum,* col. 403)

Post sanctus, Ordo de Missa unius penitentis: usque ad dignitatem glorie celestis adsumptus homo de massa nature corruptibilis glorietur in sede Patris et regnet. (*Ibid.,* col. 354)

VI. Albar: Deus qui ipsis notitiam dedisti fidei quos credituros ante mundi initium nosti. (PL 399B)

Augustine, *Liber de praedestinatione sanctorum,* c. 9, nn. 17f.: Et ab exordio propagationis humanae usque in finem, quibusdam ad praemium, quibusdam ad judicium praedicatur (sc. vera religio). Ac per hoc et quibus omnino annuntiata non est, non credituri praesciebantur; et quibus non credituris tamen annuntiata est, in illorum exemplum demonstrantur: quibus autem credituris annuntiatur, hi regno coelorum et sanctorum angelorum societati praeparantur . . . Quid enim est verius, quam praescisse Christum, qui et quando et quibus locis in eum fuerant credituri? Sed utrum praedicato sibi Christo a se ipsis habituri essent fidem, an Deo donante sumpturi, id est, utrum tantummodo eos praescierit, an etiam praedestinaverit Deus, quaerere atque disserere tunc necessarium non putavi. Proinde quod dixi: " Tunc voluisse hominibus apparere Christum, et apud eos praedicari doctrinam suam, quam sciebat et ubi sciebat esse qui in eum fuerant credituri," potest etiam sic dici: Tunc voluisse hominibus apparere Christum, et apud eos praedicari doctrinam suam, quando sciebat et ubi sciebat esse qui electi fuerant in ipso ante mundi constitutionem. (PL 44:974)

VII. There are three scattered passages in the *Confessio* that ought to be studied together, as they are all related to the Te Deum.

(1). Deus qui auctor es luminis, fluvius pietatis; dulcis es te firmo corde credenti: caecorum oculus, *debilium* animus,

infirmantium verissima salus, pes claudorum, lingua mu-
torum, fortitudo omnium saeculorum: Tu vitae via, Tu
salutis *vita,* Tu omnium te postulantium invictissima
dextra, Tu divitia pauperum, Tu consolatio tribulantium,
Tu erector humilium, Tu destructor extollentium. A te
incrementum accipit justus, per te sanctificatur perfectus,
a te coronatur in bono opere consummatus. (PL 399C)

(2). et REDIME me nunc etiam specialiter a diro praedone,
QUEM jam generaliter PRETIO SANGUINIS TUI REDEMISTI.
(PL 402A)

(3). Esto dux itineris servulo, *via regia erroneo profugo,*
medicina variis languoribus saucio, quia tu es lux omnium
saeculorum, dulcedo sanctorum, *firmitas infirmorum,*
curatio leprosorum, *vita mortuorum,* fortitudo justorum,
subditorum exemplum, via *credentium,* gaudium angelorum; per te príncipes regnant, TIBI ANGELI famulant,
Te archangeli nuntiant, Te *virtutes adorant,* TE CHERU-
BIM AC SERAPHIM INCESSABILI VOCE Trinum Dominum,
caelis hominibus nuntiant. Tu requires *patriarcharum,*
Tu laudatio PROPHETARUM, Tu exultatio MARTYRUM, *Tu*
hymnus *virginum, Tu* praemium *confessorum,* Tu vere
Sabbatum electorum; quia tuum est et in te est regnum
caelorum. (PL 407C–D)

The Te Deum is contained in the Mozarabic Breviary as printed
by Cardinal Ximenes in 1502,[6] but it is hard to say when it was
adopted by the Mozarabic liturgy. It is of course not in the
Liber sacramentorum, nor is it in the *Liber ordinum,* nor in the
Mozarabic Psalter as edited by J. P. Gilson, nor does Férotin's
index of formulas appended to the *Liber ordinum* show it occurring anywhere but in the 1502 text. Still it must have been
current before Albar's day, and that would suggest that it had been
accepted before the Moslem conquest. The words in these
passages printed in capitals are clearly based directly on the
Te Deum, and other phrases adjoining them are equally clearly
only the expansions of thought so dearly loved as embellishment
by the early writers of the Peninsula.

A similar influence makes itself known in the Mozarabic
liturgy. The *inlatio* of the Mass of Easter is famous; a long form
is given in the *Missale mixtum* of Cardinal Ximenes;[7] the first

---

6 PL 86:944.
7 PL 85:484f.

half of the same text is given for the same Mass in the *Liber sacramentorum*,[8] but it is the second half that is especially apposite:

> Unde merito illi omnes angeli: omnesque sancti non cessant clamare quotidie, ita dicentes. TE CELI celorum. TE POTESTATES. Te throni *et virtutes laudant.* TIBI cetus ANGELORUM in excelsis concinunt hymnum. TIBI CHERUBIM ET SERAPHIM INCESSABILI VOCE PROCLAMANT dicentes. Agios. Agios. Agios. Kyrie Otheos. SANCTUS. SANCTUS. SANCTUS: DOMINUS DEUS SABAOTH. PLENI SUNT CELI ET TERRA GLORIA MAJESTATIS TUE: osanna filio David: Benedictus qui venit in nomine Domini: osanna in excelsis. Agios. Agios. Agios. Te Domine laudat omnis virtus celorum: et exercitus angelorum. Tibi hymnum depromunt meliflua carmina sanctorum. *Tibi* psallant choree *virginum:* et cetus *confessorum.* Tibi genua curvant celestia, terrestria, et inferna. Laudant te regem omnium seculorum. Osanna in excelsis.

Two other passages from the Spanish liturgy may be given:

> Inlatio, Missa SS. Fausti, Januarii et Martialis: . . . Sit credentibus *vita;* sit confitentibus venia; sit tristibus letitia; *sit egrotantibus sanitas; sit malagma valetudinis laborantibus.* Sit *mortem timentibus vita;* sit *ab errore redeuntibus bona via,* et *languori* anime, atque *infirmitati* carnis a te Domino nostro confecta, sancta et perpetua *medicina. (Lib. sacramentorum,* col. 444, formula 960)

> Post sanctus, Missa quotidiana tertia: Vere sanctus, vere benedictus Dominus noster Ihesus Christus Filius tuus. Ille *patriarcharum* fides: ille plentitudo legis: ille umbra veritatis: ille predicatio *prophetarum.* Ille *apostolorum* magister; ille omnium *credentium* pater. Ille *debilium* firmamentum: ille *infirmantium* virtus. Ille redemptio captivorum: ille hereditas redemptorum. Ille viventium salus: ille *morientium vita.* Qui sacrificandi novam legem sacerdos Dei verus instituit . . . (*Ibid.,* col. 517, formula 1127)[9]

---

[8] Col. 256, formula 615.

[9] Briefer passages of the same type are an inlatio (*Lib. sacram.* col. 17), and an Ad confractionem (*Lib. ordinum.,* col. 358).

The special type makes clear the use of a common stock of materials for prayer. In style, they consist of short phrases, typically possessing something of the character of exclamations. Some are familiar to us as incorporated in the Te Deum; others are similar, but either expand the Te Deum forms (e.g., adding phrases about virtues, patriarchs, virgins, and confessors), or supplement them with considerations of God's merciful relations with men (e.g., caecorum oculus, debilium animus, tu divitia pauperum). The origins of this style of prayer do not concern us here.[10] For us it is enough to note that they have an unmistakable liturgical character, that much of Albar's phrasing in the two longer passages is paralleled in the Mozarabic liturgy, and that some phrases are from the Te Deum.

The shortest of the Albar passages (n. 2 above), besides its relation to the Te Deum, has many parallels in the Mozarabic liturgy, where, in fact, it may be said to be a commonplace.

Albar: et redime . . . quem . . . pretio sanguinis tui redemisti.

Te Deum: Te ergo quaesumus tuis famulis subveni, quos pretioso sanguine redemisti.

Ad orationem dominicam, Mass for Vigil of Easter: et qui nos redemisti pretio tui sanguinis . . . (*Lib. sacram.*, col. 251)

Inlatio, III Sunday after Pentecost: cujus sanguine omnium corda mundante . . . (PL 85:633A)

Inlatio, IV Sunday after Pentecost: quem unici Filii tui redemisti sanguine . . . (PL 85:636C)

Inlatio, V Sunday after Pentecost: qui nos unigeniti tui sanguine redemisti . . . (PL 85:639C)

Inlatio, Mass for several dead: qui nos sui sanguinis pretio redemit. (PL 85:1026C)

Lauds of Lent: Laus tibi Domine, rex eterne glorie. Salva plebem tuam Domine rex. Rege eam Domine rex.

---

[10] Cf. P. Cagin, *Te Deum ou Illatio?*, pp. 247–264.

Quam redemisti tuo sanguine rex. (*Mozarabic Psalter,* ed. Gilson, p. 292)

Hymn: Christe immense dominator sancte / conserva gregem quam tu redemisti / sanguine sacro tuo pretioso / ipse salvasti. (*Ibid.,* p. 292)

Benedictio of None: Salva plebem tuam Domine, quam tu ipse creasti: R) Amen. Benedic hereditatem tuam, quam pretioso sanguine redemisti: R) Amen. (PL 86:959C)

The fact that the phrase is so common means that Albar is less copying some single text than using a thoroughly familiar locution. The way in which he not only uses certain clauses directly, but creates naturally his own personal elaborations of familiar texts along the same lines as those followed by the Mozarabic liturgy, is a witness to the way in which in former times the liturgy became a familiar part of the mental equipment of the faithful.

VIII. Another example of the same kind comes at the close of the first section of the *Confessio.*

Albar: Qui frigidas mentes igne tui amoris incendis . . . (PL 400A)

The *Liber sacramentorum* offers the following parallels:

Ad pacem, Mass of St. Eulalia: quod ex flamma tui amoris uri repromeruit. (col. 47)

Post pridie, of the same Mass: tu e celis ignem illum tui amoris emitte. (col. 49)

Alia, Mass of St. Columba: atque per ipsius Sancti Spiritus donum cor martyris ac virginis tue Columbe tanto ardore tue dulcedinis inflammasti. (col. 76)

Post nomina, the same Mass: ut sicut illa igne amoris tui flammas penalis superavit incendii. (*loc. cit.*)

Inlatio, Mass of St. Fructuosus: Quos . . . non minus

charitatis divine quam persecutionis inimicae flamma con-
flavit . . . Libenter enim fidelium animarum ardor tuo
amore succensus sanctificatorum corporum ferebat incendium . . . Et cum illo acrius Sancti Spiritus calore
ferventes . . . . (col. 109)

Also the following formulas of the *Liber sacramentorum:* 295,
767, 769, 786; and the inlationes, *Liber ordinum,* cols. 283, 278.[11]

It may be useful to add a few quotations from individual
authors wherein the same expression is found.

Eulogius, *Documentum martyriale:* Domine Deus omnipotens . . . accende igne amoris cor nostrum, et flammae
tuae caritatis pectoris nostri exure recessum. (PL
115:834A)

Ildefonsus, *De itinere deserti,* c. 15: quia quidquid
fluidum fuit ignis caritatis exurit, quidquid fragile amoris
incendium roboravit. (PL 96:176A)

Verecundus, *De satisfactione,* lines 79ff.: Da misero
aethereum flamme coelestis amorem / Ossibus implicitum.
Tua me, tua semper inurant / Vota, tuoque meae con-
flagrent igne medullae. / Sentiat interior vividos homo
cordis amores, / Inflammerque pio carae dulcedinis aestu.

Gregory, *Hom. in Ezech.,* PL 76:799f., 824, 1223.

Jerome, *Homilia in die dominica Paschae:* Illi (sc.
Judaei) non accendebant ignem in die sabbati: nos e
contrario accendimus in nobis ignem Spiritus Sancti . . .
de quo igne Dominus ait: Ignem veni mittere in terram,
et quam volo ut ardeat. Desiderat Dominus ignem istum
ardere in nobis, et secundum apostolum Spiritu nos
Sancto fervere, ut non refrigescat in nobis caritas Dei.
(Anecdota Maredsolana, III, ii, 414)

While the doctrine of this expression is of course Scriptural,

---

[11] In the early Roman liturgy the same phrasing occurs; cf. *Gelasian
Sacramentary,* ed. Wilson, p. 124; *Gregorian Sacramentary,* ed. Wilson,
pp. 80f., 95, 120, 276f. It does not seem to appear in the Leonine Sacramentary. For the familiar modern Roman antiphon, "Veni Sancte
Spiritus" (the Alleluia of the Pentecost Mass), cf. Wilmart, *Auteurs
spirituels,* p. 43, n. 2.

the actual wording does not occur in the Bible; the nearest approach is Ezech. 20: 47, where the prophet speaks of a literal destruction by fire. It was already known to Jerome; but if its appearance in the Roman liturgy may be taken as an indication, (not in the Leonine, once in the Gelasian, six times in the Gregorian sacramentary), it was not in the earliest stratum, and only gradually made its way, becoming popular in the Gregorian and Mozarabic sacramentaries.

IX. In two kindred passages, where he laments his slavery to the devil, Albar admits that this slavery is his own fault, and that he himself supplied the weapons which have overcome him. In this there is a reminiscence of Wisdom 11: 17, ut scirent quia per quae peccat quis, per haec et torquetur.

A. Albar: Satis est Domine . . . quod contra me ipse inscius ejus tela portavi, etiam me ipso illi quasi ex debito bajulum feci, quia ejus arma unde me totum elisit, in me hactenus quasi in teca recondere numquam cessavi. (PL 400B–C)

Isidore, *Synonyma*, I, 33: Omnis enim adversitas rerum delictorum tuorum meritis excitatur, tua contra te dimicant arma, sagittis tuis confoderis, telis tuis vulneraris; per quae enim peccasti, per haec et torqueris. (PL 83:835)

Augustine, *Sermo* 216, c. 2: Humanus sermo, quia ideo Verbum caro factum est, ut sicut exhibuistis corpora vestra arma iniquitatis peccato, ita nunc exhibeatis membra vestra arma justitiae Deo. In perniciem adversus vos vester oppugnator vestris jaculis armabatur. (PL 38:1077)

B. Albar: Hanc inclementiam, hanc voracitatem, hanc crudelitatem ego mihi caecatus a diabolo spontanea mente elegi. Ego equuleum hunc dirum mihi invexi; ego gladium gutturi meo immersi; ego morti totum me ipse commisi. (PL 400f.)

Gregory, *Homil. in Evangel.*, 15, n. 3: Notandum vero est quod exponens Dominus dicit quia sollicitudines, et voluptates, et divitiae suffocant verbum. Suffocant enim, quia importunis cogitationibus suis guttur mentis strangulant. (PL 76:1133A)

—————— *Moralia*, VI, 22, n. 38: Iniquorum quippe hominum mentes cum quaedam a proximis bene gesta conspiciunt, in extenso livoris sui equuleo torquentur, et gravem malitiae suae poenam sustinent. (PL 75:749)

Augustine, *Sermo* 13, 6, n. 7: Si bene audisti, si recte audisti, si in audiendo te justus fuisti, si tuae mentis tribunal ascendisti, si te ipsum ante te ipsum in equuleum cordis suspendisti, si graves tortores adhibuisti timoris; bene audisti si sic audisti. (PL 38:110)

X. Next we come to a bit of popluar belief, where imagination has ornamented the more sober facts. It is the age-long notion that the devil is of a black, or at least of some color different from that of our own skins. The idea has roots in both the Old Testament and in pagan antiquity.[12]

Albar: ut ab optimo Domino et a pio Patre bonis multis ditatus, crudeli et horribili ethiopi existam addictus. (PL 400D)

Gregory, *Dialogues*, II, 4: the devil as "quidam niger puerulus" tugs a monk from choir. (PL 66:142)

Augustine, *De civitate Dei*, XXII, 8: Modicum quemdam podagrum in eadem urbe fuisse scimus; qui cum dedisset nomen ad baptismum et pridie quam baptizaretur in somnis a pueris nigris cirratis, quos intelligebat daemones, baptizari eodem anno prohibitus fuisset. (CSEL 40, ii, 601)

Jerome, *Tractatus de Psalmo VII:* sed secundum spiritalem intelligentiam interpretari, Chusi istum Aethiopem non alium nisi diabolum interpretamur. (Anecdota Maredsolana, III, ii, 21)

---

[12] Cf. F. J. Dölger, *Die Sonne der Gerechtigkeit und der Schwarze,* esp. pp. 49-64; also H. Leclercq, "Démon, démoniaque," *DACL,* IV, i, 578ff. In St. Athanasius' *Life of St. Anthony* the devil appears to the hermit as a little black boy (PG 26:849A); the same happened to St. Teresa of Avila (*Autobiography,* c. 31); and cf. the *Passion of SS. Perpetua and Felicitas,* n. 10.

XI. Albar: Gaudet hostis meus (sc. diabolus) quod te iratum videt; exultat cum me a tanto patre expulsum sentit; tripudiat cum me ita destitutum cognoscit. (PL 401B)

The word *tripudium, tripudiare,* meaning a solemn religious dance, is classical Latin, but it strikes one who is familiar with only the Roman liturgy as an odd word in Christian usage. However it was used in the Mozarabic liturgy, and so is not a sign of classicism in Albar.

Inlatio, Mass of I Sunday after Pentecost: Pro quibus beneficiis cherubim exultant: seraphim quoque pennigera tripudatione augustius gloriantur. (PL 85:624B)

Inlatio, Mass of St. Lawrence' Day: Archangelorum quoque exercitus in tuo nomine letantes tripudiant. (PL 85:817A)

Eulogius uses the word more often than Albar; cf. *Mem. SS.,* I, 15, 37; II, 1, n. 4; *Doc. mart,* n. 24.

XII. Albar: Noli spernere Deus meus quem mirabiliter condidisti, quemque sine comparatione mirabilius redemisti. (PL 401C)

This is another liturgical passage with which Albar is familiar enough to enable him to quote with a variation, the *sine comparatione* certainly not being in the original as it destroys the balance and rhythm of the sentence, and because it is another characteristic superlative. Unfortunately, nothing of this kind was discovered in the Mozarabic liturgy. In the modern Roman rite it occurs in two places:

(1). The collect following the first Prophecy of Holy Saturday: Deus qui mirabiliter creasti hominem et mirabilius redemisti. . . . This collect in the same place goes back to the Gregorian sacramentary (ed. Wilson, p. 54; ed. Lietzmann, p. 51), but is not in the Gelasian.

(2). The blessing of the water at the offertory: Deus qui humanae substantiae dignitatem mirabiliter condidisti et mirabilius reformasti. . . . This is a Christmas collect in the older Roman liturgy: *Gregorian Sacramentary* (ed.

Wilson, p. 13; PL 78:32) ; *Gelasian Sacramentary*, (ed.
Wilson, p. 5) ; *Leonine Sacramentary* (ed. Feltoe, p. 159)

It is possible that the phrases in question may appear in some
other connection and with some other incipit in the Mozarabic
liturgy, or it may be contained in some patristic source; but if
so, they have eluded the present writer's search. Since both col-
lects are early enough to have been known in Spain before 711,
it is probable that Albar knew them in some Spanish book, or
perhaps in some patristic writing, rather than directly from Roman
liturgical books.

XIII. Satan is a prominent character in the *Confessio*. We
next come to a passage that is thoroughly Augustinian in substance, and affirms Satan's subjection to God.

> Albar: Numquid hostis iste versutus et callidus tibi
> Domino vero valet existere obvius? Absit. Neque ille
> subsisteret nisi a te subsistendi statum acciperet. Quem
> qui a te creatus in beatitudine fuit, in qua stare elationis
> tumore non voluit, a te etiam hodie regitur, licet tibi ad-
> versare conetur. Quia quodquod voluntate impia in nos
> exercere putat, tibi et in hoc etiam invite inscius ser-
> viendo concordat. Ipsius enim voluntatem malam tua
> potestas coercet justa. Et illud quod nos caecati iniquum
> putamus, justum permissum a justo Judice non negamus.
> (PL 401C–D)

In this quotation we can distinguish three leading thoughts:
(1) that the devil was created by God with a good nature and is
still wholly under divine control, (2) that he fell through pride,
(3) that his power over men is completely subject to God's will.

1. The devil created by God with a good nature, and still under
his control.

> Isidore, *De ordine creaturarum*, c. 8, nn. 9f.: Iste autem
> angelus (sc. Satan) cum a Conditoris beatitudine recessit,
> omne suae naturae bonum, quod in conditione sua habuit,
> totum amisit; sed semetipsi malus, Deo semper bonus
> perseverat, dum obedienter dominicae jussioni, quamvis
> non sponte, propter potentiam Dei tamen obtemperat.
> Ex omni enim naturae bono quod habuit hoc nunc tantum

modo habet, quod Deo creatori ad cuncta obedit imperata.
Sed hoc bonum non in diabolo et ministris ejus bonum
est, qui idcirco obediunt, quia non obedire non possunt;
sed haec eorum obedientia in Deo bona est, cujus bonae
quidem voluntati invita diaboli mala voluntas, cum bene
operari praecipitur, resistere non potest. (PL 83:933)

Gregory, *Moralia,* XVI, 38: Cujus videlicet voluntati
(sc. divinae) nec illa obsistunt, quae contra voluntatem
illius fieri videntur, quia ad hoc nonnumquam permittit
fieri etiam quod non praecipit, ut per hoc illud certius
impleatur quod jubet. Apostatae quippe angeli perversa
voluntas est, sed tamen a Deo mirabiliter ordinatur, ut
ipsae quoque ejus insidiae utilitati bonorum serviant,
quos purgant dum tentant. (PL 75:1144)

Augustine, *De Trinitate,* XIII, 12: quia nec ipse diabolus
a postestate Omnipotentis alienus est, sicut neque a
bonitate. Nam et maligni angeli unde qualicumque
subsisterent vita, nisi per eum qui vivificat omnia? (PL
42:1026)

——— *Contra Julianum Pelagianum,* VI, 9, n. 25: qui
eos quos novit, non ad tempus sub diabolo futuros, sed
cum illo semper arsuros, non desinit creare, nutrire,
vestire, eisque pertinacissima iniquitate peccantibus vitam
salutemque subministrare. Sed facit hoc Deus quomodo
sciens bene uti et bonis et malis; cujus majestatis usibus,
non solum eas quos premit aut decipit, sed nec se ipsum
malignitatis ullius arte diabolus subtrahit. Ac per hoc
non pertinent ad diabolum qui eruuntur de diaboli
potestate: qui vero ad eum pertinent, in Dei, sicut ipse,
sunt potestate. (PL 44:837) This is a part of one of
Augustine's favorite doctrines—that every substance is
good, evil being not a substance but a deordination—and
occurs repeatedly through his works (cf. *De civitate Dei,*
XI, 17; *Contra Julianum Pel.,* III, 18; *De Genesi ad
litteram,* XI, 13); when it reappears in Gregory and
Isidore, we can discover the trace of their use of the
bishop of Hippo.

2. The devil fell by pride. Some early writers were inclined
to think Lucifer fell into sin through envy upon learning that God
intended to add human beings with their lower nature to the society of heaven. But Augustine and his followers are among

those who hold their sin was pride, self-will rebelling against God. The idea is another of those occurring constantly through Augustine's works.

> Isidore, *Sententiae*, I, 10, 7f.: Prius de caelo cecidisse diabolum (creditur) quam homo conderetur. Nam mox ut factus est in superbiam erupit, et praecipitatus est de caelo . . . Uno superbiae lapsu, dum Deo per tumorem se conferunt, et homo cecidit et diabolus. (PL 83:555)

> *Ibid.*, I, 9, 1: Non quia alicubi aut aliquando erat malum, unde fieret diabolus malus, sed quia vitio suo, dum esset angelus bonus, superbiendo effectus est malus. The same passage occurs in Taio *Sententiae*, I, 15 (PL 80:748)

> Augustine, *Enarratio in Ps. 58*, sermo 2, n. 5: Quamdiu exaggerem quid mali sit in superbia? Diabolus inde solum puniendus est. Certe princeps est omnium peccatorum; certe seductor est ad peccandum: non ei imputatur adulterium, non vinolentia, non fornicatio, non rapina rerum alienarum; sola superbia lapsus est. (PL 36:709)

> —— *De civitate Dei*, XI, 15: et illud, quod " ab initio diabolus peccat," non ab initio ex quo creatus est peccare putandus est, sed ab initio peccati quod ab ipsius superbia coeperit esse peccatum. (CSEL 40, i, 534) Cf. also *ibid.*, XIV, 11, n. 2.

> —— *De vera religione*, c. 13: Ille autem angelus magis seipsum quam Deum diligendo, subditus ei esse noluit, et intumuit per superbiam, et a summa essentia deficit, et lapsus est. (PL 34:133)

3. Satan's power is completely subject to God's will. This again is typically Augustinian.

> Isidore, *Sententiae*, III, 5, 3–6: Non amplius tentat electos diabolus quam Dei voluntas permittit. Tentando autem, sanctorum profectibus servit. Etsi nolens, utilitati tamen sanctorum servit diabolus, quando eos tentationibus suis non dejicit, sed potius erudit. Nam tentationes quas ille ad humanum interitum movet, interdum Spiritus Sanctus ad exercitium virtutum salubri utilitate convertit. In·

sidiae diaboli atque astutiae, quamvis huc atque illuc quaerentes quem devorent diffundantur, a potestate tamen divina non egrediuntur, ne tantum noceant quantum malitiose contendunt. Nam quomodo sanctorum virtus tanta tolerare posset si superna dispensatio pio moderamine nequitium daemonum non frenaret? Et licet diabolus tentationem justis semper inferre cupiat, tamen si a Deo potestatem non acceperit, nullatenus adipisci potest quod appetit. Unde et omnis voluntas diaboli injusta est, et tamen, permittente Deo, omnis potestas justa. Ex se enim tentare quoslibet injuste appetit, sed eos qui tentandi sunt et prout tentandi sunt, non nisi tentare Deus juste permittit . . . Sed duobus verbis comprehensa est, et Dei potestas justa et diaboli voluntas injusta. (PL 83:660f.) Cf. *ibid.*, I, 10, 18.

Gregory, *Moralia*, XIV, 38: Maligni quippe spiritus ad nocendum nos incessabiliter anhelant; sed cum pravam voluntatem ex semetipsis habeant, potestatem tamen nocendi non habent nisi eos voluntas summa permittat. Et cum ipsi quidem injuste nos laedere appetunt, quemlibet tamen laedere non nisi juste a Domino permittuntur. Quia ergo in eis voluntas injusta est, et potestas justa. (PL 75:1063f.) Cf. *ibid.*, II, 10; XVIII, 2; XXXII, 24.

Augustine, *In Joannis Evangelium Tractatus VII*, n. 7: Nolite timere, nec tentat ille nisi permissus fuerit: constat illum nihil facere nisi permissus fuerit aut missus. Mittitur tamquam angelus malus a potestate dominante; permittitur, quando aliquid petit: et hoc fratres non fit nisi ut probentur justi, puniantur injusti. Quid ergo times? (PL 35:1440). Cf. *Enarratio in Ps. 26*, enar. 2, n. 5 (PL 36:201); *De Genesi ad litteram*, XI, c. 27, n. 34 (CSEL 28, i, 360; PL 34:444)

Cf. Isidore, *De ordine creaturarum*, c. 8, nn. 12–14: Sed nec in hominibus nec in rebus quae hominibus subditae sunt, aliquid absque Dei permissione facere valet . . . Quod in beato Job et in rebus quas possidebat et amiserat similiter manifestatur . . . Et haec ita esse sentiens Job, cum suarum rerum damna comperisset, ita respondit: Dominus dedit, Dominus abstulit. Quomodo voluit, Dominus fecit; sit nomen Domini benedictum. Non dixit: Dominus dedit, diabolus abstulit; certissime enim absque Dei permissione in rebus aut hominibus nihil

omnino facere posse adversarium sciebat. (PL 83:933f.)
This is based on Augustine, *Enarratio in Ps. 90,* sermo
I, n. 2 (PL 37:1150)

A passage from Caesarius of Arles may be added here, not so
much as a source for Albar, but to show how much of Augustine
became common property of theological writers:

> Caesarius, *Sermon* 54, n. 4: Et illud ante omnia scitote,
> fratres, quod nec vos ipsos nec eos qui ad vos pertinent,
> nec animalia vestra, nec reliquam substantiam vel in
> parvis rebus diabolus potest laedere, nisi quantum a Deo
> potestatem acceperit: quomodo nec sancti Job facultates
> ausus fuit subvertere nisi Domino permittente. . . . Per-
> mittit autem hoc Deus duabus ex causis: ut aut nos
> probet, si boni sumus, aut castiget, si peccatores . . . Et
> hoc attendite, fratres, quia cum omnem substantiam
> diabolus evertisset beati Job, non dixit Job, Dominus
> dedit, diabolus abstulit, sed: Dominus dedit, Dominus
> abstulit. Vir enim sanctus noluit istam gloriam diabolo
> dare, ut aliquid potuisset tollere quod Dominus non per-
> misisset auferre. (ed. G. Morin, I, 228)

XIV. Albar: fecisti me ut rectus conspicerem caelum. (PL
401C)

> Augustine, *De Genesi ad litteram, inperfectus liber:* Nisi
> forte quod ad intuendum caelum figura humani corporis
> erecta est . . . (CSEL 28, i, 501; PL 34:243)

XV. (a) Albar: Ecce enim Domine puro corde delicta mea
confiteor, sicut tu ipse verissime nosti, et ab eorum inlecebra me tota mente cupio retrahere, sed vinculorum
praeditione connexus, quod promitto nequeo adimplere.
(PL 402B)

> Isidore, *Synonyma,* I, 66: Ut bene viverem ultro promisi,
> quod pollicitus sum numquam servavi.

(b) Albar: Non narrationem indiges, sed oris professionem
inquiris (*loc. cit.*).

> Isidore, *Etymologiae,* VI, 19, 76: delictum nostrum
> Domino confitemur; non quidem ut ignaro, cujus cog-
> nitioni nihil occultum est; sed confessio est rei scilicet
> ejus quae ignoratur professa cognitio.

(c) Albar: Nam quae scienda sunt scire, et ea nequaquam opere adimplere, non est vocari scientiam sed certe fatuitatis magnae dementiam (PL 403A)

Isidore, *Sententiae,* II, 1, 9: Ad majoris culpae cumulum pertinet scire quemquam quod sequi debeat, et sequi nolle quod sciat. Cf. *ibid.,* III, 36f.; Gregory, *Moralia,* XXII, 5 (PL 76:217)

XVI. Here it is a matter of the turn of a phrase rather than of doctrine, though that is close too; Jerome and Albar were alike in relishing bits of fine style.

Albar: Dixisse enim tuum Domine Jesu fecisse est. (PL 404C)

Jerome, *Ep.* 121 (ad fiin.): . . . (Deus) cuius iussisse fecisse est . . . (CSEL 56: 54)

Cf. Albar: Et hoc est verissime scire quod est amarissime flere . . . Et item novi quod praepotens es in majestate, et ut velle, ita tibi subjacet posse. (PL 403A)

XVII. A curious parallel is the following, though there is no reason for supposing that Albar was acquainted with Cicero in the original, or would have been interested if Cicero had been available. Albar was not a Renaissance humanist.

Albar: Quid enim gravior libidine? quid onerosior fraude? quid ponderosior jactantia vana? quid pejus homicidio? quid malum (sic) testimonio falso? quid iniquius miserorum spolio? (PL 405A)

Cicero, *De legibus,* I, 51: quid enim foedius avaritia, quid inmanius libidine, quid contemptius timiditate, quid abjectius tarditate et stultitia dici potest?

XVIII. Albar has a long passage (PL 405C–407A) which is interesting but hard to trace. He is sick with sin and in need of healing. God has given Scripture and the sacraments (*tuae sacrae lectionis historia . . . deifica sacramenta*) designed to heal the sicknesses of our soul; but in how many ways has Albar misused them! Meant to cure our ulcers, they have only made his wounds worse. O Lord, your presence, your grace, is needed to make the medicines useful; would Peter have wept had you not looked upon him? Without you, there is nothing good in the world. Wherefore we must needs believe that you are present in these readings (i.e., in Scripture), and that through them you cure only those worthy of you. For the Bible does not cure him who in pride opens it not to obey but to argue, who does not submit himself to your word; when he is puffed up towards you, he deludes himself and is his own enemy; so the more he thinks to study (discutere), the worse becomes his disease. We are truly unfortunate and miserable, we who believe them to be the words of our Creator and yet wish to weigh them rationalistically in the balance, as if there were any other *ratio* in nature than your just commandment, and as if man could have the power of reasoning from any other source unless you gave it with no antecedent merit of his own. But if he truly had reason, and not a reason partly corrupted by human sin, he would never seek a reason in those things that have been set forth by his Creator. Our foolishness is immense to direct our efforts to knowing forbidden things, for then we offer ourselves to the enemy to make sport of. We cannot even understand what goes on within ourselves. We have complete mastery over the animal creation and can use them as we will without having to answer for it to the animals; yet we ask for the reason for your works, we who do not know what it is to be reasonable unless we learn it from you.

These sentiments harmonize with what we should expect from Albar, a deeply religious, but somewhat fideistic temperament. Much that it says is true, but it is given a one-sided development without the balance of compensating truths. It is quite likely that similar passages are present in Augustine's works, though he would also have held supplementary doctrines to modify them; but the present writer did not find them. The nearest thing that came to light is a section of Isidore's *Sententiae* (III, cc. 8–12) which deals with the reading of Scripture; but the two authors run independent if vaguely parallel courses which seldom or never actually touch. Isidore writes: The reading of the Bible brings God's voice to us, and with it comes the obligation of practising its teachings in our lives. Assiduous study is needed. Doctrine without the aid of grace enters the ears but not the heart; it enters the heart when God's grace touches the mind enabling it to understand. For as God enlightens some with the flame of his love so they may have a living understanding, so some who are cold and torpid he abandons so they may remain without judgment. There are many who use their acquired knowledge of Scripture not for God's glory but their own praise, and are puffed up by their knowledge, sinning where they ought to cleanse their sins. The arrogant by their reading never attain to perfect knowledge. For though on the surface they seem wise, in their hearts they never touch the secrets of truth, being hindered by the cloud of pride. The proud are ever reading, seeking, and never finding. The hidden things of the divine law lie open to the humble and those who come rightly to God, but are barred to the proud and evil. For though the arrogant can read the divine words, the mystery is hidden from them. God's word is light to the faithful, but it is in a manner darkness to the proud and reprobate, and where some are enlightened others are blinded. The carnal-minded reader misses the sense of Scripture; heretics pervert its meaning, and even falsify its text.

Isidore is the moralist giving practical spiritual advice; light, truth, knowledge are the terms he uses for the effects of Bible reading; he is crisp, clear, and " sententious." The subjective Albar thinks in terms of sickness and wounds, and of the Scriptures as healing medicines. Due only in part to the difference of literary type of the two books, Albar is less clear and orderly in thought; but also he tries to go deeper. Isidore is content to insist that the proud miss the point in Scripture; Albar in his more Augustinian manner advances beyond this to consider the nature of human reason, its absolute dependence upon God, and its helplessness in the face of divine wisdom. It is probable that some writing of St. Augustine lies behind these pages of Albar.

XIX. Albar: et in tam innumerabiles formas dividitur (sc. iniquitas mea) ut ex una superbia matre multae robustiores filiae quotidie oriantur . . . Certe enim ex superbia omnis iniquitas captat principium. (PL 409C–D)

Ecclus. 10:15, Quoniam initium omnis peccati est superbia.

Oratio pro correptione vitae, n. 37: Mater et regina septem principalium vitiorum superbia non ingrediatur.

Isidore, *Sententiae,* II, 27, 8: Principalium septem vitiorum regina et mater superbia est, eademque septem principalia multa de se parturiunt vitia.

Gregory, *Moralia,* XXXI, c. 45, n. 87: Ipsa namque vitiorum regina superbia cum devictum plene cor ceperit, mox illud septem principalibus vitiis, quasi quibusdam suis ducibus devastandum tradit. (PL 76:620)

XX. Albar: Certe enim ex superbia omnis iniquitas captat principium, quia omne quod agitur vitium ex contemptu mandatorum tuorum habet exordium. Et ideo bene superbiae adscribitur quidquid ab homine contradicenti tibi perpere agitur. (PL 409D)

Isidore, *Sententiae,* II, 38, 2: Omnis peccans superbus est, eo quod faciendo vetita contemptui habeat divina praecepta. Recte ergo " initium omnis peccati superbia."

XXI. Albar: (a) Tu hymnus virginum, tu praemium confessorum, tu vere Sabbatum electorum, quia tuum est et in te est regnum caelorum. (PL 407D)
(b) ita totus a te in futuro professus, et perenni dominatione tua satis suavi addictus, merear te donante tua dona, quae nec oculus vidit, nec auris audivit, nec in cor hominis ascendit (I Cor. 2: 9), percipere: teque pro omni munere verum sabbatum perfruere. (PL 412C)

In Scripture the word *sabbatum* is used only in its literal sense, the seventh day of the week. In the figurative sense of the eternal rest of heaven the derivative form *sabbatismus* occurs once (Heb. 4: 9) ; otherwise, the figurative use is a patristic development. Especially famous is the extended use Augustine makes of it in the concluding chapters of his two best-known works, the *Confessions,* and *The City of God.* Albar also employs it in his peroration; and we know he had *The City of God,* as it was among the books Eulogius brought home from Navarre.

Augustine, *Confessiones*, XIII, 35f.: Domine Deus, pacem da nobis—omnia enim praestitisti nobis—pacem quietis, pacem sabbati, pacem sine vespera. Omnis quippe iste ordo pulcherrimus rerum valde bonarum modis suis peractis transiturus est: et mane quippe in eis factum est et vespera. Dies autem septimus sine vespera est nec habet occasum, quia sanctificasti eum ad permansionem sempiternam, ut id, quod tu post opera tua "bona valde," quamvis ea quietus feceris, requievisti septimo die, hoc praeloquatur nobis vox libri tui, quod et nos post opera nostra ideo " bona valde," quia tu nobis ea donasti, sabbato vitae aeternae requiescamus in te. (CSEL 33:386f.)

———— *De civitate Dei*, XXII, 30: Ibi perficietur: vacate et videte quoniam ego sum Deus; quod erit vere maximum Sabbatum non habens vesperam, quod commendavit Dominus in primis operibus mundi, ubi legitur: Et requievit Deus die septimo. Dies enim septimus etiam nos ipsi erimus, quando eius fuerimus benedictione et sanctificatione pleni atque refecti. (CSEL 40, ii, 668) . . . haec tamen septima erit sabbatum nostrum, cuius finis non erit vespera, sed dominicus dies velut octavus aeternus, qui Christi resurrectione sacratus est, aeternum non solum spiritus, verum etiam corporis requiem praefigurans. Ibi vacabimus et videbimus, videbimus et amabimus, amabimus et laudabimus. Ecce quod erit in fine sine fine. (*Ibid.*, p. 670)

C. SCRIPTURE IN THE CONFESSIO

The Scriptures supply far the largest share of the material of the *Confessio*, especially after the philosophical opening section which draws so much from Augustine. Albar seldom quotes directly; normally he weaves the quotation into his own context; often he changes a word or so, or more particularly expands the text in the interest of what his civilisation thought elegance. Often again, especially when he refers to Biblical narratives, it is only an allusion:

A close quotation:

Albar: Fiat Domine misericordia tua super me.
Ps. 32: 22, Fiat misericordia tua Domine super nos.

A freer citation:

Albar: sed iniquitates meae sicut onus gravatae sunt super me.

Ps. 37: 5, Quoniam iniquitates meae supergressae sunt caput meum, et sicut onus grave gravatae sunt super me.

Still freer:

(a) Albar: Neque enim tenebrae communitatem fruuntur lucis.

II Cor. 6: 14, Quae enim participatio iustitiae cum iniquitate? Aut quae societas luci ad tenebras?

(b) Albar: atque ex lateribus aquilonis saepius civitatem Sanctam tibi Regi magno fecisti.

Ps. 47: 3, Mons Sion, latera Aquilonis, civitas Regis magni.

Mere allusion:

Albar: Quia et cutis lurida pristinam colorem recepit, dum velle tuum audivit; et paralyticus . . .

Cf. Leviticus 13 for rules on the diagnosis of leprosy.

In places he brings the quotations close together and makes a Scriptural mosaic; a good example of this is the following:

Dirge Domine gressus meos, et sit lucerna verbum tuum pedibus meis, ut luce tua inluminatus, et dexterae tuae tutatione munitus, valeam in portis filiae Sion dulces psallere hymnos. Domine Deus meus miserator et misericors respice me respectu pietatis, et intuitu misericordiae tuae quo soles peccatores respicere, eosque ad te ex devia revocare. Miserere Domine, miserere, et veniam tribue te oranti. Exaudi Domine exaudi, et iniquitates meas tu dimitte. Disrumpe Domine vincula peccatorum meorum, ut sacrificem tibi hostiam laudis.	Gressus meas dirige. Ps. 118: 133. Lucerna pedibus meis verbum tuum. Ps. 118: 105. Ut annuntiem omnes laudationes tuas in portis filiae Sion. Ps. 9: 15, cf. Ps. 72: 28. Et tu Domine Deus miserator et misericors . . . respice in me et miserere mei. Ps. 85: 15f. Miserere mei Deus, miserere mei, Ps. 56: 2; cf. Ps. 122: 3. Exaudi me Domine, exaudi me. III Kings 18: 37. Exaudi eos in caelo, et dimitte peccata servorum tuorum. *Ibid.*, 8: 36. Dirupisti vincula mea, tibi sacrificabo hostiam laudis. Ps. 115: 16f.

The Psalms are more used than any other book of the Bible; clearly they were second nature to him, whether through participating in the public offices of the Church, or through private devotional reading. But apart from the Psalter, the New Testament is more in evidence than the Old,[1] though many of the New Testament citations might not show in a tabulation as they are allusions rather than quotations, for instance, to Zacheus, the Good Samaritan, and the cure of a paralytic.

So many of Albar's quotations are indirect, and modified in wording that it is somewhat difficult to be sure what Latin version of the Scriptures he used. But in eight cases he is definitely closer to the Vulgate, and in four he is closer to the Old Latin as given by Sabatier.

A. Closer to the Vulgate.

1. Albar: Qui *lassis roborem* tribuis operandi, operantibus intentionem adcommodas perficiendi, torpentibus votum ingeris inchoandi. (PL 400A)

   Isaias 40: 29. Vulgate: Qui dat *lasso* virtutem, et his qui non sunt, fortitudinem et *robur* multiplicat.

   Old Latin: Qui dat *esurientibus fortitudinem,* et non dolentibus moerorem.

2. Albar: unde me debui lacrymis *inrigare* . . . (PL 402C)

   Luke 7: 44. Vulgate: haec autem lacrymis *rigavit* pedes meos.

   Old Latin: haec autem lacrymis *lavit* pedes meos.

3. Albar: Sed numquid *adbreviata* est manus tua *ut salvare nequeas?* aut auris tua adgravata est ut non exaudias? Absit. *Sed iniquitates* meae multiplicatae sunt, et peccata mea adgravaverunt me nimis. (PL 404B)

   Isaias 59: 1, 2. Vulgate: Ecce non est *abbreviata* manus Domini *ut salvare nequeat,* neque aggravata est auris eius

---

[1] It is not easy to see why some, e.g., Polheim, *Reimprosa,* p. 360, and Ebert, *Gesch. Lit. Mittelalters,* II, 308, speak of Albar as predominantly Semitic in mind; they base their judgment on his passionate and pompous style.

ut non exaudiat. *Sed iniquitates* vestrae diviserunt inter
vos et Deum vestrum, et peccata vestra absconderunt
faciem eius.

Old Latin: Numquid non potest manus Domini salvos
facere? aut aggravata est auris eius ut non exaudiat?
Sed peccata vestra separant inter vos et Deum, et
propter peccata vestra avertit faciem eius a vobis ut non
misereatur.

4. Albar: Aspice Domine, et me *haerentem in vepribus* vide.
(PL 406A)

Gen. 22: 13. Vulgate: viditque post tergum arietem *inter
vepres haerentem* cornibus.

Old Latin: ecce aries unus tenebatur *in arbore Sabech*
cornibus.

Albar here is closer in wording to Genesis than to Verecundus
and the pseudo-Isidore, though like Albar they apply the allusion
figuratively to a human sinner. (See n. XIII, p. 132 above)

5. Albar: Ecce Deus meus *fons* iste *patet* omnibus habitantibus Hierusalem *in ablutione peccatorum et menstruatae.* (PL 409A)

Zach. 13: 1. Vulgate: In die illa erit *fons patens* domui
David, et habitantibus Ierusalem *in ablutionem peccatoris
et menstruatae.*

Old Latin: In die illa erit omnis *locus apertus* in domo
David et habitantibus Jerusalem et *in transmutationem
et in aspersionem.*

6. Albar: quia portas eius *occupavit salus,* et muros ipsius
laudatio. (PL 409A)

Isaias 60: 18. Vulgate: et *occupavit salus* muros tuos, et
portas tuas *laudatio.*

Old Latin: sed *vocabuntur salutare* muri tui, et portae
tuae *sculptura.*

7. Albar: tolle me a me, *et conloca juxta te, et cujus vult
manus pugnet tunc contra me.* (PL 412A)

Job 17: 3. Vulgate: Libera me Domine, *et pona me iuxta te, et cuiusvis manus pugnet contra me.* ·

Old Latin: Quis es iste? ad manum meam ligetur.

8. Albar: Subveni Domine perdito *vago et profugo.* (PL 412A)

Gen. 4: 12. Vulgate: *Vagus et profugus* eris super terram.

Old Latin: *gemens et tremens* eris in terra.

B.   Closer to the Old Latin.

1. Albar: Qui mortem *peccatoris* numquam *desideras,* sed ad vitam delinquentes semper verissime vocas. (PL 400A)

Ezech. 33: 11. Vulgate: Vivo ego, dicit Dominus Deus, *nolo* mortem *impii,* sed ut convertatur impius a via sua et vivat.

Old Latin: Vivo ego, dicit Dominus, quia non *desidero* mortem *peccatoris,* sed desidero ut avertatur peccator a via sua pessima et vivat.

Ezech. 18: 23 is similar in thought, but the wording in both versions is a little farther from Albar.

2. Albar: Numquid est aliud noli peccare *deinceps,* nisi ulterius non peccabis? (PL 404C)

John 8: 11. Vulgate: Vade, et iam *amplius* noli peccare.

Old Latin: Vade, et *ex hoc* iam noli peccare.
Cf. Augustine: Vade, iam *deinceps* noli peccare.[2]

3. Albar: *Qui* sitit veniat, et bibat. (PL 408D)

John 7: 37. Vulgate: *Si quis* sitit, veniat ad me, et bibat.
Old Latin: *Qui* sitit, veniat ad me, et bibat.

---

[2] The only authority given by Sabatier, and by Wordsworth and White, for *deinceps* in the Biblical text is Augustine, who uses it several times (e.g., PL 33:660; 36:590); so his use is evidently not a casual personal variation. Albar may have gotten it from Augustine.

4. Albar: Peccavi Domine, peccavi, et iniquitates meas ego *ag*nosco. (PL 412A)

Ps. 50: 5. Vulgate: Quoniam iniquitatem meam ego *cog*nosco.

Old Latin: iniquitatem meam ego *ag*nosco.

Cf. Augustine: iniquitatem meam ego *ag*nosco.[3]

C. In one place it is possible Albar is combining the two versions.

Albar: Pie Deus et misericors, *patiens, longanimis* . . . (PL 404A)

Ps. 102: 8. Vulgate: Miserator et misericors Dominus, *longanimis* et multum misericors.

Old Latin: Miserator et misericors Dominus, *patiens* et multum misericors.

The evidence is strongly in favor of Albar's using the Vulgate text; its witnesses are both more numerous and more conclusive. The four passages favoring the Old Latin can be plausibly explained as due to patristic influence, or, as was often the case, to Vulgate manuscripts containing a certain mixture of Old Latin readings. One or two of the cases are so tenuous that the variations may be fortuitous.

---

[3] So Augustine writes it twice, *Enarratio in Ps. 50*, n. 8, PL 36:589f. *Agnosco* is also the reading in *Oratio Manasse* as given in the Mozarabic liturgy, *Mozarabic Psalter*, ed. Gilson, p. 153, PL 86:859. Again, Albar could have found the text without the Old Latin Bible.

CHAPTER IV

LITERARY STYLE OF THE CONFESSIO

The *Confessio* is decidedly a self-conscious work of art, and in writing it Albar proves that a ninth-century Mozarab could still use the Latin language with facility and have many of the resources of rhetoric under his control. We cannot put too much weight on details of spelling and grammar, as the editor has done much to normalize these; but we can obtain a fair idea of Albar's command of Latin and his literary formation from the larger matters of his style.

Albar was one of those who by nature love the richly decorated. The simple directness of most of Isidore's writings is not for him. Writing for publication must have seemed a solemn business, requiring the observance of a formal ritual. He expresses himself forcefully, and, usually, clearly—after the second reading. But he dearly loves to develop his sentences, to beautify them with rhetorical ornaments, and at times to the best of his ability, to turn them into arabesques of complicated clauses. Others have surpassed him in this, for Albar is always serious, and his subject matter is more important to him than the decoration; we never lose the thought in mere verbiage. But we can say even more than this; even when we may wish for greater simplicity, the ornament is seldom a real distraction, and there are times when he achieves a felicity of phrase which reinforces the thought.

In an early Spaniard following in the wake of Isidore's *Synonyma* we should fear to find considerable use of the " synonymous style." In this we are happily disappointed. There are only a few places where Albar merely repeats the same thought in varied words.

Nec peccatores despicis, sed delicta condemnas; non odis

173

peccantes, sed peccata detestas; non hominem sed scelera
insectanda consumis; non creaturam sed culpam extirpas.
Iniquitas enim nostra justitiam tuam commendat; scelera
nostra te justum adfirmant; acta nostra sceleribus digna
justitiae tuae est documentum.   (PL 399D)

Much more common are passages where the thought is ex-
panded, each new clause adding some development.   At times this
becomes monotonous, but sometimes he uses it with success, adding force or feeling to the thought.

> Gaudet hostis meus quod te iratum videt; exultat cum
> me a tanto patre expulsum sentit; tripudiat cum me ita
> destitutum cognoscit.   Sed tu Deus, qui misericordia
> super opera tua largus praepotens es, qui peccatoris non
> mortem sed reversionem ad te post lapsum inquiris, qui
> plus pietatem quam ultionem diligis, nec judicium sed
> misericordiam peccantibus exhibes, adesto mihi.   (PL
> 401B)

> Repelle dominum consuetum, disrumpe vincula per-
> plexionum, restaure Domine opera tuae fabricae, et
> similitudinem tuam quam inimicus invasit mihi restitue.
> (PL 401B–C)

> Numquid justitia tua injustitiam probat? aut veritas tua
> mendaces coronat? aut sanctitas tua iniquos remunerat?
> ut me iniquum, impium, et mendacem impunitum evadere
> credam?   Absit.   (PL 403B)

Examples of balanced sentences:

> Verum quia diversa arte et vario deceptionis articulo me
> inimicus volentem ligavit, cui non mens ut debuit repug-
> navit, sed velut obediens manus vincturae dedit; inde
> piissime Deus; adsiste jam misero poenitenti et sere sua
> delicta plangenti, et redime nunc etiam specialiter a diro
> praedone quem jam generaliter pretio sanguinis tui re-
> demisti.   (PL 402A)

> Tu certe es qui cordis occulta vides, qui latentia pro-
> spiciendo cognoscis, qui cogitationes discutis atque
> ulciscis; qui enim universa consilio salutari creasti, uni-
> versa etiam cognoscendo librasti, sed confessionem pec-
> catoris expectas.   (PL 402B)

Pie Deus et misericors patiens longanimis, et super malitias hominum valde placabilis; comesum a bestiis erige, et a latronibus vulneratum oleo misericordiae fove. (PL 404A)

A less usual spiral development is this in which a Trinitarian invocation is three times repeated. It is the opening of the second section and thereby introduces the main body of the *Confessio:*

Adesto, adesto pauperi Pater, adsisto fesso o Emanuel, juva contritum Spiritus Sancte; erige dejectum Creator juste, sana aegrotum Jesu bone, visita languentem Paraclite alme; largire vires Agie [1] Deus, praebe virtutem o lux Nazarene, solida comessum Donum Tu Patris; atque vitiorum dominio usquequaque possessum, Tu Trinitas Deus, tibi effice servum devotum. (PL 400B)

Alliteration is seldom noticeable; two or three phrases such as *de sublimissima solii tua sede* occur.

But rime, prose rime,[2] is one of Albar's most cherished ornaments; it occurs on every page; never is it missing for more than a very few sentences at a time. Being attached to prose clauses of varying length it is not blatant when read silently; but if it were read aloud by one conscious of the author's intention, it could not help being wearisome. Its frequency is by itself proof of the great pains Albar took to make the *Confessio* a work of art.

The rime may be carefully exact and for two or three syllables, as: amas: damnas; praecedente: patescente; voluisti: noluisti: praetulisti; or only the final syllable, as: occulta: omnia; justa: vera: extenta. Ordinarily it is the final words of clauses that are rimed, but it may also be a series of words within the same clause, as: cibas atque sustentas. A case of assonance and rime used together within a clause is: Imo corde puro et ore patulo firmiter confitendum est. A continuous passage may be given to show how it runs:

---

[1] This use of *Agios* is no proof of a knowledge of Greek as it was not uncommon in the Mozarabic liturgy; cf. the inlatio for Easter (PL 85:484), and Férotin, *Lib. sacramentorum,* p. xxxiii.

[2] Polheim, *Reimprosa,* pp. 36off. mentions the use of prose rime by Albar and Eulogius.

Quod si haec omnia, quae a me dige*sta sunt,* et alia major*a,* quae a me omis*sa sunt,* quotidie in non merentibus oper*as;* me, Rex reg*um,* exigu*um* et pene pro nihilo computat*um,* quare non mund*as?* Hic *enim* mundationem inquir*o,* hic misericordiam posc*o,* hic veniam peccatorum efflagit*o,* quia in inferno nullam professionem profectuosam esse confid*o.* Quod si forsitan expectaris ut ext*endam* pusillitatem meam ad magnitudinem tuam intu*endam,* quaeso largire vires tend*endi* et praebe statum in anterioribus ampli*andi,* vel potius in sublime pedes erig*endi;* quia et pusillus statura Zachaeus, licet se extend*eret,* te videre minime poss*et,* si sicomori altitudinem non adir*et.* Et vere te ipse oculis vid*et,* qui praecepti altitudinem ten*et,* qui mundo corde in arborem vitae conscend*et.* (PL 410D–411A)

The first sentence contains an unusually complex rime scheme: a b a b c d d d c.

The mediaeval pronunciation of *ae* is evident in another example: meae: durissimae: eluendae: rore. In another place the rime enables us to see that a bit of bad grammar in the manuscript is due to the scribe, not to the author:

Satis est Domine quod hucusque diabolum milit*avi* (MS militavit); quod hostis orbis servitium sponte impl*evi;* quod inimico famulatum iniquitatis opere praeb*ui;* quod latentes insidias ejus licet intelligerem non devit*avi* . . . port*avi* . . . fec*i* . . . cess*avi.* (PL 400B–C)

Cursus, or accentual clausulae,[3] is the other ornament which Albar uses most constantly; and is probably the one that would most quickly strike a reader's attention. He handles them with apparent ease, fitting a great variety of different words into the rhythmic patterns: it is not a matter of the tiresome repetition of a few clichés. Choosing arbitrarily the third division of the *Confessio,* which fills four columns of Migne's text, a count was made of all the cursus occurring at the end of phrases and clauses, with the result that 230 were discovered. Internal cursus, that

---

[3] On the nature and forms of clausulae see: Sister Mary Emmanuel Mann, *The Clausulae of St. Hilary of Poitiers;* Thomas A. Kelly, *Sancti Ambrosii liber de consolatione Valentiniani.*

is, the same patterns occurring in the interior of a clause and not leading to a pause, are more elusive and often uncertain; but fifty-two reasonably clear cases were noted. The results can be seen most readily in tabular form.

	Planus	Tardus	Velox	Trispondaic	Medius	Ditrochaic	Dactylic Dispondee
Final	110	53	23	20	10	6	8
Internal	36	10	4	1	1		

Planus / x x / x. rodendo contrado. piissime clamo. sensu sentire. tu solus purgas.

Tardus / x x / x x. tremendo contabui. esse non dubito. bene perpenderet.

Velox / x x \ x / x. valeam enarrare. lectionibus non curantur. deifica sacramenta.

Trispondaic / x ϡ x / x. confabulatione. quis dinumerare. ipsa medicina. premimus reddamus.

Medius / x / x x. si sanguinibus. quis elicere. Dic jam Domine. tua super me. partim opere. miserorum spolio.

Ditrochaic / x / x. tunc jam laetus. aguntur nescit. in mundo bonum.

Dactylic dispondee / x ϡ x / x x. pejus domicidio. recte cogitavero. gravior libidinem.

The final two sentences of this third division may be given as an outstanding example of how densely the cursus can be packed into the text:

Planus   Tardus
/ x x / x   / x x / x x
Si enim homo seipsum bene perpenderet, ex seipso ra-

Velox
/ x x \ x / x
tionem quam inquirit utiliter compensaret; quoniam qui

Tardus   Tardus   Ditrochaic
/ x x / x x   / x x / x x   / x / x
ea quae infra se, vel in se quotidie aguntur nescit, stulte

Planus   Ditrochaic   Planus   Planus
/ x x / x   / x   / x   / x x / x || / x   x
Domini sui opera librare cupit, qui sui ignarus perpetim

                                                    Velox
/ x   / x x
manet. Et cum nos miserrimi in bestiis et quadrupedibus

            Trispondaic   Planus
\ x / x || / x   \ x / x   / x x / x
voluntates nostras impleamus, et etiam ipsis avibus et

            Trispondaic   Planus
            / x \ x / x   / x x / x
piscibus ex tuo dono imperemus, et partim in cibum,

            Planus   Planus   Planus
            / x x / x || / x x / x || / x x /
partim in adjumentum ex ipsis vel capiamus, vel occida-

            Planus   Trispondaic
x   / x x / x   / x x x
mus, nec pro hoc rationem illis quos premimus red-

        Tardus   Planus   Planus
/ x || / x   x / x x   / x x / x || / x
damus, quare hoc facimus, vel cur illi et illi non sunt

            Planus   Planus
x / x   / x x / x   / x x / x
occisi; quare isti et isti sunt ad adjumentum ab oc-

Planus   Tardus
/ x x / x   / x   x
cisione servati; rationem miseri factorum tuorum in-
                    Medius
/ x x   / x / x x
quirimus, qui rationabiliter quid sit sapere, nisi per te

    Dactylic dispondee
    / x x x / x x
addiscere non possumus. (PL 406D–407A).

The three forms common in the Middle Ages are well in the lead, the *planus* alone accounting for nearly half; but the less usual types occur clearly enough to make it certain Albar was using them consciously. All of these forms are used by patristic writers like Augustine and Jerome. The various placing of word-divisions within each pattern have not been separately counted, but the examples chosen to illustrate the types show some of the variety.

In a number of cases there occur longer rhythmical phrases which fall between a single and a double cursus; perhaps they might be thought of as two *plani* telescoped together, or as a reminiscence of the last half of an hexameter, or merely as an extra flourish on the part of the author.

> / xx / x x / x
> Domini mei mundatus. qualiter saepe proruat. usque
> delatam dedisti.

The reader will notice that prose rime is also used in the selection given, the author with no small skill writing his text with these two ornamental patterns interweaving.

Though much of the *Confessio,* especially the latter part, is written in a fairly direct style, Albar admired one of greater elaboration and tried when possible to use a more complex word order. At times he succeeds in achieving a rhetorical arrangement of words. For instance, there is the figure called hyperbaton, or the separation of related words:

> et erue Te corde contrito quaerentem. (PL 401B).
> et libera me ab isto qui me furatum tenet saevo dracone.
> (PL 403C).
> et per sanctorum pede trita deinceps incede vestigia. (PL
> 404C). .
> et tuo eum sancto munire praesidio. (PL 412A).

The following sentence is a curious example of the gathering together of verbs at the end; it is perhaps an accident that, in addition, the last part can be read as an accentual hexameter:

> Tu vero, Deus meus, qui paralyticum non habentem qui
>   se in piscinam dúm turbáta fuísset mítteret vérbo
>   curásti. (PL 409A).

Twice in the same sentence, at the end of his book, Albar uses anadiplosis, which is the doubling of a word, either immediately or after an interval; here both forms are employed:

> Et sicut ex *me me* tremulum vides, nihilque nisi ex te
>   praesumentem cognoscis; ita *me* pie Opifex *totum*
>   defende, quia me *totum totum* commisi. (PL 412C).

A variant of this is the juxtaposition of words which are different but of similar sound. There is one notable occurrence of this in the *Confessio;* it also appears in other writings of this group, and in the Mozarabic liturgy.

> Albar: et etiam non merentibus viam *salutis solitus* es
> tribuere . . . (PL 408A).
> *Oratio pro correptione,* n. 27: ex *indigentina indulgentiam*
> afferens.
> Augustine, *Soliloquia,* I, 1, 3: Deus per quem improbamus
> *eorum errorem.*
> *Lib. sacramentorum,* col. 153, lines 26f.: Quo et nobis
> serviendi tibi concedatur cum *affectu effectus* . . .

Albar loves double negatives, or litotes. These three specimens appear in the same passage: non nescio; non nolens, imo volvens involvo; non inscius, sed ut scita (PL 402C–D).

There are a few cases, apart from the longer passages already discussed, where there are locutions reminiscent of the liturgy:

> et ea quae dixero tu ipse *acceptare dignare.* (PL 402A).
> ut obediam voci tuae tu clemens inspirare dignare corde
> meo. (PL 408C).
> Cf. *Oratio pro correp. vitae,* n.2: . . . intende placatus
>
> *ibid.,* n.41: . . . te meditetur, te delectetur . . .

A certain affection for the nominal use of infinitives may also be noted:

> Et hoc est verissime scire, quod est amarissime flere.
> (PL 403A).
> Et item novi, quod praepotens es in majestate, et ut velle,
> ita tibi subjacet posse. (PL 403A).
> Dixisse enim tuum, Domine Jesu, fecisse est. (PL 404C).

Rhetorical questions are so common throughout the *Confessio* that some are included within the examples already given. The following is typical of his use:

> Sed numquid non vocasti? numquid non ad tuam gratiam
> invitasti? numquid non quotidie nobis vocem vocationis
> tuae misisti? (PL 408C).

Albar's temperament was emotional and extremist, prone to exaggeration. Thus, though we do not know his sins, some of his self-recrimination may strike us as a bit over-vivid. Such is the *foetidissimus hircus* already mentioned; his statement that he receives his food from God in a viperous mouth (PL 410B); his speaking of his sins as ulcers, in which however he follows his predecessors. With these may be associated the epithet applied to others, *Judeorum foetores* (*loc.cit.*).

Two expressions used in the *Confessio* have parallels in the *Vita Eulogii.* (Notes are given on them in the translation.)

> Aedifica Domine in corde meo urnam *candore* vitae *nitentem.* (PL 403C). cf. *Vita,* n.15: columba miro *candore nivescens.*
> qui *fastu superbiae* non obediendo sed discutiendo incedit. (PL 406C). cf. *Vita,* n.1: segnitiae *fastu.*

The study of vocabulary and syntax is not a part of this essay. In general, both as printed are fairly normal. Flórez[4] and Nicolas Antonio[5] give short discussions of them as they stand in the manuscript with many typical mediaeval aberrations. In the normalized form published by the editor, some common mediaeval forms survive:

> *seu* and *vel=et:* Deus qui creaturam illam quam primam dignitate *seu* fortitudine *vel* decore esse voluisti . . . (PL 399A).
> *infra= intra:* Qui sursum residendo regis, deorsum continendo ades, extra circumdas, *infra* et omnia penetrans. (PL 398C).
> *qualiter=quomodo:* Sed *qualiter* potum in te accipio, qui ad illum animi gressu non propero? (PL 409A).

Some interest attaches to adverbial phrases in which an adjective is combined with the ablative case of *mens.* Three of these occur in the *Confessio:*

> hanc crudelitatem ego mihi caecatus a diabolo *spontanea mente* elegi. (PL 400D).

---

[4] ES XI, 53-60.
[5] Reprinted PL 121:392f.

> et ab eorum inlecebra me *tota mente* cupio retrahere.
> (PL 402C).
> (crucem), quam et nobis tollere humeribus, et te sequere
> *pura mente* jussisti. (PL 408A).

While this locution goes back to the days of the Roman Empire, it was from it that Romance adverbs were formed. The first two examples the phrases could well be treated as simple adverbs, but the third not so well; all three can easily be given the full force of each word, so probably to Albar they were still phrases with the idea of *mens* yet present.

Unusual words are rare. The changed environment of the Middle Ages, and of Mozarabic Spain do not show here. Efforts to maintain the past are more in evidence than the expression of the new whether on purpose or unintentionally. *Tripudio* and *centuplico* are classical; *lucifluus* is post-classical but still imperial. *Rosifluus* seems to be the only word not in the standard dictionaries, and it is merely a poetical combination of two classical roots, without any of the interest of a Germanic or Arabic importation.

At times Albar achieves passages of real eloquence; this is particularly true of the latter part of the book where his strong and sincere feeling expresses itself in a style that is fundamentally Scriptural. In some cases we find phrases which have a deceptive Biblical ring, yet which are not to be found in Scripture. They may be taken from some Father, or they may be adaptations or creations by Albar himself. As no source has been discovered for them, with some hesitation they are put down here as Albar's own. The first two are much like the Psalms; the third suggests Job coming through St. Augustine; the last two seem more like a Christian mystic praying for complete union with God.

> (Fiat Domine misericordia tua super me [Ps. 32: 22]),
> et dirige vultum tuum in inluminatione cordis tui.
> (PL 404D).
> Adsperge me Deus dulcedinis tuae rore, et complue
> mentem meam imbribus gratiae tuae (PL 409C).
> Numquid a nobis praemii aliquid accepisti ut creares?
> aut dedimus tibi pretium operis nostri ut redimeres?
> (PL 407A).
> Tolle me Domine mihi, et redde me tibi; tolle malum
> meum, ut bonum perfruam tuum; tolle me a me, (et

conloca juxta te, et cujus vult manus pugnet tunc
contra me [Job 17: 3]). Tolle propria mea, vitio meo
concepta, et prae benignitate tua confecta. (PL
412A–B).

Exue me meis, et induar tuis. Exime totum me a me, ut
totus restituar tibi. (PL 412B).

The sources for this last quotation were given earlier. Albar
makes a real improvement over the *Oratio* of the pseudo-Isidore,
and in the opinion of the present writer is the equal of the parallel
in Augustine: Albar is less Platonically speculative than Augustine, but perhaps more thoroughly Christian.

PART FOUR

ALBAR'S VITA EULOGII

FOREWORD

THE Vita *Eulogii* is the best known of Albar's writings. Morales found it in two manuscripts and published it in his edition of Eulogius' works in 1574, and since then it has been many times reprinted. In a way it may be considered the crown of Albar's life. From youth Eulogius had been not only a friend, but a hero and ideal to him, and Eulogius' martyrdom appears as the climax of the martyr movement. How long Albar survived his friend is not certainly known; two or three of his letters and perhaps the *Confessio* may be placed after 859, but they are in the nature of an anticlimax and farewell, and after them nothing more of Albar is heard.

In writing the *Vita* Albar wished not only to do personal honor to his friend, but to build a memorial which would perpetuate Eulogius' fame down the centuries; it is a memorial upon which the author spent all his talent, " it is built of fine gold and precious stones that will survive the depredations of the tyrant," and in the words of Horace will be a " monument more enduring than bronze." Further than this, the *Vita*, or at least the Passion,[1] was meant to be read in the liturgy of " the annual recurrence of his feast." [2]

---

[1] Beginning with n. 12, and perhaps ending with n. 16 or 17.

[2] N. 11; cf. the two opening lines of the Hymn for St. Eulogius' day. A modern reader might wonder whether a man would be given official honor as a saint so soon after his death. But apart from the many cases in the later Middle Ages, there is evidence that this was done with this very group of Cordovan martyrs. Eulogius implies his readiness to call them saints when he blames some of the moderate party "qui jubent eos non recipi in catalogo sanctorum" (*Mem. SS.*, I, 18, PL 115:751C; and cf. *Ibid.*, I, 37, PL 763f.). Whenever possible their relics were collected by the Mozarabs and reverently buried in one of the churches with the

The authenticity of the biography has never been doubted, and there is no reason to question its substantial truth, though admitting that some of its praise of its hero's learning is hyperbolical. The life is wholly different from the many unhistorical legends of martyrs where the hero lacks all individuality, where the trial, sufferings and death are conventionalized, and the chief interest is in a stereotyped series of miracles.[3] To be sure, Albar speaks of the Moslem judges in terms of unmitigated condemnation as is customary in the legends—" truculent," " cruel," etc.; but he records their actions as being much more moderate and legal than the epithets suggest. The abusive adjectives are a true part of Albar's outlook, and likely enough also of the others who took part in the martyr movement. By far the largest part of the biography is given to Eulogius' life and character. The course of his life is not at all that of a conventional legend, but is at the same time natural and individual; I know of no parallel in early western hagiography to the story of his school-boy friendship with Albar, or of his journey in search of his brothers which turned into a literary pilgrimage to the monasteries of Navarre. Apart from the simple episode of the bird, and the vision of a soldier, there is no suggestion of the miraculous, and there are no post-mortem legends. There is no lingering over the gruesome details of the martyrdom; there are no preliminary tortures, and the death itself is told in less than a sentence. The personalities of the two men were poles apart, and it would be psychologically impossible for the

---

bishop pontificating. The honor paid their remains by the Christians irritated the Moslems, who thereafter tried to destroy the bodies of those executed by throwing them into the river, burning them, or exposing them to beasts of prey. When the monks of Saint Germain des Près came to Spain in 858 seeking relics of saints, they were told in Zaragoza of the new martyrs of Córdoba as though suitable for their purpose; and in Córdoba they had a hard time to get relics of two of them, so great was the devotion of the Christians. This was the year before Eulogius' death. The bishop officially sealed the relics they took, as is done with those to whom public religious honor is paid. Some years later, 884 A. D., the remains of Eulogius himself and of his fellow-martyr Leocritia were translated to Oviedo and were there met by King Alfonsus the Great and Bishop Hermenegild in formal procession (see ES X, 457).

[3] Cf. H. Delehaye, *Les légendes hagiographiques.*

highly emotional, subjective, and violent Albar fully to understand the quiet, studious, and gentle character of Eulogius. Yet this biography presents us the interesting picture of one as seen through the admiring but not wholly comprehending eyes of the other. And the Eulogius of the *Vita* is the same man we find in the saint's own writings.

The book is so personal that it is unique in old hagiographical literature. In spite of the strained rhetoric and the effort at an elegant style in a language not his mother tongue, qualities that at first may seem to detract from the sincerity, the work is clearly the genuine, deeply-felt outpouring of Albar's heart. Though he speaks of him reverently as a saint, from the first line to the last there is the tenseness of personal affection. This is not the impersonal account of a wonderworker as in Sulpicius Severus' life of St. Martin, or the picture of a remote ascetic as in St. Athanasius' life of St. Anthony, not the calm story of a great man who happened to be an old friend as in Possidius' life of St. Augustine. Albar was of too egoistic a temperament to be able to achieve such detachment; his personality is as much present as the life of Eulogius; but he humbly flings himself with all his passionate nature at the feet of his hero.

This reaches a unique climax in the last chapter (nn.16–20) where, after concluding the passion of Eulogius, Albar pours out a torrent of self-recrimination for his own shortcomings, and then turns to a direct address to his friend in heaven where he is now a saint, asking for his intercession and help that Albar, too, may have the grace of salvation. The Augustinian sense of sinfulness, apart from particular, concrete sins, is characteristic of Albar. The direct appeal to a personal friend now in heaven I do not know to occur elsewhere in so fully developed a form. It is true that some early lives of saints have something in the way of an apostrophe at the end. Thus St. Gregory Nazianzen closes his panegyric on St. Basil[4] with a brief apostrophe to his friend; and the *Passio Sancti Zoyli* ends with a similar purely rhetorical

---

[4] A Select Library of Nicene and Post-Nicene Fathers of the Christian Church, Second Series, VII, 395–422.

address.[5] The short *Acta* of St. Genesius of Arles by Bishop Paulinus do not invoke Genesius directly but urge readers to pray to him for his intercession.[6] St. Braulio of Zaragoza goes further in his *Vita Sancti Aemiliani,* directly asking the saint's intercession,[7] and St. Hilary of Arles does the same at the end of his *Sermo de vita Sancti Honorati.*[8] Yet while the theological implications are the same, even these last two fall short of Albar's outpouring. Albar may have known the Spanish Braulio's life of San Millán, and he may have known Hilary's work,[9] though both the literary style and the course of the life Hilary narrates are too different to suggest it was a source for Albar. In his chronicling of the earlier martyrs, Eulogius himself comes nearer to Albar, several times praying directly to them as saints in heaven.[10]

To beautify his style Albar weaves in phrases from Scripture and from St. Jerome, and a famous line of Horace,[11] but he does not seem to have moulded the *Vita* on any particular model. Still, it is clearly in the literary tradition; it is orderly, with a formal opening, a profession of truthfulness, disclaimers of rhetoric and studied style, an orderly narrative of the biography; then the passion in a separate section (meant for the liturgy), and finally the highly developed apostrophe, which was perhaps developed out

---

[5] ES X, 491–493; ends: O summa juvenis constantia qui . . . . O omni laude dignissimum virum qui . . .

[6] AASS, Aug. V, 135.

[7] PL 80:699–714. Vale, vale, Aemilaine beate . . . praesideo dignus inveniar in extremo judicio (*loc. cit.,* 712C–D).

[8] PL 50:1249–1272.

[9] C. Lynch, *St. Braulio,* pp. 152f., says that Braulio had a copy of the life of St. Honoratus; if so, then perhaps Albar knew it too.

[10] In the first book of *Mem. SS.* Eulogius several times addresses the martyrs, and in closing asks their prayers as saints, PL 115:766A. Again, he closes his long account of St. Columba with a prayer to her: caeterum tu sacratissima, quae . . . , esto memor cultoris tui; erue me laqueis mundi, abstrahe perturbationibus saeculi, et confer post mortem requiem paradisi. Per Dominum nostrum Jesum Christum . . . (PL 115:811D).

[11] The "satires" of Horace was part of the treasure Eulogius had brought back with him from Navarre; this citation suggests that "satire" meant, or at least included, the Odes. In the Middle Ages the hexameter poems of Horace were more valued than his lyrics; cf. J. E. Sandys, *History of Classical Scholarship,* 2nd ed., pp. 636f.

of a simple rhetorical form in classical composition. In spite of passages of cumbrous rhetoric, it is well constructed and true to life. It is no mean achievement. The only place where interest flags is in the prologue, where he repeats too often that it is better to tell the truth than to concoct what is not so. As a composition, it is perhaps the best biography written in early Spain.

TRANSLATION

PREFACE

1. In beginning to write the passion of the blessed martyr and doctor Eulogius, I have thought that an orderly account should be given of his life before describing the glorious combat of his end, to let readers first know who and what he was, and then to show clearly that he worthily obtained the palm of victory. Confident in the aid of our Lord and Redeemer, at the beginning of this work I protest [1] that I am putting down not doubtful things I have heard but what I have myself seen and experienced; for by God's grace we were joined together from the first flower of youth with one uniting bond in the sweetness of charity and in love of the Scriptures, and we led our lives, if not with equal rank, still with mutual affection in all things. For he, adorned with the office of the priesthood and raised aloft on the wings of virtue, flew the higher; while stained with the mire of luxury and concupiscence I am still creeping on the earth. And so it is that I have set out to tell things, not uncertain and learned from the lips of other men, but which were done in my company and which I myself have known. For as I confess that it would be dangerous to make statements rashly about unsure matters, so I think it is not without peril to withhold my knowledge of those things that ought to be known. Moreover, laudable truth should be published as an example to all, while the artificial falsehood of the rhetoricians is to be despised. [2] For it is better to say nothing about many noble exploits than from

---

[1] With this passage cf.: obsecro autem eos qui lecturi sunt, ut fidem dictis adhibeant, neque me quicquam nisi conpertum et probatum scripsisse arbitrentur: alioquin tacere quam false dicere maluissem, Sulpicius Severus, *Vita sancti Martini,* I, CSEL I, III.

[2] Cf.: melius siquidem est ut vera minus erudite quam ut ficta enarrentur eloquenter, Braulio, *Vita sancti Aemiliani,* praefatio, n. 5, PL 80:702f. More remote is Cicero's: Nam quis nescit primam esse historiae legem, ne quid falsi dicere audeat? deinde ne quid veri non audeat? *De oratore,* II, 62. Eulogius himself had already expressed similar sentiments: Preface to *De vita et passione SS. virginum Florae et Mariae* (= *Mem. SS.,* II,

petty good deeds to elaborate many things falsely; it is safer to pass over all that has been done than to concoct some that were not done. It is a more pardonable error to suppress the truth, not through wilful malice, but through carelessness,[3] than to fabricate eloquently things that are not so. For when spoken from a zeal for truth and not from vainglory, truth awards[4] a crown to the speaker, but falsehood destroys anyone who engages in it. And as I am happy to say that I ought to be rewarded telling the truth, so I do not deny I ought to be condemned if I should speak falsehood. Therefore I have not thought I should plunge into weaving falsehood, as I know that truth in all things and not lying is rewarded.

CHAPTER I

2. Sprung from a noble line, born in a senatorial family of Córdoba, dedicated to the ecclesiastical ministry, serving the

---

8): (as the cult of the martyrs redounds to God's praise) . . . ergo nostrarum virginum Florae et Mariae tropaea digesturi insignia non facundiae lepori, non tonantibus euphoniis verborum serviamus; sed quod fidelibus simpliciter rei gestae veritatem insinuet, observemus: quia sufficere nostris credimus veritatem pura simplicitate digestam, quam vano infulatam cultu fallaciam. Et sat nobis est fideliter referre quod fuit; quia non congruit sub venustate sermonis rem quae non exstiterit adhibere. Illibata namque veritas, quoquo modo proferatur, firmiori gressu constitit, et ornatissime fictum mendacium paululum perseverat. Nec patitur Christus assertorem justitiae immunem esse benedictionis praemio, cum tamen reatu homicidii astringatur prolator mendacii. (end of pref.) (PL 115:835A–B.) In the long prayer that closes the second book of *Mem. SS.*: Numquid si ego mentior, tu testis non es? si falsum astruo, nonne vides? si aliter quam fuit affirmo, tu poteris ignorare? Si non profero veritatem, non latere te potest, qui omnia nosti. Certe tu cuncta consideras, penetras universa, secretum intelligis, vides profundum, omneque tibi patet arcanum, et totum in praesenti tibi manens, praeteritum et futurum in tuo cuncta volumine ascribentur. (PL 115:798D)

[3] Segnitiae fastu. This unusual phrase also occurs in canon 13 of the Council of Mérida: In ecclesia Dei sancta congregatio clericorum fit non modica, et sunt aliqui quorum intentio non pauca est in sancto Dei officio, atque multi quos *segnitudinis fastus* minime perducit ad bonum perfectum. (PL 84:621A; Mansi, *Concilia,* XI, 83) Mansi gives the date of the council as 666 A. D.

[4] Implodit.

Church of San Zoylo and living in the community of its clergy, the blessed martyr Eulogius flourished in many outstanding virtues and was mighty in great and praiseworthy deeds. He devoted himself to ecclesiastical learning from the very cradle, and growing daily through the study of good works he reached perfection; outshining all his contemporaries in the knowledge of doctrine, and flourishing in the light of learning, he became the master of his teachers. Indeed, having a mature mind in his small body,[5] he surpassed all in knowledge though not in age. For he was a most studious searcher of the Scriptures [6] and earnest investigator of its teachings; so that he preferred nothing to the Bible, and liked nothing better than to " meditate on the law of the Lord day and night " (Ps. 1: 2). Not resting content with the instruction of his own masters, he sought out at a distance such others as he heard of; and not to offend his own, he went out secretly at such hours as he could. Often he went to see Abbot Speraindeo of holy memory, a man renowned [7] and heralded for the fame of his teaching, and as an auditor hung on his eloquent lips. At that time Speraindeo was enriching all Baetica with the streams of his wisdom. It was there first I had the good fortune to see him, there I entered into his sweet friendship, there I was bound to him in inseparable sweetness. For I was one of the disciples of the same illustrious man; and while I was constantly frequenting his light and sharpening my raw mind, at last by divine providence [8] I became acquainted with Eulogius. Gradually we [9] were not only

---

[5] Albar: mentem senilem parvissimo corpore gerens. Cf. Gregory, *Dialogue,* II, praefatio: ab ipso suae pueritiae tempore cor gerens senile (of St. Benedict), (PL 66:126A).

[6] Albar: studiosissimus Scripturarum scrutator. Cf. John 5: 39, scrutamini Scripturas; Acts 17: 11, quotidie scrutantes Scripturas.

[7] opinabilem. Schott's regularly quoted note that this word in the sense of "famous" is an Hispanicism is wrong. Cf. Cassiodorus, *Institutiones,* II, 20: Plato et Aristoteles, opinabiles magistri, (ed. Mynors, p. 130); and cf. Du Cange.

[8] respectio. For examples of its use in the late sense of Divine favor, grace, providence, cf.: *Leges visigothorum:* tandem superne respectionis adflatu nobis est divinitus inspiratum ut . . . (ed. Zeumer, MGH, *Leges nationum,* I, 49, lines 11–12); mihi . . . et cuncto populo regiminis mei respectio divina semper opituletur (*ibid.,* p. 481, lines 36–38).

[9] The Latin text in both Flórez and Lorenzana has verbs in the first

joined but united in an unshakable bond; we became disciples of the same man, searchers for truth, and devoted to each other; so much so that our inexperienced youth presumed in fields beyond its power. Together we studied the Scriptures with the zest of a game,[10] and not knowing how to handle an oar on a lake we ventured on the raging of the Euxine Sea.[11] For we carried on in letters to each other the childish disputes on matters where we differed, not contentiously but with delight, and in accentual verses we affectionately praised each other. This exercise was sweeter to us than honey and more enjoyable than the honeycomb,[12] and daily pressing onward our boyish and immature eagerness to learn [13] drove us into tackling many inaccessible things of Scripture. And thus we composed volumes which in mature age we destroyed so they would not go down to posterity.

3. When Eulogius reached manhood [14] he ministered as a deacon, and, in a short time deservedly raised higher, he was honored with the rank of the priesthood and quickly both by order and character was associated with the masters. The affection of every one showed how great were his humility, his goodness, and his charity. Henceforth he set out to restrict himself in a greater

---

person singular, but no direct object. The passage must be corrupt, and the translator has the choice of supplying the object, or making the verbs plural reflexives.

[10] Cf. Jerome *Ep.* 110, n. 8 (Augustine to Jerome) : . . . dum cogito inter vos, quibus Deus hoc ipsum, quod uterque nostrum optavit, largum prolixumque concesserat, ut coniunctissimi et familiarissimi mella Scripturarum sanctarum pariter lamberetis . . . (CSEL 55:363). *Ep.* 115 (Jerome to Augustine) : In Scripturarum, si placet, campo sine nostro invicem dolore ludamus (*ibid.*, p. 397). *Ep.* 116, n. 2 (Augustine to Jerome) : Petis . . . ut in Scripturarum campo sine nostro invicem dolore ludanus . . . tamquam ludentem in campo Scripturarum . . . (*ibid.*, p. 398). These three epistles are in Escorial & I.14, a manuscript that Millares Carlo thinks of Cordovan origin.

[11] Albar: et scalmum in lacu nescientes regere, Euxini maris credebamur fragori. Cf. Jerome, *Ep.* 1, n. 2: qui necdum scalmum in lacu rexi, Euxini maris credor fragori (CSEL 54:1f.).

[12] Albar: nobis melle suavius, favis iucundius. Ps. 18:11, dulciora super mel et favum; Ecclus. 24:27, hereditas mea super mel et favum.

[13] docibilitas.

[14] juventus.

austerity of life, to adorn all his actions by following the rules of modesty, to apply himself to the sacred Scriptures, to chastise his body with vigils and fasting, to frequent monasteries, to visit religious houses, and to compose rules for the brethren. In each place he so conducted himself that it seemed that, had it been possible, he would have lived in both states: bearing himself so in his own clerical state that he did not put aside the regular order as something alien; so associating with the monks that it was clear he belonged to the clergy; so living in the clergy that he seemed a monk; moving an adept in both groups, and completely fulfilling in himself both ideals. Often he ran out to the holy communities of the monasteries, but then again returned to the clergy so that none would think he disdained his own order; then after staying there for a time he returned to the monasteries to keep his soul from being enervated by worldly cares. Here adorning the Church with his teaching, there beautifying his own life by mortification, possessed of such great virtues, he trod the world's road sad and anxious; and longing daily to fly to heaven, he was weighted down with the burden of his body. So much so that he planned to go to Rome in order to subdue by tears and pilgrimage the faults of youth, or rather to efface faults that were already overcome. But all of us surrounded him and held him back in body rather than in spirit.

Chapter II

4. While these and other things were happening, Bishop Reccafred[15] descended upon churches and clergy like a violent whirlwind, and threw as many priests as he could into jail. Among whom Eulogius was included as an elect ram, and was imprisoned along with his own bishop and other priests. In this confinement he gave more thought to prayer and reading than to his bonds. There for the holy virgins Flora and Mary, imprisoned for their faith, he wrote his *Documentum martyriale* in one book, in which with strong encouragement he fortified them for martyrdom, and both in person and by correspondence taught them to despise

---

[15] Formerly bishop of Córdoba, now metropolitan, or archbishop of Seville; Saul had succeeded him as bishop of Córdoba.

death; he asked their prayers that he and his companions might be released from jail—which he obtained the sixth day after their passion. For they were martyred on the twenty-fourth day of November,[16] and the priests of the Lord were set free on the twenty-ninth. There is a letter [17] about this, written in elegant style and sent to me at the time, recounting the passion of those virgins and the release of the priests through their merits. While there he became a master of Latin metrics,[18] which until then Spanish scholars did not know, and explained them to us after his release. From there also he wrote me a letter in eloquent style about the books he had written in defense of the martyrs. For while the other priests who were with him relaxed in ease and quietness, he did not cease from reading night and day, working [19] both night and day, drawing out the honey of the Scriptures, and ruminating it in mouth and heart.

5. I think it worth while to write a little more fully of how he conducted himself in the time of persecution. For while bishops, priests, and clergy, and the wise men of Córdoba trod a devious path in the persecution [20] which had recently broken out, and driven by fear almost denied Christ by sign if not in words, he was unshakable and was never seen to suffer even a tremor of vacillation. But going to meet all who were advancing to their death, giving all stout hearts, venerating and burying their bodies, he was so on fire with the flame of martyrdom that he seemed to be the inspirer of martyrdom [21] in those days. For this zeal for uprightness he was attacked with many insults and wearied with great threats. For one of the notables who assailed and injured him with threats,

---

[16] In 851 A. D., cf. Eulogius, *Mem. SS.*, II, 8; this chapter is not dated, but those before and after are.

[17] "Magnificavit Dominus misericordiam . . . ," Lorenzana, *SS. PP. Tolet.*, II, 533-535; PL 115:841-844.

[18] perfectissime docuit. "Docuit" must be an error of scribe or printer, for it is clear that Eulogius *learned* the subject in prison, and *taught* it later.

[19] noctes diesque ingeminans. *Ingemino* properly means to double; is Albar thinking of working "double time"? or may it be a mistake for ingemiscens, sighing? The latter would fit the context.

[20] martyrio nuper exorto. An odd use of *martyrium*.

[21] MS. martyrii; Lorenzana, martyrum.

turned to a reprobate sense [22] by a just judgment of God, was soon so unhappy and foolish as to lose the faith which he had ignorantly fought against while he still held it; the blessed Eulogius wrote more fully of him in the third book of the *Memoriale sanctorum*.[23] In these books he described in a distinguished style the passion of each martyr, and with considerable fulness he published for future generations all that was done and said in the case of the martyrs of God. How great and how outstanding was his learning is shown more clearly than day by the writings which he composed with Attic salt and beauty of prose style,[24] I may even say with divine inspiration.

6. But let us go back to the times of Bishop Reccafred, and tell how cleverly Eulogius suspended himself from saying Mass in order not to become entangled in his error. For in those days all, delivered to him by force and power and subjected to him by royal command, seemed to be joined to the evil enemy; and those who in the earlier revolt had stood upright against him now, prostrated by terror, clung to him like a retinue, not in mind but in body, not from love of the heart but driven by fear, and lest he should have an excuse [25] for injuring them further. Also the king who was raging against us made constraining laws,[26] and doing away with free will, subjected all to our savage enemy. This story will be told more clearly in another work.[27]

7. But now we wish only to explain the holy stratagem of this

---

[22] Albar: in reprobum sensum conversus; Eulogius on the same event: in deteriora conversus (*Mem. SS.*, III, 2); Romans 1:28, tradidit illos Deus in reprobum sensum.

[23] *Mem. SS.*, III, 2. PL 115:801. cf. *ibid.*, II, 15, n. 2. The person concerned held the important position of exceptor, or tax-collector for the Christians. His name is thought to have been Gomez.

[24] Albar: sale Attico et prosatico lepore; Jerome, *Ep.* 57, n. 12: hic lepos Atticus et Musarum . . . eloquio (CSEL 54:525); Jerome, *Ep.* 125, n. 6: qui Asianum tumorem Attico siccabant sale (CSEL 56:123); Martial, *Epigr.*, III, 20, lines 8f.: an otiosus in schola poetarum lepore tinctos Attico sales narrat.

[25] aditus.

[26] legibus necessitatem induxerat.

[27] This promised writing was either unwritten or lost.

admirable man. For with a heavy sense of grief, when he saw that the bishop's sorry plottings were spreading all around him, and noticed that others of his circle were in communion with the bishop, and when he could see no possibility left him of resisting, nor yet had any freedom to move elsewhere as he had given sureties, he began as we said to exhaust himself with deep groaning and to be overwhelmed by great sorrow. But by the will of God it happened that one day there was read in the presence of the bishop a letter of blessed Epiphanius, Bishop of Salamis in Cyprus, to Bishop John of Jerusalem,[28] a letter I had told a certain deacon to read. In it that holy bishop, reproving the nonsense of Origen, and defending the ordination of a priest he had consecrated in a certain [29] monastery of the said bishop of Jerusalem, explained the cause of the ordination, and praised the action of the blessed priests, Jerome and Vincent, in refraining from saying Mass.[30] Eagerly jumping at, rather than receiving this, and recognizing an opening given him by God, Eulogius fetched a deep sigh from the

---

[28] For a general discussion of this episode, see F. Cavallera, *Saint Jérôme*, I, 210ff. The letter of Epiphanius to John of Jerusalem, translated by Jerome into Latin, is n.51 in the corpus of Jerome's letters, CSEL 54:395-412, only pp. 396-399 concerning this episode. Albar misinterprets the action of the two priests. Jerome and Vincent had left their dioceses to live in solitude as monks, and were unwilling to perform priestly functions in their new home. In 393 the other monks had complained of their lack of a priest to administer the sacraments, and in 394 Epiphanius to supply this seized an opportunity to ordain Jerome's brother, Paulinian, against his will. This was one of a series of improprieties and importunities which a little later led to an open breach between the Bishop of Jerusalem and Epiphanius, Jerome, and the monks of Bethlehem, involving excommunication for the monks. But the abstention of Jerome and Vincent from saying Mass was not because of their disagreement with John of Jerusalem: (1) Epiphanius says it was "propter verecundiam et humilitatem," i.e., for ascetical reasons (in which that age would differ from our own); (2) it was before the open breach between the two parties who were still in communion with each other; (3) Epiphanius' action in ordaining Paulinian was precisely so there would be a priest to do what Jerome and Vincent were not doing; (4) Albar says that Epiphanius praised the action of the two priests; but Epiphanius merely calls them "holy priests" and says that they abstained "propter verecundiam et humilitatem," without further praise.

[29] adsignato.

[30] Hieronymi et Vincentii continentiam sacrificandi laudando.

bottom of his heart as if he had received a great wound, and
glancing at me he turned to the bishop and said: " If the lights of
the Church and pillars of our faith acted so, what does it become
us to do who are heavily weighted down and afflicted by the burden
of sin? So may your paternity know that I suspend myself from
offering sacrifice." And so by this artifice he voluntarily bound
himself in the days of Reccafred. In this way, although he had
assumed the rank of the priesthood, nevertheless having given up
its delightful use, he was afterwards unwilling to take up again
the state he had laid aside. But his own bishop [31] was so insistent
that he return to his rightful office of sacrificing that he did not
hesitate to threaten him with anathema if he would not promise
to return to it quickly.

CHAPTER III

8. He was a man not passably but outstandingly adorned with
all accomplishments, equally developed in them all; and although
he surpassed all in learning he seemed more lowly than even the
least. He was distinguished in appearance, foremost in honor,
brilliant in eloquence, and luminous in the actions of his life;
inspirer and eulogist of the martyrs, a most accomplished writer
and author. Who with a whole [32] river of talent [33] could tell the
flame of his genius, the beauty of his speech, the glory of his
learning, his constant courtesy in the ministry? What volumes
were unknown to him? What writings could be hidden from him,
whether of Catholics, of philosophers, of heretics, or of the
heathen? Where were the books of metred poetry, or prose, or
history which escaped his study? Where were the verses whose
music he did not know? Where were the hymns, or the books
from other lands [34] which his fair eye had not perused? Daily he
brought to light hidden treasures like one who digs up new and

---

[31] I.e., Bishop Saul of Córdoba. Albar blames Saul for this in his *Ep.* 13,
n. 4 (PL 121:477D): . . . et Eulogio in primo persecutionis impetu sacri-
ficare jusistis . . .

[32] quocumque poterit prudentiae dicere flumine.

[33] prudentiae.

[34] peregrina opuscula. Or does he mean books about pilgrimages?

wonderful things from fields [35] and ditches. No sage could understand with how great capacity [36] his beautiful soul was endowed, or how great and endless was his devotion to industry. O the admirable kindness of his heart! Never wishing to know anything merely for himself, he offered everything to us. Correcting what was faulty, mending what was broken, restoring what had fallen into disuse, renewing [37] what was ancient, renovating what was neglected, and whatever feats he could find done by the men of old he labored to perform in his own life. He combined in himself the severity of Jerome, the sobriety [38] of Augustine, the mildness of Ambrose, the patience of Gregory in correcting errors, in supporting the lowly, in mollifying [39] the great, in enduring persecutions.[40]

9. He was not satisfied with seeing the monasteries of his own land, but because of his brothers who were at that time travelling in the farther parts of Frankland, he set out on the road,[41] and going beyond into the country of Pamplona, he stopped at the monastery of St. Zachary, and moving about with growing enthusiasm among the other religious houses of those parts, he was favored with the friendship of many fathers. He wrote an account of their manner of life, giving names and places, in the letter that he wrote from prison to the bishop of Pamplona. In those places he found many books, hidden and almost unknown to many,[42] and these he placed in his bosom for us on his return.[43] There he enjoyed talking with blessed Odoarius, who was abbot over 150

---

[35] MS., iugeribus; Lorenzana, ruderibus (debris, ruins).

[36] Docibilitas.

[37] repriorans. This unusual word occurs several times in Albar and Eulogius.

[38] modestiam.

[39] demulcendo.

[40] MS., in sufferendos orores; Schott, in sufferendo sorores; Flórez and Lorenzana, in sufferendo horores.

[41] indeptam viam arripuit. On this journey see the letter that Albar will mention in a moment, Eulogius' *Epistola ad Wiliesindum*, PL 115: 845–852.

[42] abstrusa et pene a multis remota.

[43] The translation is based on the MS text given in Lorenzana's footnote: hic remeans suo nobis in sacratissimo pectore conlocavit.

monks. He brought back with him Augustine's City of God, and Vergil's Aeneid, the metrical works of Juvenal, the satirical works of Horace, the ornate treatises of Porphyry, the collection of Aldhelm's epigrams, Avienus' fables in meter, glorious verses of Catholic hymns, with many small things on religious matters collected by the efforts of various men;[44] these he brought back not just for his own use but for all eager students. Thereafter[45] by his brilliant work and dazzling genius he constantly opened up glorious trails with clear sign posts and led the way down them with luminous footsteps—doing this in person for all of his own day, and by establishing a custom he did it for those to come. Everywhere he went forth resplendent, from everywhere he returned refulgent, clear, sweet, like nectar, he shone forth to everyone as the crowned servant of Christ.

10. I must not fail to mention that Eulogius was elected by all the bishops of the province as one thought worthy to succeed Bishop Wistremirus[46] of holy memory in the see of Toledo, and was approved by the testimony of all. But Divine Providence, which was saving him for martyrdom, placed obstacles in the way. Yet since by common consent they had agreed to consecrate him as their bishop, now that this was prevented by opposition, they refused to elect another while he was alive. But although by manipulation he was held back from this rank, he was not deprived of the honor of the order. Indeed, he received a heavenly episcopate when he was joined to Christ through the glory of

---

[44] cum multis minutissimarum causarum ex sanctis quaestionibus multorum ingenio congregatis.

[45] Item praeterea fulgorem operis et coruscationem ingenii resplendentibus semitis praesentialiter cunctis praesentibus, et usualiter sequentibus, specificis semper ostentans indiciis, et luminosis deducens vestigiis. Albar displays his wares!

[46] The date of Wistremir's death and Eulogius' election is unknown. Flórez with inadequate proof (ES V, 365f.; X, 424), and Gomez Bravo (*Catálogo de los obispos de Córdoba*, I, 143) with no proof at all give the date as 858. Gams (*Series episcoporum*, p. 80) gives a list of names for Toledo, but no date for death of Wistremir and election of Eulogius. It is certain that Wistremir was still living when Eulogius wrote to Wiliesind of Pamplona in 851.

martyrdom. For all saints are bishops, but not all bishops are saints. Attaining sanctity through the shedding of his blood, he was endowed with episcopal order when having been received into heaven he was rewarded with the eternal promises.

11. Since he was made remarkable by these virtues and teachings, and since like a lamp placed on a pedestal and like a city set on a mountain top (Mt. 5:14f.) he gave light to all far and wide, and since like a learned scribe he provided from his master's treasure things new and old for all the household (Mt. 13: 52),— being first among the priests, highest of the confessors, and holding not the last seat among the judges,—at last he obtained his desire, and the divine mercy co-operating with him, by an unexpected judgment yet by his deliberate choice, he was raised to heaven. And those things which he had asked with tears of the martyrs, and which he had scattered as a prayer through all his writings, he won by his life of holiness. Anyone who will read his noble works can verify this. And as it is expedient, and as it seemed to us proper for the convenience of readers, and for the annual recurrence of his festival, to set forth his passion briefly, therefore in a separate part we have described truly and sincerely the beautiful end of his combat.

CHAPTER IV

(THE PASSION)

12. At the time when the savage rule of the Arabs miserably laid waste all the land of Spain with deceit and imposture, when King Mohammed with unbelievable rage and unbridled fury determined to root out the race of Christians, many terrified by fear of the cruel king and hoping to allay his madness, by a cruel use of evil will endeavored to assail Christ's flock with various and ingenious temptations. Many by denying Christ threw themselves into the abyss; others were shaken by severe trials. But others were established and confirmed in flourishing virtue. In his time, as we have said, the martyrdom (or, testimony) of the faithful shone gloriously, and the error of the gainsayers was as

shifting as waves (cf. James 1: 6). For some who were holding
the Christian faith only in secret by God's grace brought out into
the open what they had concealed, and without being searched out
they sprang forward to martyrdom and snatched their crown from
the executioners. Among these was blessed Christopher, of an
Arab family, the story of whose passion we plan to write in
another place.[47] Among them also were blessed Aurelius and holy
Felix, who having practised Christianity in secret, came forward
with their wives to the glory of martyrdom.[48] Another of them
was the blessed virgin Flora,[49] who indeed flowered with virtues,
and despising the transitory pomp of the world won an eternal
crown. Our holy doctor Eulogius described the combat of each
of these and wrote their lives and acts in a brilliant style.

13. At this time there was a certain girl named Leocritia, of
noble family, but nobler in soul, begotten of the filth of the
Moslems and born from the womb of wolves, baptized some time
earlier by a Christian nun, Litiosa, who was of her kindred.
Secretly she blossomed in the Christian faith she had adopted, and
knowledge of her spread abroad as a sweet odor. For as in her
childhood she visited the nun as relatives do, and Litiosa daily
instructed her as well as she could, at length by divine grace [50]
Leocritia received Christian faith and preserved it in her breast
with the fire of love. When she came to years of wisdom and
attained the lights of knowledge, that faith which she had secretly
learned in her earliest childhood, increased by spiritual food day
by day, she nourished to still greater growth, at first in secret,
then publicly and openly. Her parents gave her earnest warnings,
but as this had no effect, they tried to assail her with whipping
and beating in order to coerce her by punishment, since she was

---

[47] This promised book, also, was either unwritten or lost. This lack of
two promised books would harmonize well with the supposition that
Albar's illness (*Epp.* 9, 11–13) followed soon after the writing of the *Vita*,
and that he died not long after.

[48] They were born and married in families of secret Christians; Eulogius
tells their story at length, *Mem.SS.*, II, 10.

[49] *Mem.SS.*, II, 8.

[50] respectione caelesti.

not to be moved by gentler means. But that flame which Christ
sent into the hearts of the faithful cannot yield to any threats.
When in this conflict she was beaten day and night, and saw
herself attacked with severe punishments and tied with heavy
bonds, and fearing that if she did not profess her faith publicly
she would be burned in hell for her infidelity,[51] she made her case
known through messengers to blessed Eulogius, who was already
much esteemed in many such cases, and to his sister, Anulo, a
virgin dedicated to God. She explained that she wished to go
to safer places among the faithful where she might without fear
make her faith known. Thereupon blessed Eulogius recognized
his accustomed office, and as he was a zealous partisan of the
martyrs, he directed her through the same messengers to leave
home secretly. She quickly planned a stratagem, and pretending
to yield to her parents, and attacking our faith in words, according
to plan she donned all her best ornaments and appeared in the
manner of those who are out to please and marry in the world;
she set out to change their minds by attiring herself in a way she
hated. When she saw that everything was now safe for her,
pretending to go to the wedding of some of her kindred which was
then being celebrated, beautifully dressed as befitted the occasion,
she hurried off to the protection of blessed Eulogius and his sister
Anulo. At once they received her with joy, and turned her over
to trusted friends to be kept in hiding. Her father and mother
awaited her, and when they did not see their daughter, wailing
that they had been deceived and torturing themselves into an
unheard of rage and grief never before seen,[52] they upset everything, confused[53] everything, running about among friends and
strangers, using force and the authority of the judge, they loaded
into prisons and chains all whom they suspected;[54] they afflicted
with stripes and imprisonment men, women, confessors, priests,
nuns, and whom they could, hoping that by these and other measures they might in some way get their daughter back. But the
saint unmoved changed her from place to place, taking every

---

[51] cauterio ureretur perfidiae. It might also mean, branded with infidelity.
[52] rabie inaudita et dolore inviso.
[53] contaminant.
[54] quoscumque impetendos putabant.

precaution that the sheep should not fall into the hands of wolves. Meanwhile she austerely wore down her body, being constant in fasting and vigils, wearing haircloth and sleeping on the ground. The blessed man Eulogius, whose name is to be spoken with reverence, applying himself to nocturnal vigils, and praying prostrate on the ground in the basilica of San Zoylo, spent nights without sleep, beseeching the Lord for help and strength for the maiden, and consecrating her [55] to the Lord by these exercises.

14. Meanwhile the serene maiden wished to see Eulogius' sister, whom she loved with warm affection, and came by night to their dwelling, moved by a revelation of the Lord and led by her desire of consolation, to spend just one day with them and then return to her usual hiding place. She told them that twice while praying her mouth had been filled with honey, that she had not dared to spit it out but had swallowed it, wondering at the nature of the thick substance. The saint interpreted this to her as a presage that she would enjoy the sweetness of the heavenly kingdom.

CHAPTER V

15. The next day when the maiden prepared to go back, it happened that her attendant did not come at the accustomed hour but only when dawn was breaking. She could not set out, for she used to travel at night to avoid being caught. So it was arranged that the virgin of God should stay where she was that day until the sun should put a term to its light for the earth and the shades of night should grant again the desired quietude.[56] It was indeed by human counsel, but really by God's decree that she was held back, in order that he might give her her crown, and bestow the diadem of glory on the blessed Eulogius. For on that day, I know not at whose suggestion nor by whose plottings and betrayal, the hiding-place was made known to the judge, and

---

[55] se . . . consecrans. *Se* must here refer to Leocritia, as Eulogius at this time had little reason to expect speedy death.

[56] A purple passage: usquedum sol metam sui luminis terrae subduceret, et nocturnae tenebrae quietudinem optatam indulgeret.

suddenly their whole dwelling was surrounded by soldiers sent for the purpose. It happened that the elect and predestined martyr was there in person. Bringing Leocritia into Eulogius' presence they arrested both together, and beating them and treating them with disrespect, they brought them to the unjust and infamous judge. The judge at once thought to kill them by scourging, and roused to vehement fury, with truculent face and impatient mind he questioned Eulogius in furious words, and inquired with threatening why he had detained the girl at his house. Eulogius answered him patiently and with good grace, as he commonly spoke, and splendidly made clear the truth of the matter as follows: " Sir, the office of preaching is laid upon us, and it is a part of our faith that we should hold out the light of faith to those seeking it of us, and that we should deny it to no one who is hastening to the highways of life which are holy. This is the duty of priests, true religion demands it, and this also Christ our Lord taught us: that whoever is athirst and wishes to draw from the rivers of faith will find double the drink that he sought. And as this girl asked us for the rule of our holy faith, our purpose necessarily applied itself to her the more gladly as her desire was the more ardent. It was not proper to turn away a person asking this, especially not proper for one who for this purpose was endowed with the office of Christ. Hence as I was able I have enlightened and taught her, and I have shown her that the faith of Christ is the road of the kingdom of heaven. In the same way I should be glad to do it for you, if you should care to ask me." Then the judge with stormy visage commanded rods to be brought in, threatening to put him to death by scourging. The saint said to him: " What do you intend to do with those rods? " He replied: " I mean to put you to death with them." Eulogius said: " Sharpen and prepare the sword with which you may send my soul, released from the bondage of the body, back to Him who gave it. Do not imagine that you will cut my body apart with scourges." And straightway reproaching with clear invective and much eloquence the falseness of their prophet and law, and redoubling what he had said,[57] he was hurried off to the palace and brought before the

---

[57] praedicationis verbum ingeminans.

king's councillors. One of them who was very well known to him addressed him sympathetically: " Even though fools and idiots are borne to this miserable ruin of death, you who are girt with the beauty of wisdom, and famous for your excellent life, what madness drove you to commit yourself to this fatal ruin, forgetting the natural love of life? Please listen to me, and do not rush into this headlong destruction, I beg you. Say only a word in this hour of your need, and afterward practise your faith where you will. We promise not to search for you anywhere." The blessed martyr Eulogius answered him smiling: " If only you could know what things are laid up for those of our faith! Or if I could place in your breast what I possess in my own; then you would not try to hold me back from my purpose, but even more gladly would you yourself think of giving up your worldly position." And he began to offer them the teaching of the everlasting Gospel, and with bold freedom to pour forth the preaching of the Kingdom. But not wishing to hear him, those present ordered him to be put to the sword. While he was being led away, one of the king's eunuchs slapped him. Turning the other cheek, Eulogius said: " Please strike this too, and make it equal to the other." When this had been struck, he patiently and meekly turned the first again. But the soldiers hurried him out to the place of execution, and there kneeling in prayer and raising his hands to heaven, making the sign of the cross and saying a few words of prayer silently, he stretched out his neck for the blade, and, despising the world, by a swift blow he found life. He was martyred in mid-afternoon of Saturday, the eleventh of March.[58] O blessed and wonderful man of our age, who in many martyrs sent the fruit of his work ahead of him, and in the virgin Leocritia left another to follow! Raising in his hands the standard of victory, and dedicating to the Lord the

---

[58] Albar does not give the year, but scholars generally agree that it was 859, which is the date given in the ancient notice of the first translation of his relics (ES X, 562; PL 115:722B). The other years in which the eleventh of March fell on Saturday are 853, 864, and 870. He could not have died in 853, for in his *Liber apologeticus* he chronicles the martyrdom of SS. Roderick and Salomon which occurred in 857 (PL 115:868C). The adoption of one of the later dates would leave that many years during which nothing is known of any activity of Eulogius.

sheaf of his labor for himself, offering a pure oblation and peaceful sacrifices,[59] and what things he had taught others, now in himself he presented to Christ the Lord of all things. As soon as his body was thrown from the upper level onto the river-bank, a dove of snowy whiteness,[60] gliding through the air,[61] in the sight of all flew [62] down and sat on the martyr's body. They all tried to drive it away by throwing stones from all sides, but being nevertheless unable to move it as it sat there, they sought to put it to

---

[59] This is an echo of liturgical language, but the nearest I have found in the Mozarabic liturgy is: spiritales victimas inmolantes offerimus tibi, Deus, hostiam inmaculatam (Missa de Nativitate Domini, Post nomina, *Liber sacramentorum,* col.55).

[60] Albar: colûmbă mĭrō cāndŏrĕ nĭvĕscĕns. This could be part of a metrical hexameter, and come bodily from some unidentified source; the following are the nearest parallels I have found:

Dracontius, *De laudibus Dei,* I, 246 (= Eugenius, *Hexaemeron,* line 129): hae niveo candore nitent, has purpura vestit (of birds at Creation).

Mozarabic liturgy: nivei candoris (*Lib. sacramentorum,* col. 49, form. 100).

Juvencus, III, 321f.: Continuo Christus faciem fulgore corusco / mutatur, vestemque nivis candore nitescit. (CSEL 24:92).

Vergil, *Aeneid,* III, 537f.: equos in gramine vidi / tondentes campum late, candore nivali.

ibid., XII, 84: qui candore nives anteirent, cursibus auras.

cf. Albar, *Confessio,* n.3: Aedifica Domine in corde meo urnam candore vitae nitentem.

[61] Albar: secans aera pennis. This also is a poetical echo.

Dracontius, *op.cit.,* I, 254: et rudibus tenuem subtexunt aera pennis (cf. Eugenius, *op.cit.,* line 136)

Eugenius, *op.cit.,* line 148: temptant et rudibus librantur in aera pennis (cf. Dracontius, *op.cit.,* I, 266).

Dracontius, *op. cit.,* I, 243: aera concutiens pennis crepitante volatu (= Eugenius, *op.cit.,* line 126).

Prudentius, *Psychomachia,* line 305: dixit et auratis praestringens aera pinnis.

ibid., Hamartigenia, line 816: libera sideream plaudens super aera pinnis. line 849: concretum celeri relegens secat aera lapsu.

Vergil, *Georgics,* I, 406: quacumque illa levem fugiens secat aethera pinnis.

Ovid, *Metamorphoses,* VII, 354: Hic ope nympharum sublatus in aera pennis.

[62] aligerans.

flight directly with their hands. But the dove, fluttering rather than flying around the body, came to rest on a tower overlooking the corpse, with its beak pointed towards the blessed man's body. And I must not be silent about the miracle that Christ worked for the glory of his name over the body of the martyr. A native of Ecija, while performing with others his monthly service in the palace and taking his turn with the watch, at night desiring a drink of water arose and went to the projecting water outlet [63]

[63] The key texts here are: (1) Mox vero ut projectum est cadaver e loco eminentiori in ductum alvei . . . (2) nocte aquam potare desiderans, surrexit et ad prominentem canalis ductum, qui super illa loca producitur, pervenit, ubi vidit desuper super corpus ejus quod deorsum jacebat . . . The correct translation depends upon knowing the locality of the martyrdom. Though Albar is vague, it is commonly agreed that Eulogius, and many others of the martyrs, were put to death somewhere in the vicinity of the Alcázar. In modern times there is a place behind the Seminario de San Pelagio called Campo santo de los mártires, but scholars like Castejón y Martínez (*Córdoba califal,* p. 27, n. 1) and Levi-Provençal (*Espagne musulman,* p. 222) say it is not the real site of the martyrdoms; it would seem from a comparison of maps that this Campo santo is too far back from the river and on ground that would have been within the former emir's palace. Except for fragments, the still existing Alcázar is of later date and Christian origin, and covers only a part of the area of the old palace.

The following description is based chiefly on Castejón y Martínez (*op.cit,* pp.27f., 57), and for the modern site on Baedeker and various photographs. The Moslem Alcázar, or emir's palace, was on the north side of the Guadalquivir, and just west of the great mosque. Between it and the river was a spacious terrace or esplanade called Hassá. At the southern edge of the hassá there was a stone wall, and then a drop of a number of feet to the level of the river. However, between the wall and the river there was a bank, and along this Abd ar-Rahman II (d. 852 A.D.) had built a stone-paved road (Levi-Provençal, *op. cit.,* p. 223, n. 1), called the arrecífe, which was therefore new in Albar's day. In front of one of the gates on the south side of the Alcázar opening onto the hassá was a strong wooden post to which were hung the heads of executed criminals.

Assuming that Eulogius was martyred on the hassá, his body was thrown over the wall, e loco eminentiori in ductum alvei. Does this mean that it was thrown into the river or onto the river bank? Pérez Urbel assumes it was into the river for he pictures the body floating gently down the stream, while members of the hostile populace used boats in their efforts to drive off the dove (*San Eulogio,* pp. 429f.). Indeed, in the next paragraph Albar says the body of Leocritia was thrown into the water and was carried down

which comes to that place. There he saw above Eulogius' body, which lay lower down, priests glistening white as snow, holding dazzling lamps, and earnestly reciting psalms. Frightened by this vision he went back to his station, fleeing rather than returning. After telling a companion all about it, he decided to go with him again to the place; but this second time he was unable to see it. On the next day the effort of the Christians obtained the blessed man's head, and on the third day they gathered the rest of the body, and buried it in the church of the blessed martyr San Zoylo.

16. As for the blessed virgin Leocritia, though they tried to

---

with the current. In the case of Eulogius, Albar's words could well mean water; *ductus* is frequently used of water, both in aqueducts, and more generally in water "courses"; *alveus* can mean a ditch, canal, channel, or river-bed. But the context seems to make it clear that the body was actually lying on the ground, for while Eulogius was martyred in mid-afternoon, his body was still readily visible below the wall to the Ecija soldier during his watch the following night, many hours later. His vision of the priests about the body also implies the river-bank or the roadway rather than the river. Nor does Albar say anything about boats being used to drive away the pigeon.

What was the *prominentem canalis ductum* to which the soldier went to get his drink, and from which he could look down and see Eulogius' body lying beneath him? It was not a canal in the modern sense, for there has never been such at this place, nor is there room for it. Both the word *ductum* and the general situation suggest an aqueduct. Castejón y Martínez (*op.cit.,* pp. 62ff.) says Abd ar-Rahman II was the first to bring drinking water into Córdoba, and it may be supposed that his own palace and its environs were the first to profit by it. Unfortunately, it is hard to trace the old aqueducts, and the one that went to the Alcázar was perhaps subterranean. Another possibility is the Albolafía which is thus described by Ramírez de Arellano (*Historia de Córdoba,* III, 400): it is an old building at the river's edge in front of the former hassá, which formerly housed a wheel which by a chain-pump with buckets raised water from the river to an aqueduct 687 feet long, which went over arches and then along the wall of the Alcázar. Queen Isabella the Catholic had the apparatus dismantled as it was so noisy that it prevented her sleeping. No part of the existing remains go back before the tenth century at the earliest. But if there were some similar water supply in Albar's time, it would explain Albar's wording about the soldier's drink, and would also furnish a tower upon which the pigeon could perch with its beak pointing to Eulogius' corpse on the bank below.

seduce her with many delights and move her with many promises, she was by God's grace strengthened in the firmness of faith, and on the fourth day after Eulogius' martyrdom was herself beheaded and thrown in the Guadalquivir. But she could not be submerged nor hidden in the water, for moving with body erect she presented an astonishing sight to all. So she was taken out by the Christians and buried in the basilica of the martyr St. Genesius, which is in the place called Terzos.[64] Such was the end of the blessed doctor Eulogius, this his admirable departure, such his crossing over after many labors.

CHAPTER VI [65]

17. Now at the end of the volume it remains to give thanks to the King of ages [66] who from the beginning of the faith has adorned his Church with martyrs, has given strength to the weary,[67] and has brought to eternal glory those who put no trust in themselves. To our God be glory and dominion for ever and ever. Amen.[68]

18. And now that we have unfolded in halting and unpolished speech the combat of our doctor and martyr, it remains for us to address our beloved patron as one who hears and is present to our prayers, and to remind him of our old friendship. Surely he is able to hear us praying and to be a patron of the unfortunate and afflicted,—if our own merits assist us, if grave sins do not block the way, and if a pure affection asks it. And so, great martyr of God bearing the sweet name of Eulogius, hear your

---

[64] Terzos was a suburb at the third milestone southwest of Córdoba.

[65] With this final burst of praise, cf. what Albar had written to Eulogius during his lifetime: Egisti autem, beatissime pater, carmen sonorum, quo mortis metus excantatus effugiat, et antiqua glacie duratus animae stupor, frigusque pellatur: quo calor vitae . . . Splendesce, et ampliori lumine, quo fulges, claresce: quia reposita tibi sunt praemia, et centuplicata te manet corona, nosque tuo suffragio, quo semper fovisti, tuere. (Letter prefixed to *Mem.SS.*, PL, 115:736).

[66] Cf. I Tim. 1:17.

[67] Cf. Isaias 40:29.

[68] Cf. I Pet. 5:11 and Apoc. 1:6; Jude, verse 25.

Albar calling to you; and as here on earth you held me fast in
your heart [69] with love, so make me your servant in heaven. I
shall urge no words but your own as intercession. I am the one
you said was united with you, to whom and of whom you spoke
in this way: " Let there be no other Albar but Eulogius, and may
the whole love of Eulogius be settled nowhere but in Albar." [70]
Let it be strong. O Lord Christ, let this sweet and loyal love be
strong between them. Let it be strong in the unending height
of holiness, may it go forth as a shining light and increase unto
the perfect day.[71] Behold, master,[72] I have your testimony here
at hand inscribed in golden letters and with sentences like jewels,
but I desire it to be completed by your patronage. As when
on earth you unceasingly prayed that our love might flourish,
now that you have been taken to heaven you can by your suf-
frage procure in me what has been completed in you. For as
you used to say, true love faithfully keeps its affection for one
who is absent, and what it can [73] it holds forth to its lover.
Therefore, noble martyr and dear friend, while it is possible
and the season of mercy still continues, grant your friend the
gift of your intercession, that here an improvement of life may
be conceded to me, that I may have the gift of frequent tears,
that the love of virtue may be impressed on my unstable [74] mind,
that I may have a continual affective compunction and a pure
affection of repentance, may the desired place be happily granted,
may my speedy entrance not be hindered by any obstacles. May
the chains of all obscurities be loosed; may the mass of all
hindrances spring away; may the ensnaring obstacles by the change
of the right hand of the Most High [75] be transformed into help for
the obedient. May the gates of the heart be opened to receive
the kingdom of the most high God; may the haughty shoulders
bend and the neck be tamed to bear the sweet yoke of Christ. I

---

[69] MS. animo.

[70] nec alibi quam penes intima Alvari totus sit conlocatus amor Eulogii.

[71] Prov. 4:18.

[72] domine; here it refers to Eulogius.

[73] quod sibi poterat hoc exhibet.

[74] labili.

[75] Ps. 76:11.

should like to ask still greater things, but I fear to incur the note of presumption. But, O great servant of God, you who have your fill of the Lord's presence and are made happy with his endless gift, grant to an unhappy man by your worthy mediation what you know purges a thousand faults. I also long for eternal life and thirst for the repose of the heavenly kingdom. So with no matter what torment or affliction strive to provide a remedy for your servant, and deign [76] to purify your friend with that ardent fire with which you were bound to us here on earth; as that love may now blaze with a purer light, when it shines with fuller brightness, and with more powerful intercession is able to pray for [77] what we ask.

19. Now, my dear Eulogius, to the best of my power I have done honor to the memory of your name, I have described your life, I have set forth your doctrine, I have recounted your glorious passion; and in order that the memory of your dear name may ever flourish on earth, and that as your life in heaven so its renown here may gleam with undying splendor, I have written this down,[78] if not in the clearest speech at least with obvious efforts as I was able. I have built to your glory a monument more enduring than bronze [79] which no whirlwind nor hailstones may destroy nor funeral pyre melt with any flames. I have built to your name a memorial of refined gold [80] and all kinds of precious stones which no ruthless tyrant will be able brigand-like to destroy. I have put together the fabric of your temple and have raised the tower of your dwelling on high that you may be a bright beacon giving light to all travellers on every side. I have adorned the epitaph of your beauty with great pearls of snowy whiteness [81] and with blazing topaz that it may sparkle to all the ends of the earth. I have

---

[76] desidera.

[77] prorogare.

[78] dedicavi.

[79] Albar: Construxi enim aere perennius monumentum gloriae tuae. Horace, *Carmina*, III, 30, 1: Exegi monumentum aere perennius.

[80] ex auro obrizo. This name for gold is common in the Scriptures, but Albar seems to have no particular passage in mind.

[81] unionibus miro candore niventibus. Cf. note 60 above.

strewn your holy ashes with nectar-like flowerets that wither in no
heat and wilt at no approaching [82] flame. I have anointed your
precious body with right spikenard [83] and with divers kinds of
perfume, mixing them with amomum, balsam, and besem,[84] that
the ardent and sweet odor of your holiness, blown abroad and
carried through all ages, may never grow faint. I have fulfilled
the duty of friendship, I have been unwilling to send the name of
your charity out naked to the world, so that, as in heaven you are
resplendent in life and work, in the world you may be glorious in
tongue and name, in order that the coming generation may find
you have been praised and see you are to be imitated, and that
it may learn by our poor talent how great you were in doctrine.
Nor will the age to come revere you because the care of earlier
men has heaped you with worldly benefits, with images [85] and
flowers which always are consumed with the passing of time; [86]
but it will venerate you adorned with spiritual gifts and glorified
with undying memorials.[87]

20. Therefore, venerable master, give us a reward in return,
that as your remains are honored by our labor, and your funeral
adorned, so henceforth we may be blessed with a favorable
regard [88] and be visited with a celestial gift, so that I, who so far—
flowing unsmoothly through a downward and broken course—have
failed by my sin, and who until now remaining corrupted in my
evil ways have withdrawn from the face of my God and adhered
to the malignant enemy, so that I, enlightened by prevenient grace
and made whole whenever the end of life may come, may merit

---

[82] indito.

[83] Cf. John 12:3.

[84] bisamoque. Morales does not know what this is; Flórez and Lorenzana, though not knowing specifically, say it must be some fragrant unguent.
It is close to a common Semitic root: Hebrew—besem, bosem (balm,
perfume); Arabic—balsam, balsan (balm, perfume, or the tree producing
it).

[85] speciebus.

[86] temporum vetustate.

[87] immortalibus sublimatum titulis venerabitur.

[88] inlustremur deinceps respectione felici. Does he mean the glance of
Eulogius? or the glance, the judgment, or the providence of God?

so to possess in common with you unbroken heavenly joys, as here tormented by earthly straits in equal weeping and groaning I have drawn prolonged and lengthy sighs; that although it is not given me to shine with equal glory, at least the forgiveness of my sins may be granted me; and that I may not suffer sunk in the pit of punishment, but forgiven, may rejoice in heavenly rest with you and with my other lords your fellows.   Amen.

CONCLUSION

THE opening chapters of this dissertation pieced together from the sources what is probably the fullest account of the life of Albar. Most of the events of his life remain unknown, yet, in view of the fact that he lacks both biography and autobiography, it is surprising how much of a picture we can get of the man. Well educated, he apparently belonged to a prominent and well-to-do family, yet so far as we can judge, he never held any office or practised any profession or business. He would seem to have been a cultured private gentleman, deeply religious, whose chief interest was theology. Though not a master, and not free from unintentional error, he acquired a measure of competence in his chosen study, and was admired by some of his leading fellow-Christians for his knowledge of " the Scriptures." The " Scriptures," however, does not mean the Bible exclusively; it means also the understanding of the Bible, and that in turn meant a knowledge of the interpretation given by the Fathers; in other words, it involved some acquaintance with patristic theology.

So the main part of the dissertation has been detailed examination of two of Albar's more important writings. The correspondence with John of Seville embodies a full-length debate on the value of heathen rhetoric to Christians, and another on the relationship of the human and divine natures in our Lord, and ends with the raising of the question of the soul's origin. On the first question, Albar held a theoretical position which, if narrower than that usually adopted today, was by no means extreme when seen against its patristic background. And if his theoretical opinion was not over-narrow, his practice throughout all his writings was to meet to the best of his power the rhetorical requirements for a fine style. Of course he follows the masters at a distance; Albar lived at a time when western Christendom was well on its way toward the Dark Age, and among a people who were cut off from regular intercourse with the rest of the Church and subject to a con-

215

queror with an alien civilisation. But his fundamental earnestness
and sincerity saved him from bombast, and usually preserved him
in real dignity.

In the Christological question both Albar and John meant well,
but both ventured beyond their depth and became entangled in
inexactness if not in error. Albar gives evidence of wider reading
than John, and also of a mind which, though not fully trained,
had a tendency toward deeper and more speculative thought. In
both these qualities he also surpassed his friend and hero, St.
Eulogius. Here the *Confessio* amplifies the evidence of his letters
to John, for in them we see Albar permeated with some of the
outstanding doctrines of St. Augustine. Jerome, especially in his
Letters and to some extent in his Biblical commentaries, was a
favorite in Albar's reading; but Augustine seems to have done
more to mould his thought. In the *Confessio* Albar is more
Augustinian than was Isidore.

It is hoped that the study of the *Confessio* has added something
to our understanding of it. The bringing together of kindred
writings, and the explanation of the background of the administration of the sacrament of penance, point to the *Confessio* as having
been written as a book of devotion, presumably for common use,
aimed to arouse compunction and thus obtain forgiveness of sins
during life without waiting to receive the sacrament on the deathbed. At the same time it is a carefully wrought work of art on
which Albar lavished all his literary resources. It is well adapted
to its purpose, is genuinely deep-felt, and at times rises to a surprising eloquence. Of his writings, only the poems are of negligi-
ble value; the rest are all worthy of attention even today. The
letters to John and to Bodo, and the *Indiculus* show us the vigor
and originality of Albar's mind when dealing with intellectual
problems; the *Confessio* and the *Vita Eulogii* bring us his greatest
depth of feeling and his most finished literary workmanship. The
present dissertation has given special attention to a specimen of
each category.

Since the search for sources, though not always successful, was
an important part of this dissertation, it will be well to bring
together here in the conclusion a list of those works which there
is reason to believe Albar used. Most of the list comes from the

letters, since in the other two works he seldom quotes directly. The many patristic passages which were given to illustrate the thought of the *Confessio* are not included here, as we have no assurance that Albar had those specific passages in mind.

Ambrose, Expositio evangelii secundum Lucam.
        De incarnationis dominicae sacramento.
Augustine, De civitate Dei.
        Confessiones.
        De doctrina Christiana.
        Enarratio in Psalmum 37.
        Epistolae 166, 169.
        Soliloquia.
Cassian, Collatio XIV. (second hand?)
Claudianus Mamertus, De statu animae. (second hand?)
Eucherius, Formularum spiritalis intelligentiae . . . liber.
Eusebius, The Ecclesiastical History. (in Rufinus'
    translation)
Fulgentius of Ruspe, De fide ad Petrum.
Gregory, Homiliae in Ezechielem. (?)
        Moralia.
Heterius and Beatus, Epistola ad Elipandum.
Isidore, Differentiae.
        Etymolgiae.
        Sententiae.
        Synonyma. (?)
Jerome, Adversus Jovinianum.
        Commentary on Daniel.
        Commentary on Galatians.
        Commentary on Titus.
        Epistolae 1, 21, 22, 51, 58, 70, 121, 126, 57
          or 125(?), 115 or 116.
Junilius, De partibus divinae legis. (second hand?)
Sedulius, Carmen paschale. (?)
Vigilius of Thapsus, De unitate Trinitatis.
Pseudo-Isidore, Lamentum poenitentiae, Oratio pro cor-
    reptione vitae.

From the *Confessio* we could not be certain Albar used the poems of Eugenius of Toledo, but he clearly used them as a model of some of his own verses. Two classic poets are represented, Vergil's *Aeneid* by a few scraps in a letter to John, and Horace who lends one line (*Carmina*, III, 30) to the *Vita Eulogii*.

It is interesting, by contrast, to see the character of the additional sources traceable in the two letters of John of Seville.

> Gennadius (or Bracharius), De ecclesiasticis dogmatibus.
> The *Hispana* collection of canon law.
> Jerome, Commentary on Matthew.
>   Commentary on Philemon (?).
> Origen, Homilies on Numbers, 13, 18 (second hand).
> Pseudo-Augustine, Adversus quinque haereses (second hand).
> Pseudo-Ambrose, Altercatio beati Ambrosii.

Albar makes a very respectable showing. It is always possible that he knew this or that passage at second hand, and a few have been so marked. But it is even more probable that he had read books of St. Augustine from which he drew the thoughts we find in the *Confessio,* but which he had made so much his own that we cannot identify them. For in spite of Bodo's parting insult, Albar was not a mere compiler; he was a zealous reader and humble follower of the Fathers, but he also had a forceful personality and a mind of his own. He was a not unworthy exponent of Christian-Latin culture during the ebb-tide between two civilisations.

APPENDIX I

The Manuscripts of Albar

An extensive search of printed manuscript catalogues has failed to bring to light the existence of any ancient manuscript of Albar other than the two which have long been known, and which were used in preparing the printed editions. The *Vita,* with its attendant poems, survives in one manuscript, the remaining works in the other.

The *Vita Eulogii* is contained in Madrid, Biblioteca Nacional, MS. 10029.[1] This has often been called the "Azagra" or the "Corippus" codex. It measures 16 by 23 cm., and contains 159 folios written in Visigothic script by several hands, mostly of the ninth or tenth century. It is largely an anthology of Christian poets, especially of St. Eugenius of Toledo, Dracontius, Corippus, and Juvencus. The last twenty leaves become more miscellaneous as various early scribes added things that struck their fancy. It is here, on folios 145-158, that we find the *Vita.*

Someone in the sixteenth century wrote out a table of contents, at the end of which he tells us that the codex was bought at Valladolid by Miguel Ruiz de Azagra, a talented young secretary of the princes of Bohemia,[2] and after his death was obtained in 1587 for the library of Toledo by Juan Bautista Pérez. Meanwhile, Azagra had lent the manuscript to Ambrosio de Morales, who used it in publishing the works of St. Eulogius at Alcalá de Henares in 1574.[3]

It is said that Juan Bautista Pérez was the first to assert that this codex had once belonged to the cathedral of Oviedo.[4] Partsch says that there is no doubt that he based this opinion upon identifying the codex as the one for which the so-called "Oviedo book-list of 882" is an index.[5] Partsch implies that he himself accepts the identification. But Ewald[6] opposed the identification because the titles of the list are not in the same order in which they appear in this codex, and because the list does not refer to a single

---

1 Formerly Toledo 14.22, by which number it is best known. It is described by: Ewald, "Reise," *NA,* VI, 316-318; Hartel, *Wiener SB,* CXII, 712-718; Traube, MGH, *Poet. lat.,* III, i, 125f.; C. U. Clarke, *Collect. hisp.,* pp. 46f.; *García Villada, Paleogr. esp.,* I, 114; Millares Carlo, *Paleogr. esp.,* p. 460; *ibid., Cód. visigót. cated. toled.,* pp. 23f.

2 Morales, *Corónica general,* V, 300.

3 Morales' preface, reprinted by Migne, PL 115:705f; cf. his *Corónica general,* VII, 396.

4 J. Partsch, MGH, *Auct. ant.,* III, ii, pp. l–li; Beer, *Wiener SB,* CXXVIII, Abh. 12, p. 14, n. 1.

5 This is a list of titles appearing on the last leaf of Escorial codex R.II.18. The text is printed by: G. Becker, *Catalogi bibl. ant.,* p. 59f.; Beer, *op. cit.,* pp. 12–15; Antolín, *La Ciudad de Dios,* CX (1907), 59ff. J. Tailhan, *Nouv. mélanges,* IV, 301–303 identifies some of the titles.

6 "Reise," *NA,* VI, 316.

volume; this latter point ought to be obvious when the first title alone is a complete Bible. However, it is possible that the Azagra codex was made where the "Book-list" library was available. A. Millares Carlo,[7] has recently pointed out that, in spite of general acceptance, there is no proof that the "Book-list" refers to Oviedo. An inscription on the first folio of the codex containing the list reads: "de la yglesia mayor de Oviedo"; Clark[8] says the inscription is of the twelfth century, Antolín[9] calls it sixteenth century. In either case, the inscription is centuries later than the codex, and Millares Carlo now urges on palaeographical grounds that the manuscript was written in Córdoba, and that the list may well refer to some library in that city.

There are various modern copies of this codex. One is in Madrid, Biblioteca del noviciado de la Universidad central, no. 130; it is a copy made in the sixteenth or seventeenth century.[10] Another transcript is Berlin, Staatsbibliothek, cod. lat. fol. 448; this was made by John Heller in 1878 when the original codex was lent by the Spanish government to Berlin for the edition of Corippus which was being prepared for the MGH.[11] In addition to these copies, textual variations between the original codex and Morales' edition, made by or for Father Burriel in the middle of the eighteenth century, form a part of Madrid, Bibl. Nac., cod. 13062.[12] Rome has a transcript of a different kind. Father Antonio Gallonio of the Roman Oratory collected lives of some of the less known saints. Twenty volumes of these, dating from the late sixteenth or early seventeenth century, are preserved in the Biblioteca Vallicellana; that numbered Codex H. 4 (Galonii D) contains Albar's *Vita Eulogii;*[13] but I do not know whence he copied the text.

Finally, Madrid, Bibl. R. Acad. Hist. (MSS from San Millán and San Pedro), no. 13, is a large tenth-century codex containing many lives of saints.[14] On fol. 169[v] it has a "Vita S. Eulogii," but Pérez Pastor does not say whether this is the Cordovan saint, nor whether it is Albar's life; since it fills no more than one side of a single leaf, it could not be Albar's complete text, but might be the part containing the Passion. It would be interesting to know, for it might be a *legendarium* from which saints' lives were read in the liturgy; and if it is Albar's, we could see how it was used.

Morales claimed[15] to have had, in addition to the Azagra, a codex from

---

7 *Cód. visigót. cated. toled.*, p. 50.

8 *Collect. hisp.*, p. 120.

9 *Catál. cód. lat. Escor.*, III, 481ff.

10 "Reise," *NA*, VI, 323; Hartel, *Wiener SB*, CXIII, 572.

11 Ewald, *op. cit.*, p. 316; Vollmer, MGH, *Auct. Ant.*, XIV, xxxviii; Traube, MGH, *Poet. lat.*, III, i, 126. Unfortunately I have been unable to locate this in Valentine Rose, *Verzeichniss der latein. Hss. d. k. Bibliothek zu Berlin*, in which no. 448 is assigned to a fifteenth-century MS.

12 Millares Carlo, *Cód. visigót. cated. toled.*, p. 23.

13 A. Poncelet, *Cat. cod. hagiogr. lat. bibl. Roman.*, p. 409.

14 Pérez Pastor, *BRAH*, LIII, 479.

15 Preface to edition of Eulogius, reprinted PL 115:705B; cf. *Corónica general*, VII, 396; also cf. Traube, *op. cit.*, p. 126.

Oviedo, also in Visigothic script. But in more recent times there has been no trace of it.

The other writings of Albar also come down to us in a single early manuscript, preserved in the Archivo de los Canónigos in Córdoba. It is a quarto volume [16] of 221 leaves, measuring 16 by 24 cm. The script is Visigothic minuscule, single column, filling a space of 12 by 18 cm. on each page. The volume falls into two main parts: first, fols. 1–164 contain the works of Albar, and are written neatly by a single scribe, 28 lines to the page; second, fols. 165–221 are in a poorer hand using larger letters, 24 or 25 lines to the page; the contents are four unidentified theological tracts, and a spurious letter of Jerome.[17] Ewald says that the main codex is preceded by four pages in a twelfth century hand, giving St. Augustine's Sermon no. 350. The binding and the leaves at each end are damaged by fire and water, and were already so in the eighteenth century. The date of the leaves containing Albar's works is usually given as the tenth century,[18] but Artiles places it in the eleventh century, and thinks it was written in Andalucia. Two inscriptions, one of the sixteenth century and one of the eighteenth, show the volume was in the same library at those dates.

This codex has long been known, but usually at second hand, for it has been amusingly elusive. Ambrosio de Morales described it,[19] mentioning the works of Albar and a letter of Speraindeo; he thought it was written in Córdoba and had remained there continuously since. Bernardo Aldrete illustrated Visigothic script by a facsimile of parts of fols. 69r and 70r [20] The great Nicolas Antonio, in writing his *Bibliotheca Hispana vetus,* says [21] he had used only a transcript. But it was not until Enrique Flórez was publishing the *España sagrada* in the eighteenth century that the works of Albar were finally edited and printed; and then not from this manuscript, but from a copy made at royal command for Flórez' use. On comparing this transcript with the facsimile of Aldrete, Flórez discovered that Aldrete had "corrected" spelling and syntax in his "facsimile," so Flórez had a new specimen facsimile made [22] and printed with Albar's works.[23] But the original codex was becoming elusive. Andrés Merino tells of his inability to find it.[24] In 1846 Heine published a little *Reise* to the libraries of Spain and

---

16 J. Artiles, " El códice visigótico de Álvaro Cordobés," *Revista de la Biblioteca, Archivo y Museo del Ayuntamiento de Madrid,* IX (1932), 201ff.; P. Ewald, " Reise," *NA,* VI, 382f.

17 Printed PL 30:122–142.

18 Ewald, *loc. cit.;* Ewald and Loewe, *Exempla script. Visicot.,* p. 26; Flórez, ES, XI, 53.

19 " De los libros antiguos . . .", *Crónica general,* V, 300.

20 *Del origen de la lengua Castellana,* Bk. III, p. 252, according to Flórez, ES, XI, 52.

21 Rome (1696), I, 350; Madrid (1788), I, 475.

22 Of the beginning of *Ep.* 12.

23 ES, XI, facing p. 52.

24 *Escuela de leer letras cursivas antiguas y modernas,* Madrid 1780, cited by Clark, *op. cit.,* p. 14.

Portugal,[25] which closes with a description of the Capitular Library of Córdoba. He found the library neglected and full of dust and worms, but containing two hundred manuscripts and about a thousand incunabula; he made a list of seventy-two important manuscripts, but the Albar is not among them. A dozen years later Valentinelli [26] was not allowed access to the library, but says many books had been removed to the Escorial by Carlos III, and hints that the Albar is among the missing—apparently because it is not on Heine's list, which he cites. Dümmler says that the codex " scheint nicht mehr vorhanden." [27] Paul Ewald rediscovered it, and includes the story in his *Reise nach Spanien im Winter von 1878 auf 1879.*[28] The Biblioteca Capitular, in the famous Mosque or Cathedral, is very hard to get entrance to, but through a Spanish friend he succeeded; however, he could not find the Albar codex mentioned by Valentinelli. At the last moment an obliging seminarian in charge of the books remembered that a long time before some volumes had been taken to the Archivo de los Canónigos, which is a staircase deeper than the Biblioteca Capitular. Here Ewald found the Albar codex, the 1751 copy of it made for Flórez, and a thirteenth-century chronicle. Not having the *España sagrada* volume with him, he did what he could from memory in making some notes of where Flórez' text differed from the manuscript. Ewald and Loewe give a sample facsimile of it in their *Exempla scripturae visicothicae,* and in the text [29] say that Morales and some who followed him thought the date to be 854; this, however, is the year in which Albar composed the work, while the present manuscript is later. Ewald later published a little note [30] on three small bits of secret writing that appear in the midst of the codex. These give the name " Sisvertus," two of them asserting " Sisvertus pres(byterus) scripsit." Since the only other similar cryptographic writing known to him was the work of north Spain, Ewald thought this proved the present volume was written there, only later wandering back to Córdoba. He took for granted that these notes of Sisvert refer to his being the scribe of the codex; but he does not specifically say that the penmanship is the same, and his facsimiles of the cryptograms do not show any of the surrounding text and their relation to it, but they come oddly at the beginnings of Albar's Letters 16, 18, and 19, and ground is given for wondering if they are not the work of some early owner or reader rather than of the scribe. Even if by the scribe, they need not prevent the codex having been written in Andalucia, if other reasons urge it.

In 1907 Charles Upson Clark visited Córdoba while gathering materials for his *Collectanea Hispanica.* He did not see the Albar codex, but a manuscript of Smaragdus which is also of the tenth century. The archivist

25 *Serapeum,* VII, 193–204.
26 Wiener SB, XXXIII (1860), 93f.
27 *NA,* IV, 515.
28 *NA,* VI, 382f.
29 *Op. cit.,* p. 25f.
30 *NA,* VIII, 359f.

informed him that he knew of no other Visigothic manuscript there.[31] So Clark has caused confusion by identifying the two, giving five facsimiles of Smaragdus, and attributing to it what earlier scholars had said of the Albar. Actually the contents of the two manuscripts are totally different.

The manuscript was again in hiding. In a book published in 1923 Ramírez de Arellano writes [32] that he looked for the codex in company with the canon archivist, but they did not find it. In the same year García Villada [33] lists two tenth-century manuscripts in Córdoba, the Smaragdus for which he cites Clark, and the Albar which latter he explicitly says he has not seen but describes on Ewald's authority.

Finally, while looking for things to send to the Exposición Hispanoamericano at Seville, the codex was again discovered, still in the Archivo of the cathedral, and described by J. Artiles in an article [34] which gives us our most detailed account, with long table of contents, reproductions of Aldrete's and Flórez' facsimiles, and four new facsimiles—two from the works of Albar, and two from the tracts at the end of the codex. The author is not aware of the work done by German scholars in the nineteenth century, and that Ewald actually found the volume; also there are a number of slips in the printed form of the article, both in the transcriptions of the facsimiles and in omissions in the table of contents. But we are grateful for his information, and not least for his assurance that the Albar is still with us.

There are two or three modern transcripts of this manuscript. One was made in the early seventeenth century by the royal chronographer, Tomás Tamayo de Vargas, and given by him to Cardinal Francisco Barberini when the latter was legate of Urban VIII in Madrid. It was this transcript that Nicolas Antonio used; [35] it is preserved in the Barberini Library in Rome.[36] A second transcript was made at royal command for the use of Enrique Flórez in 1751; it is kept together with the original in the Archivo of Córdoba.[37] Artiles mentions a third, once in the possession of Lorenzo Ramírez de Prado, but gives no further information.

A manuscript described as containing Albar's *Indiculus luminosus* was in the Escorial library at the beginning of the seventeenth century when Alaejo made a catalogue.[38] But Fernandez in 1902 was unable to find any trace of it, and probably it was lost in the Escorial fire of 1671.

---

[31] *Op. cit.*, p. 31.

[32] *Ensayo cat. biogr. Córdoba*, II, 267, (no. 3256).

[33] *Paleografía española*, (1923), p. 96.

[34] *Loc. cit.*

[35] *Loc. cit.*

[36] Cod. Barberini XI, 121, according to Traube, *op. cit.*, p. 125.

[37] ES, XI, 51f.; Artiles, *op. cit.*, p. 202.

[38] Published by Fernandez, *Antigua lista de manuscritos latinos y griegos inéditos del Escorial*, Madrid 1902, p. 23. The list also appears in *La ciudad de Dios*, 1901–1902.

I

In the printed editions as in the manuscripts, the *Vita Eulogii* has a different history from the rest of Albar's works. It was first published by Ambrosio de Morales in his edition of Eulogius' works.[1] This volume was a monument of local piety by two native sons of Córdoba. Pedro Ponce de León, Bishop of Plasencia, was, he says, given to delving in old libraries, and in the Cathedral of Oviedo he found a codex containing the works of St. Eulogius. For editing and printing he turned it over to another native Cordovan, the royal chronicler Ambrosio de Morales.[2] Morales prepared valuable scholia and appendixes which have been reproduced in several subsequent editions. He had finished his work and written and dated his dedicatory letter in November 1572,[3] but the death of the bishop who was going to pay the costs of printing delayed publication until 1574.[4] Morales was enthusiastic, and in his continuation of Ocampo's *Corónica general,* which he published about the same time, he not only retold at great length from Eulogius the stories of the ninth-century martyrs, but also gave a free Spanish translation of Albar's *Vita.*[5]

The second edition is due to the Flemish Jesuit, Andreas Schott, whose *Hispania illustrata* was published in four volumes at Frankfurt in 1603–1608. The fourth volume was brought out by his brother Francis, and this contains Albar's *Vita,* and also its four pendants, the *Hymn,* the prose *Translatio,* the *Epitaphium,* and *Oratio Alvari.*[6] Morales' scholia are reproduced. The main text is for the most part that given by Morales; however, many new readings are given, usually as marginal notes, but occasionally incorporated into the text. Schott's text is better and closer to the manuscript than Morales', though, according to Flórez, it is a less elegant volume.[7]

---

1 There seems to be no copy of this in the United States. The *Catalogue général des livres imprimés de la Bibliothèque Nationale* (Paris) gives the title as follows: Divi Eulogii . . . opera, studio et diligentia . . . reverendissimi domini Petri Poncii . . . reperta. Ejusdem sanctissimi martyris vita, per Alvarum Cordubensem scripta, cum aliis nonnullis sanctorum martyrum Cordubensium monumentis, omnia Ambrosii Moralis . . . scholia illustrata, ejusque cura et diligentia excussa . . . Compluti, 1574. fol. 132ff. and index.

2 The bishop's dedicatory letter to the Church and City of Córdoba, PL 115:913D–914D.

3 PL 115:916D.

4 Flórez, ES, X, 452.

5 *Op. cit.,* VII, 359–380.

6 *Op. cit.,* IV, 213–372.

7 Flórez (ES, X, 452) is worried, thinking the Bollandist Du Sollier may refer to the existence of a second edition of Eulogius by Schott, distinct from that in *Hisp. illust.*

It is said that the *Vita* was included in the 1618 edition of the Carthusian Lawrence Surius' *De probatis sanctorum historiis.*[8] The only edition of Surius available is that published at Turin, 1875–1880, and in this there is no mention of Eulogius or Albar.

Marguerin de la Bigne, a forerunner of Migne, published the first great collection of patristic works, *Bibliotheca veterum patrum et auctorum ecclesiasticorum,*[9] which was constantly enlarged in succeeding editions for a century, reaching twenty-eight folio volumes in the Lyons edition in 1677. Eulogius' works were added in the third edition,[10] reproducing Morales' text. But Albar's *Vita* and three poems are omitted.

The Bollandists included the *Vita* and poems in the eighth volume of the *Acta sanctorum,*[11] first published in 1668. The editor says nothing about his text, though the title implies it is Morales' edition. A comparison of variant readings shows that this edition usually follows Morales, but that occasionally a reading is adopted from Schott, and once in a while a new emendation is offered. Morales' notes and scholia are not given, but a few brief notes are added by the Bollandist editor.

Juan Tamayo de Salazar produced the *Martyrologium Hispanum* in six volumes, 1651–1659.[12] Under the eleventh day of March he reproduces the *Vita* and the three poems. He omits the rhetorical preface and the personal conclusion of the *Vita.* The text usually follows Morales, but here and there adopts a reading of Schott, or gives a conjecture of the editor's own (unless perhaps he got it from Surius, to whom and to Schott he directs the reader who might wish the complete text of the *Vita*).

Enrique Flórez re-edited the *Vita* and pendant verses in 1753.[13] He gives variant readings of Morales and Schott, but does not reproduce Morales' scholia and appendixes, writing instead his own life of Eulogius and explanatory material.

Finally, in 1785, Cardinal Lorenzana issued the last edition of the *Vita* and of Eulogius' writings in his *Sanctorum patrum Toletanorum quotquot*

As one of his reasons he says that Du Sollier affirms that Schott always calls a certain martyr, whose history is given by Eulogius, Natalia and not Sabigotho, whereas in the *Hisp. illust.* the reading is Sabigotho. But this is based on a mistake made by Flórez himself: reading *ac* in place of *at* in a note of Du Sollier (AASS, VI July, p. 453C, note d.); Du Sollier actually says that Schott used Sabigotho, and this is the reading of *Hisp. illust.* For the rest, it is easier to suppose that Du Sollier attributed Morales' notes which he found reproduced in *Hisp. illust.* to Schott, than to suppose another edition which would seem uncalled for, and of which no one has found a trace.

8 E.g., Gams, *Kirchenges. v. Span.,* II, ii, 328, n.2; the Bollandist *Bibl. hagiographica latina,* no. 2704, gives the reference, Surius, III, 95–99.

9 First ed., Paris, 8 Vols. fol., with appendix Vol. 9, 1579.

10 Paris, 1609–1610, Eulogius in Vol. 8, according to Brit. Museum *Catal. Printed Books* (1881). The present writer has had access only to the 1677 edition.

11 AASS, II March, eleventh day; in third ed., pp. 89–95.

12 *Anamnesis, sive commemorationis sanctorum Hispanorum . . . tomus secundus,* part I, pp. 167–175. Lyons, 1652. He omits §§ 1, 6, 18–20 of the *Vita.*

13 ES, X, 543–563.

extant opera.[14] He explains that he has had no new manuscripts, and has limited his editorial work to checking one edition against another to eliminate their errors, and adding notes of his own. He reprints the variants, notes, and scholia of his predecessors, and so his edition is considered the standard. It was reprinted by Migne.[15]

2

The rest of Albar's works have not been so highly favored. Though already known to Ambrosio de Morales, they were not published[16] until Flórez edited them in the *España sagrada*[17] with a long introduction but with only brief notes. As was said above, he did not see the original codex but had to work from a copy made for him. Since he believed that most of the many grammatical mistakes in the manuscript were due to the copyist and not to Albar, Flórez corrected the smaller faults such as spelling, agreement of noun and adjective, of subject and verb, but the larger passages of difficult or uncertain meaning he printed as he found them.[18] This is not only the first, but remains the only complete edition of Albar, and was reproduced in Migne.[19]

Ludwig Traube made a new critical edition of Albar's poetical production, supplying it with a very useful introduction and notes.[20]

Finally, Clemens Blume included one poem, the Hymn to St. Eulogius, in his *Hymnodia gotica*.[21]

---

14 Madrid, 3 vols., 1782–1793.

15 The *Vita*, PL 115:705–720.

16 Gomez Bravo (*Catál. obisp. Córd.*, 2nd ed., I, 145ff.) prints the text of *Epp.* 11–13 and a large part of *Ep.* 10. If, as seems probable, this was already in the first edition of 1739, he gave the first edition of these letters. Being a canon of Córdoba, he had direct access to the MS, and prints from it unchanged the mediaeval spellings and forms not appearing in Flórez.

17 Vol. XI (1753), 62–299.

18 *Ibid.*, pp. 54ff.

19 PL 121:397–566.

20 MGH, *Poet. Lat. aevi carol.*, III, i (1886), 122–142.

21 *Analecta hymnica medii aevi*, XXVII, 169–171.

APPENDIX III

The Liber Scintillarum [1]

Ambrosio de Morales discovered a manuscript [2] containing a *Liber scintillarum* with a title which attributed it to Albar. Since then, many Spanish writers have followed Morales in accepting this attribution.[3] But it is now generally agreed that it cannot be his,[4] at least in its original form, for old book-lists show that in 822 it was at Reichenau,[5] and another copy at St. Riquier in 831.[6]

The book is purely an anthology of selections from Scripture, and from such Fathers as Isidore, Augustine, Gregory, Cyprian, Cassian, and Caesarius—Isidore being far·in the lead—without any original contribution from the compiler. The material chosen is almost wholly moral and ascetic, and is divided into about eighty chapters [7] according to subject. The choice of this kind of material does not harmonize with Albar's tastes as we find them in his own writings; Albar's mind was rather given to dogmatic and theological topics, and had a strong Augustinian tinge; the *Liber scintillarum* reflects a quiet, and fairly sunny moral earnestness, even more so than that of Isidore.

The work was very popular in many countries throughout the Middle Ages. The MSS. assign it to various authors—Bede, Defensor of Ligugé, Caesarius, Eligius, and others—but most resisted the temptation and left it anonymous. Early in the eleventh century an Anglo-Saxon version was made.[8] In the sixteenth century the Latin text was published with the works of St. Bede.

The following list of manuscripts was made while searching printed catalogues of manuscript collections. It does not pretend to be complete;

1 The text can be found most conveniently, PL 88:597–718.

2 Now Madrid, Bibl. Nac., 112; formerly A 115; Flórez and others following him call it A 110.

3 E.g., Flórez, ES, XI, 47–50; Ballesteros y Beretta, *Hist. de Esp.*, II, 158; García Villada, *Hist. eclés. Esp.*, III, 108.

4 Millares Carlo, *Nuevos estudios*, p. 138; Manitius, *Gesch. d. latein. Lit. d. Mittelalters*, I, 422f.; C. H. Beeson, *Isidor. Studien*, pp. 124f.; A. E. Anspach, *Misc. Isidor.*, pp. 329ff.

5 Becker, *Catalogi bibl. ant.*, p. 8, list 6, no. 131.

6 *Ibid.*, p. 27, list 11, no. 176.

7 The manuscripts differ in their inclusiveness, and may represent more than one redaction.

8 It was an interlinear translation of the Latin text; both the Latin and the Anglo-Saxon have been edited by Ernest Rhodes, *Defensor's Liber scintillarum*, EETS, O.S. 93, London, 1889.

still other MSS. are mentioned by Manitius, Beeson, and Anspach in the references already given.

AVIGNON, Bibliothèque, 235. Late 14th century. Fragment.

AVRANCHES, Bibliothèque, 108, fols. 1–58. 10th cent.

BAMBERG, Staatsbibliothek, B.V. 18, fols. 1–78. 9th cent. Attributed to Isidore.

———, ———, B. V. 25, fols. 1–101. 9/10th cent.

BARCELONA, Archivo general de la corona de Aragon, MS. Ripoll. 138, fols. 2–71. 14th cent.

———, ———, MS. Ripoll. 199, fols. 2–156. 11/12th cent.

BERLIN, Königliche Bibliothek, Theol. fol. 152.

BOURGES, Bibliothèque, 97(87), fols. 99–169. 13th cent.

BRUGES, Bibliothèque publique, no. 12, fols. 93–136. 13th cent.

BRUSSELS, Bibliothèque royale, 1337 (II. 1069), fols. 11–58. 13th cent. Attributed to Augustine.

CAMBRAI, Bibliothèque, 485(453), fol. 55. 9th cent. Fragment.

CAMBRIDGE, Fitzwilliam Museum, McClean Collection, 107, fols. 1–102. 12th cent. Attributed to Bede.

———, Corpus Christi College, 190, pp. 265–280. 11th cent. Excerpts.

———, ———, 337, fols. 26–36. 13th cent. Attributed to Bede.

———, ———, 439, fols. 1–48. 12/13th cent.

———, Pembroke College, 275, fols. 83–101. 13th cent.

———, St. John's College, 42, fols. 121–130. 12th cent.

———, Trinity College, O. 3.50, fols. 61ff. 13th cent.

CHARTRES, Bibliothèque, 291(349), fols. 228–257. 14th cent.

———, ———, 352(457), fols. 65–231. 13/14th cent.

CHICAGO, Univ. of Chicago Library, 482, fols. 141–183. Cir. 1440 A. D.

CLEVELAND, Otto F. Ege, 58, fols. 1–158. 12th cent.

COPENHAGEN, Kongelige Bibliotek, Gl. kgl. S. 1378, fols. 1–61. 14th cent.

CREMONA, Biblioteca governativa, L. 2. 17–4005. 12th cent. Attributed to Bede.

DIJON, Bibliothèque, ancien fonds 207(169), fols. 1–87. 13th cent.

ENGELBERG MONASTERY, codex 161, fols. 76–159. 13th cent.

ERFURT, Amplonius-Sammlung, quarto no. 102, fols. 6–59. 12th cent. Attributed to Bede.

ESCORIAL, d. IV. 32. 14th cent.

FLORENCE, Biblioteca Laurenziana, plut. XXI, cod. XIX. 11th cent.

———, ———, Plut. XXV, cod. V, pp. 1–24. 13th cent. Attributed to Alcuin.

GLASGOW, University of Glasgow, Hunterian Museum, S. 2. 20, fols. 1–75. 12th cent. Attributed to Bede.

GRENOBLE, Bibliothèque, 257, fols. 1–101. 12th cent. Attributed to Bede.

THE HAGUE, Koninklijke Bibliotheek, 72/J24, fols. 1–63. 14th cent.

LONDON, British Museum, Add. MSS. 15,122. 15th cent.

L<small>ONDON</small>, British Museum, Harley 406, fols. 144ff. Attributed to Bede.

——, ——, Royal and Kings Collections: 7C.IV; 6D.V; 12B.IV; 5A.VIII; 7C.VII; 8A.XXI; 8B.XVIII;8C.IV; 7C.I; 8F.IV.

——, Lambeth Palace, $\left\{\begin{array}{l}\text{(L. } \Theta \text{ 2 or 3)} \\ \text{8 vo. 16} \\ \text{V.21}\end{array}\right\}$ fols. 155–174. 13th cent.

L<small>OUVIERS</small>, Bibliothèque publique, 3. 9th cent.

L<small>YONS</small>, Bibliothèque, 444(373), fols. 2–67. 12th cent.

M<small>ADRID</small>, Biblioteca Nacional, 112 (formerly A 115), fols. 1–81. 11th cent. Attributed to Albar.

——, ——, A 118, fols. 1–106. 12th cent.

——, ——, B 19, fols. 44ff. 1432 A. D. Attributed to Paternus.

——, ——, P 73, fols. 75–126. 14th cent. Attributed to Bede.

——, ——, P 113, fols. 1–95. 1434 A. D.

——, ——, 6222. 11th cent. Excerpts.

——, Biblioteca de la Real Acad. de Hist., 26 (aemil. 13), fols. 147–211. 10th cent. Attributed to Albar.

M<small>ONTE</small> C<small>ASSINO</small>, 214, pp. 1–73. Pp. 1–8 of 15th cent., the rest of 11th cent.

M<small>UNICH</small>, Bayerische Staatsbibliothek, 2535. 12th cent.

——, ——, 4582. 8th cent.

——, ——, 4654, fols. 76–112. 12th cent.

——, ——, 7982, fols. 1–93. 13th cent.

——, ——, 11334. 12/13th cent.

——, ——, 11726. 1447 A. D. Attributed to Paterius?

——, ——, 16472, fols. 130–157. 14th cent.

——, ——, 18557. 12th cent. Attributed to Paterius.

——, ——, 18619. 1465 A. D. Attributed to Paterius.

——, ——, also 16515; 17181; 17202; 18326; 18535B; 22377; 23836.

O<small>PORTO</small>, Bibl. Publica Municipal, 80.

O<small>SIMO</small>, Biblioteca del Collegio, 4. 15th cent.

O<small>XFORD</small>, Bodleian Library, Canonicianae, Script. eccles. 44, fols. 1–79. 14th cent.

——, ——, ——, misc. 552. 14th cent.

——, ——, Digby 158, fols. 7–90. 12th cent. Attributed to Cassiodorus.

——, ——, Laud misc. 112, fols. 274–316. 13th cent. Attributed to Cassiodorus.

——, ——, ——, 372, fols. 3–151. 14th cent. Attributed to Cassiodorus.

——, ——, ——, 631. 14th cent.

——, ——, Rawlinson, C. 23. 12th cent.

——, ——, ——, C 288, fols. 22–81. 15th cent. Excerpts.

——, All Souls College, 19, fols. 85–109. 14th cent.

——, Corpus Christi College, 212. 12th cent.

P<small>ARIS</small>, Bibliothèque Mazarine, 692(1127). 12th cent.

——, Bibliothèque Nationale, fonds latin, 12402, fols. 105ff. Attributed to Bede.

——, ——, ——, 13404. Attributed to Bede.

——, ——, ——, 13575.

——, ——, ——, 17400, fols. 94ff. 12th cent.

——, ——, nouv. acquis. lat. 202, fols. 157–189.

——, ——, ——, 664, fols. 1–125. 15th cent.

——, ——, ——, 1605, fols. 44–110. 9/10th cent.

——, ——, ——, 2169. (From Silos).

PRAG, Oeffentliche u. Universitäts Bibl., IX, E, 8. 14/15th cent.

——, ——, XII. A. 24. 15th cent. Attributed to Bede.

——, ——, XII. B. 14. 15th cent.

REIMS, Bibliothèque. (Contains two copies.)

RODEZ, Bibliothèque, 23, pp. 111–239. 13th cent.

ROME, Vatican Library, cod. vat. lat. 1042, fols. 50–65. 13/14th cent.

——, ——, ——, 1046, fols. 1–69. 13th cent.

ROUEN, Bibliothèque, A289, fols. 105–166. 13th cent.

——, ——, A468, fols. 4–83. 13th cent.

——, ——, A557, fols. 458–510. 13th cent.

——, ——, A561, fols. 11–93. 14th cent.

ST. GALLEN, Stiftsbibliothek, cod. 124, pp. 133–306. 8/9th cent.

——, ——, cod. 230, pp. 441–498. 9th cent. Attributed to Eligius.

——, ——, cod. 426, pp. 1–252. 9th cent.

——, ——, cod. 776, pp. 80–96. 1381 A. D.

SOISSONS, Bibliothèque, 128(119), fols. 3–80. 15th cent. Attributed to Bede.

STUTTGART, Landesbibliothek, cod. theol. 4°, 213. 12th cent.

SUBIACO, Bibl. dell' Abbazia, 154. 15th cent.

TOURS, Bibliothèque, 331, fols. 23–37. 14th cent. Excerpts.

——, ——, 337, fols. 1–84. 14th cent. Attributed to Bede.

TRIER, Bischöfliches Seminar-Bibliothek, R. IV, 14, fols. 1–71. 1253 A. D.

VALENCIA, Bibl. Univ. Valencia, 206, fols. 3–75. 15th cent.

VALENCIENNES, Bibliothèque, 302(292), fols. 52ff. 9/10th cent.

VIENNA, Nationalbibliothek, 14892 (Suppl. 2073). 15th cent.

——, ——, 4231 (Univ. 46). 15th cent.

——, Schottenkloster, 50 h. 10, fols. 1–80. 1423 A. D.

BIBLIOGRAPHY

ABBREVIATIONS

AASS. Acta sanctorum bollandiana.
BRAH. Boletín de la Real Academia de la Historia, Madrid.
CB. Die griechischen christlichen Schriftsteller der ersten drei Jahrhunderte, Berlin. (Berlin Corpus.)
CSEL. Corpus scriptorum ecclesiasticorum Latinorum, Vienna.
DACL. Dictionnaire d'archéologie chrétienne et de liturgie.
DHGE. Dictionnaire d'histoire et de géographie ecclésiastiques.
DTC. Dictionnaire de théologie catholique.
ES. España sagrada.
MGH. Monumenta Germaniae historica.
PL. Migne, Patrologia Latina.
RHE. Revue d'histoire ecclésiastique, Louvain.

PRIMARY SOURCES

AIMOIN. *De translatione SS. martyrum Georgii monachi, Aurelii et Nathaliae ex urbe Corduba Parisios,* ES X, 511–523; PL 115:941–948.
ALBAR, PAUL. *Vita Eulogii,* ES X, 543–560; PL 115:705–720.
—— Other writings, ES XI, 62–299; PL 121:397–566.
Annales Bertiniani, ed. G. Waitz, MGH, *Scriptores . . . in usum scholarum,* 1883.
BLUME, CLEMENS, S.J. *Hymnodia Gotica. Die mozarabischen Hymnen des alt-spanischen Ritus,* Analecta hymnica medii aevi, XXVII, Leipzig, 1897.
DRACONTIUS. *Carmina,* ed. Friedrich Vollmer, MGH, *Auctores antiquissimi,* XIV, 22–228.
EUGENIUS. *Carmina et epistolae,* ed. Friedrich Vollmer, *ibid.,* pp. 231–270.
EULOGIUS. *Opera,* Lorenzana, *Sanctorum patrum Toletanorum opera,* II, 391–642; PL 115:731–870.
FELTOE, CHARLES LETT. *Sacramentarium Leonianum,* Cambridge, England, 1896.
FÉROTIN, MARIUS, O.S.B. *Le Liber Ordinum en usage dans l'église wisigothique et mozarabe d'Espagne du Ve. au XIe. siècle,* Monumenta Ecclesiae liturgica, V, Paris, 1904.
—— *Le Liber Mozarabicus Sacramentorum et les manuscrits mozarabes, ibid.,* VI, Paris, 1912.

231

Fragmentum chronici Fontanellensis (841–855), Bouquet, Recueil des historiens des Gaules et de la France, VII (2nd ed., 1869), 40–43; MGH, *Scriptores,* II (1829), 301–304.

GILSON, J. P. *The Mozarabic Psalter,* Henry Bradshaw Society, XXX, London, 1905.

ISIDORE. *Sententiae,* PL 83:537–738.

―――― *Synonyma,* PL 83:825–868.

LIETZMANN, HANS. *Das Sacramentarium Gregorianum nach dem Aachener Urexemplar,* Liturgiegeschichtliche Quellen, Heft 3, Münster, 1921.

LORENZANA Y BUTRON, FRANCISCO ANTONIO CARDINAL. *Breviarium Gothicum,* PL 86.

―――― *Missale mixtum,* PL 85.

―――― *Sanctorum patrum Toletanorum quotquot extant opera,* 3 vols., Madrid, 1782–1793.

MORIN, GERMAIN, O.S.B. *Liber Comicus, sive lectionarius missae quo Toletana ecclesia ante annos mille et ducentos utebatur,* Anecdota Maredsolana, I, Maredsous, 1893.

―――― *Sancti Hieronymi presbyteri: Commentarioli in Psalmos, Tractatus,* Anecdota Maredsolana, III, in three parts, Maredsous, 1895–1903.

PSEUDO-ISIDORE. *Exhortatio poenitendi* and *Lamentum poenitentiae,* ed. Karl Strecker, MGH, *Poetae Latini aevi carolini,* IV, ii, 760–783; PL 83:1251–1262.

―――― *Oratio pro correptione vitae,* PL 83:1261–1274.

ROSSI, GIOVANNI BATTISTA DE. *Inscriptiones christianae urbis Romae septimo saeculo antiquiores,* 2 vols., Rome, 1857–1888.

SABATIER, PIERRE, O.S.B. *Bibliorum sacrorum Latinae versiones antiquae seu vetus Itala,* 3 tomes in 6 vols., Paris, 1751.

SAMSON. *Liber apologeticus,* ES XI, 325–516.

SCHOTT, ANDREAS, S.J. *Hispaniae illustratae; seu rerum urbiumque Hispaniae, Lusitaniae, Aethiopiae et Indiae scriptores varii,* 4 vols., Frankfurt, 1603–1608. Albar and Eulogius, IV, 213–372.

TAMAYO SALAZAR, JUAN. *Anamnesis, sive commemorationis sanctorum hispanorum . . .* (tomus), 6 vols., Lyons, 1651–1659. Albar's *Vita,* II, 167ff.

TRAUBE, LUDWIG. *Pauli Albari carmina,* MGH, *Poetae Latini aevi carolini,* III, i, 122–142.

WILSON, H. A. *The Gelasian Sacramentary,* Oxford, 1894.

―――― *The Gregorian Sacramentary,* Henry Bradshaw Society, IL, London, 1915.

SECONDARY WORKS

AIGRAIN, RENÉ. "L'Espagne chrétienne," Fliche and Martin, *Histoire de l'Eglise,* V (1938), 231–276.

ALTAMIRA, RAFAEL. "The Western Caliphate," *Cambridge Medieval History,* III (1922), 409–442.

AMANN, ÉMILE. "L'Adoptianisme espagnole," Fliche and Martin, *op. cit.*, VI (1937), 129–152.

―――― "L'Expansion chrétienne en Occident," *ibid.*, VII (1940), 367–428.

―――― "Pénitence," *DTC*, XII, i (1933), 722–948.

ANSPACH, AUG. ED. "Das Fortleben Isidors im VII. bis IX. Jahrhundert," *Miscellanea Isidoriana* (Rome, 1936), pp. 322–356.

ANTOLÍN, GUILLERMO, O.S.A. *Catálogo de los códices latinos de la Real Biblioteca del Escorial,* 5 vols., Madrid, 1910–1923.

ANTONIO, NICOLAS. *Bibliotheca Hispana vetus,* 2 vols., Rome, 1696; 2nd ed., Madrid, 1788.

ARTILES, JANARO. "El códice visigótico de Alvaro Cordobés," *Revista de la Biblioteca, Archivo y Museo del Ayuntamiento de Madrid,* IX (1932), 201–219.

AUZIAS, LÉONCE. *L'Aquitaine carolingienne (778–987)*, Toulouse and Paris, 1937.

BALLESTEROS Y BERETTA, ANTONIO. *Historia de España,* 9 vols., Barcelona, 1918–1941.

BAUDISSIN, WOLF WILHELM GRAF VON. "Alvar von Corduba," Herzog and Hauck, *Realencyklopädie für protestantische Theologie und Kirche,* 3rd. ed., I (1896), 426–428.

―――― *Eulogius und Alvar,* Leipzig, 1872.

BECKER, GUSTAV HEINRICH. *Catalogi bibliothecarum antiqui,* Bonn, 1885.

BEESON, CHARLES H. *Isidorstudien,* Quellen und Untersuchungen zur lateinischen Philologie des Mittelalters, IV, ii, Munich, 1913.

BONILLA Y SAN MARTIN, ADOLFO. *Historia de la filosofía española,* Madrid, I (1908), 289–307.

BOURRET, JOSEPH C. E. CARDINAL. *De schola Cordubae christiana sub gentis Ommiaditarum imperio,* Paris, 1855. This was not available.

BRUYNE, DONATIEN DE, O.S.B. "Un document de la controverse adoptianiste en Espagne vers l'an 800," *Revue d'histoire ecclésiastique,* XXVII (1931), 307–312.

BUTTELL, SISTER MARY FRANCES. *The Rhetoric of St. Hilary of Poitiers,* Washington, 1933.

CABROL, F., O.S.B. "Mozarabe (la liturgie)," *DACL,* XII (1935), 390–491.

CARAVACA MILLÁN, A. *Alvaro Páulo Cordobés. Su representación en la historia de la cultura y controversia con Bodo Eleazar,* 1909. This was not available.

CASPARI, CARL PAUL. *Kirchenhistorische Anecdota nebst neuen Ausgaben patristischer und kirchlich-mittelalterlicher Schriften,* Christiania, 1883.

CASTEJÓN Y MARTÍNEZ DE ARIZALA, RAFAEL. "Córdoba califal," *Boletin de la Real Academia de Ciencias, Bellas Lettras y Nobles Artes de Córdoba,* num. 25, 1929.

CAVALLERA, FERD. *Saint Jérôme, sa vie et son oeuvre,* first part alone publ., Louvain and Paris, 1922.

CLARK, CHARLES UPSON. *Collectanea Hispanica,* Transactions of the Connecticut Academy of Arts and Sciences, XXIV, Paris, 1920.

COOK, SISTER GENEVIEVE MARIE. *The Life of St. Epiphanius by Ennodius,* Washington, 1942.

COTARELO Y VALLEDOR, ARMANDO. *Historia crítica y documentada de la vida y acciones de Alfonso III el Magno,* Madrid, 1933.

DELEHAYE, HIPPOLYTE, S.J. *Les origines du culte des martyrs,* 2nd. ed., Brussels, 1933.

DÖLGER, FRANZ JOSEPH. *Die Sonne der Gerechtigkeit und der Schwarze,* Liturgiegeschichtliche Forschungen, Heft 2, Münster, 1918.

DOZY, R. P. A. *Histoire des musulmans d'Espagne jusqu'à la conquête de l'Andalousie par les Almoravides (711-1110),* new ed., 3 vols., Leyden, 1932.

EWALD, PAUL. "Mittheilungen. III. Palaeographisches aus Spanien," *Neues Archiv,* Hannover, VIII (1882), 357-360.

—— "Reise nach Spanien im Winter von 1878 auf 1879," *ibid.,* VI (1881), 217-398.

—— and GUSTAVE LOEWE. *Exempla scripturae Visicoticae,* Heidelberg, 1883.

FLÓREZ, ENRIQUE, O.S.A. *España sagrada.* Teatro geográfico-historico de la Iglesia de España, 52 vols., Madrid, 1747-1918.

FOURNIER, PAUL, and GABRIEL LE BRAS. *Histoire des collections canoniques en occident depuis les fausses décrétales jusqu'au Décret de Gratien,* 2 vols., Paris, 1931-1932.

GAIFFIER, BAUDOUIN DE, S.J. "Les notices hispaniques dans le martyrologe d'Usuard," *Analecta Bollandiana,* LV (1937), 268-283.

GAMS, PIUS BONIFAZ, O.S.B. *Die Kirchengeschichte von Spanien,* 3 vols. in 5, Regensburg, 1862-1879.

GARCÍA VILLADA, ZACARÍAS, S.J. *Historia eclésiastica de España,* 3 vols. in 5, Madrid, 1929-1936.

—— *Paleografia española,* 2 vols., Madrid, 1923.

GÖLLER, EMIL. "Das spanisch-westgotische Busswesen vom 6. bis 8. Jahrhundert," *Römische Quartalschrift,* XXXVII (1929), 245-313.

GOMEZ BRAVO, JUAN. *Catálogo de los obispos de Córdoba,* 2 vols., Córdoba, 1739; 2nd ed., 1778.

GOMEZ MORENO, MANUEL. *Iglesias mozárabes; arte español de los siglos IX à XI,* 2 vols., Madrid, 1919.

GUTIÉRREZ, C. "Alvaro (Paul) de Cordoue," *Dictionnaire de spiritualité,* Paris, I (1937), 410.

KELLY, THOMAS A. *Sancti Ambrosii liber de consolatione Valentiniani,* Washington, 1940.

LAMBERT, A., O.S.B. "Bachiarius," *DHGE,* VI (1932), 58-68.

LE BRAS, GABRIEL. "Histoire des collections canoniques. VI. Pénitentials espagnoles," *Revue historique de droit français et étranger,* fourth series, tenth year, 1931, 115-131.

LECLERCQ, HENRI, O.S.B. "Démon. démoniaque," *DACL,* IV, i (1920), 578–582.

—— "Légendes liturgiques," *ibid.,* VIII, ii (1929), 2440–2456.

—— "Lettres classiques," *ibid.,* 2885–2942.

LÉVI-PROVENÇAL, E. *L'Espagne musulmane au Xe. siècle,* Paris, 1932.

LOPEZ BAENA. *Vida y glorioso martyrio del esclarecido doctor y martyr San Eulogio,* Córdoba, 1748. This was not available.

LOS RIOS, AMADOR DE. *Historia crítica de la literatura española,* Madrid, II, 97–113.

MADOZ, JOSÉ, S.J. "El florilegio patrístico del II Concilio de Sevilla (a. 619)," *Miscellanea Isidoriana* (Rome, 1936), pp. 177–220.

MANITIUS, MAX. *Geschichte der christlich-lateinischen Poesie bis zur Mitte des 8. Jahrhunderts,* Stuttgart, 1891.

MANN, SISTER MARY EMMANUEL. *The Clausulae of St. Hilary of Poitiers,* Washington, 1936.

MENÉNDEZ Y PELAYO, MARCELINO. *Historia de los heterodoxos españoles,* 2nd. ed., 7 vols., Madrid, 1911–1932, scattered through his *Obras completas.* Vols. II and III deal with our period.

MEYER, WILHELM. "Anfang und Ursprung der lateinischen und griechischen rhythmischen Dichtung," Abhandlungen der philosophisch-philologischen Classe der k. bayerischen Akademie der Wissenschaften, Munich, XVII (1886), 265–450. Reprinted in his *Gesammelte Abhandlungen zur mittellateinischen Rhythmik,* Berlin, II (1905), 1–201.

MILLARES CARLO, AGUSTÍN. *Nuevos estudios de paleografía española,* Mexico City, 1941. This is a new edition of his *Los códices visigóticos de la catedral toledana,* Madrid, 1935.

—— *Tratado de paleografía española,* 2nd. ed., Madrid, 1932.

MORALES, AMBROSIO DE. *Corónica general de España,* new ed., 10 vols., Madrid, 1791–1792. The first two vols. are by Florian de Ocampo, the rest by Morales.

MULLINS, SISTER PATRICK JEROME. *The Spiritual Life according to St. Isidore of Seville,* Washington, 1940.

PÉREZ DE URBEL, JUSTO, O.S.B. *San Eulogio de Córdoba,* Madrid, 1928. An adaptation and translation from this is *A Saint under Moslem Rule,* Milwaukee, 1937.

POLHEIM, KARL. *Die lateinischen Reimprosa,* Berlin, 1925.

PONCELET, ALBERT, S.J. *Catalogus codicum hagiographicorum Latinorum bibliothecae Vaticanae,* Subsidia hagiographica XI, Brussels, 1910.

RAMÍREZ DE ARELLANO, RAFAEL. *Ensayo de un catálogo biográfico de escritores de la provincia y diócesis de Córdoba,* 2 vols., Madrid, 1922–1923.

—— *Historia de Córdoba desde su fundación hasta la muerta de Isabel la Católica,* 3 vols., Ciudad Real, 1915–1918. Albar and Eulogius are treated in III, 33–43.

RODRIGUEZ DE CASTRO, JOSÉ. *Biblioteca española,* 2 vols., Madrid, 1781–1786. Treats Albar in II, 446–453.

SIMONET, FRANCISCO JAVIER. *Historia de los Mozárabes de España,* Memorias de la Real Academia de la Historia, XIII, Madrid, 1903.

TAILHAN, JULES. "Les bibliothèques espagnoles du haut moyen âge," in C. Cahier, *Nouveaux mélanges d'archéologie et de littérature sur le moyen âge,* IV, Paris, 1877, 217–346.

TONNA-BARTHET, A. "Alvare de Cordoue," *DHGE,* II (1914), 856f.

INDEX

Abd ar-Rahman II, 15ff., 209.
Adoptianism, 14, 20, 61ff., 73.
Afflictions, purifying effect, 126ff.
Aimoin, 38.
Albar, Paul. (1) Name, 1; chronology, 2; ancestry, 2ff.; titles of address, 5f.; family property, 3f., 6f.; culture of family, 4ff., 14f., 19; friendship with Eulogius, 7f., 27f., 192ff.; schooling, 7ff.; layman, 9f.; verses, 10, 31f.; advice to Aurelius, 7, 9; Correspondence with Bodo, 11ff.; Correspondence with Speraindeo, 14; Correspondence with John, 18ff., 43ff.; relation to martyr movement, 23ff.; Correspondence with Eulogius, 27f.; Indiculus luminosus, 28ff.; Vita Eulogii, 31, 185ff.; sickness and reception of penance, 32ff.; death, 41f.; sainthood, 42.
(2) Use of rhetoric, 28, 43, 56, 74f., 173ff., 188; admiration for rhetoric, 28, 50, 56, 196, 198; disparagement of rhetoric, 46, 50–56, 75f.; on Christology, 60, 64–71; date of Confessio, 83, 102; Augustinian, 142f., 146ff., 158ff., 187, 216.
Amann, E., 14, 61.
Ambrose, St., 71, 73, 104.
Anadiplosis, 179f.
Ancilla, 10.
Annales Bertiniani, 11f., 16f.
Anthologies of patristic texts, 49, 52, 63, 72, 74.
Antonio, Nicolas, 1, 5, 18, 85.
Artiles, J., 1, 28, 42, 223.
Augustine, St., Attitude towards rhetoric, 45f., 54; theory of origin of soul, 76ff.; text of Scripture used, 171f.; Soliloquia, 76, 79, 130, 133, 139ff.; Confessions, 58, 75, 84f., 166f.; City of God, 15, 21, 76, 79, 166 f.; quoted, 71f., 106, 144ff., etc.
Azagra codex, 94, 96, 219f.

Basiliscus, 73.

Baudissin, W. W., x, 3, 8, 10, 14ff., 18ff., 40, 83, 85.
Beatus of Liebana, 70f.
Bodo-Eleazar, 2f., 7, 11ff.
Bracharius, 81.

Candore nivescens, 207, 212; cf. 181.
Caspari, C.P., 81.
Cassian, John, 55.
Cassianists, 14, 109f.
Charles the Bald, Emp., 11, 16ff.
Cicero, 163, 190.
Compunction, 105f., 111ff., 122f.
Cursus, 74, 176ff.

Delehaye, H., 24f.
Donatus, condemned by Albar as exemplifying rhetoric, 46, 51ff., 56.
Dozy, R., 22, 24f.

Epiphanius of Salamis, 52, 197.
Eucherius, 75, 79.
Eugenius of Toledo, St., 92f., 96f.
Eulogius, St., ixf., 2, 4, 7f., 185ff.; trip to Navarre, 15ff., 199f.; Correspondence with Albar, 27f.; scene of martyrdom, 208f.
Eusebius, 56, 59.
Evil, permitted by God 146; not a substance but deordination, 146.
Ewald, Paul, 222.

Flórez, Enrique, 1, 5, 9, 14, 20, 24, 31, 33, 37ff., 85, 226.
Fulgentius of Ruspe, St., 71.

Gennadius of Marseilles, 81.
God, enumeration of attributes, 144f.
Gomez Bravo, J., 1, 3, 5, 14, 16, 20, 33, 40f.
Gregory the Great, St., on rhetoric, 46, 53f.; on venial sin, 105f.; Moralia in Indiculus luminosus, 30; Moralia in Spain, 57; quoted also 49, 58, 133, 144, 154ff., etc.

Hermes Trismegistos, 48f.
Heterius, 70f.

237

THE CATHOLIC UNIVERSITY OF AMERICA

STUDIES IN MEDIAEVAL HISTORY

New Series